BIOGRAPHIES OF WORDS AND THE HOME OF THE ARYAS

BIOGRAPHIES OF WORDS AND THE HOME OF THE ARYAS

BY

F. MAX MULLER

GYAN

Published by

GYAN

Gyan Publishing House
5, Ansari Road
Daryaganj, New Delhi-110002
Phone: 011-47034999, 9811692060
E-mail: books@gyanbooks.com

Distribution Network
gyanbooks.com
India, USA, Canada, UK, Australia, France

ISBN : 978-81-212-3151-0 (PB)
First Published, 1888

2nd Impression 2020

Printed at: Gyan Press, Delhi.

Biographies of Words and the Home of the Aryas
Author: F. Max Muller

BIOGRAPHIES OF WORDS

AND

THE HOME OF THE ARYAS

BY

F. MAX MÜLLER

London

LONGMANS, GREEN, AND CO.

AND NEW YORK: 15 EAST 16TH STREET

1888

TABLE OF CONTENTS.

INTRODUCTION.

IF what I have tried to prove in my 'Science of Thought[1]' is true, if thought is impossible without language, as language is without thought, many things will follow, not dreamt of yet in our philosophy. But leaving aside these graver matters for the present, there is one thing which, as everybody can see, will follow by necessity from the admission of the inseparableness of language and thought, and that is that all thoughts which have ever passed through the mind of men must have found their first embodiment, and their permanent embalmment, in words.

If then we want to study the history of the human mind in its earliest phases, where can we hope to find more authentic, more accurate, more complete documents than in the annals of language?

I speak, of course, of the materials of thought only, of the words which in reasoning we add and subtract, combine and separate, whether in the daily intercourse of life, or in our speculations as philosophers, or in our flights of fancy as poets. No doubt, the way in which we reason, in which we arrange or contrast our materials, is our own, the work of our own will, our own judgment, our own genius, or whatever else we like to call it. With all the bricks, or all the marble, silver, gold, and precious stones that may be given to an architect,

[1] 'The Science of Thought,' by F. Max Müller. Longmans, 1887.

it is only a Michael Angelo that could build St. Peter's; and with all the wealth of the Greek language, it is only an Aeschylus that could create the Agamemnon. But neither could a builder build a temple without bricks and mortar, nor a poet make a poem without the materials supplied by dictionary or grammar. We are far too apt to take these bricks and mortar for granted, and to look upon our dictionary as something given, something for which no one is responsible, something for which we owe no thanks to anybody. But that is not so. Our words are not rough, unhewn stones, left at our door by a glacial moraine; they are blocks that have been brought to light by immense labour, that have been carved, shaped, measured and weighed again and again, before they became what we find them to be. Our poets make poems out of words, but every word, if carefully examined, will turn out to be itself a petrified poem, a reward of a deed done or of a thought thought by those to whom we owe the whole of our intellectual inheritance, the capital on which we live, with which we speculate and strive to grow richer and richer from day to day.

Every word therefore has a story to tell us, if only we can break the spell and make it speak out once more. It is known that every word, if we can analyse it at all, is found to be derived from a root. It is equally well known that every root is predicative, that it predicates something of something, and that what it thus predicates is in reality an abstract or general concept. This applies to all languages, even to those of so-called savages, whenever they have been subjected to a really scholarlike analysis. All words, even the most concrete, are based on abstract concepts, and what was supposed to come last, namely abstraction, has now been proved to have come first, at all events in the growth of real language and real thought.

This may sound strange particularly if we remember how often we have been told that there are savages now living in whose languages we find as yet no abstract nouns at all. These poor savages are a real godsend to our young philosophers, a kind of Utopia where they find everything which their hearts desire. If by abstract nouns we mean what Schopenhauer calls abstract nouns of the second degree, such as whiteness, goodness, kindness, this may be true. These words form a kind of second story, and may well be absent in some of the languages of so-called savages, without causing serious inconvenience. Even in our own advanced languages we could dispense with those words. We could speak of the white of the eye, instead of its whiteness; we could speak of the white of milk, chalk, and snow, and we should convey the same idea, though less definitely, as if we used the word whiteness. But what we have now learnt is that the very ground-floor of our language is made up of abstract terms, that it rests in fact on arches and pillars, and not on mere rubbish. White is an abstract term, so is good, so is kind, so are also man and woman, dog and cat, river and tree. A river is a runner, and presupposes a root meaning to run; a tree is what can be torn or peeled or hollowed out or shaped into shafts, and presupposes a root meaning to tear. There is this ancient crypt underlying everywhere the ground-floor of our language, and though that crypt is often very troublesome to explore, very slippery and full of cobwebs, no one can any longer deny its existence, or doubt that it consisted of what, for want of a better name, we call roots.

What we have more ately learnt is that these roots, or these elements, which resist further analysis, expressed originally concepts, and that these concepts can, in most cases, be traced back to simple states of consciousness of certain primitive acts of our own, which, if repeated and conceived as one, contain within themselves the first germs of general and abstract concepts.

There are, or there were, writers who try to deny these facts, or to minimise their importance. There are no such things as roots, they say, and they imagine that in saying this they have started quite a new heresy. But the question whether there ever was a time in which language consisted of roots only, is really an absurd question. A root with us is always the result of an analysis, and, as such, it cannot strictly be said to have ever existed by itself. A word, even though identical in sound with a root, has no right to be called a root, as soon as it forms part of a sentence. All this has been explained a hundred times. Sanskrit grammarians have insisted on it more than two thousand years ago; and yet it is preached again and again as a new revelation, that in real language we never meet with a root[1].

[1] 'Der Wurzel werden wir eine einstmalige reale Existenz abzusprechen nicht im Stande sein.' Schrader, 'Über den Gedanken einer Kulturgeschichte,' 1887, p. 7; Delbrück, 'Einleitung in das Sprachstudium,' p. 74.

Another discovery which likewise seems to be made periodically, is that roots, such as we can now discover by phonetic analysis, need not therefore be considered as the ultimate elements of language. Of course, if ultimate is used in the sense of existing in the beginning of all things, we can know nothing of ultimate roots. But if, as every scholar knows, we mean by ultimate the last elements within our reach, then the 800 roots of Sanskrit may be called the ultimate elements of Sanskrit. Of ultimate, in the sense of primary elements of language, we can never hope to know anything. We may, if it gives us pleasure, believe in ever so many extinct generations of roots, but real science has nothing to do with such mere dreams of possibilities. What we know is that, given about 800 roots, we can account for the great majority of words in Sanskrit. Modern languages, though richer in words, require even a smaller number of roots for their explanation, because where all the descendants of a root have become extinct, and this is frequently the case in modern languages, the very existence of such a root would be unknown to us, unless we possessed some documents of an earlier date.

The fact then that nearly the whole of the Sanskrit Dictionary can be accounted for with about 800 roots, expressing about 120 concepts, remains unaffected by all these vague surmises. All we mean when we call these roots ultimate elements is that, for the present at least, they admit of no further analysis[1]. It is

[1] If in the list of Sanskrit roots, as arranged by me for the first time under 121 concepts, there are roots of a clearly secondary character,

the discovery of these predicative roots which lie embedded in every word, which has restored life to our words, and has enabled us to read the original meaning of many of the most ancient names in our language.

Every word, if it can thus be analysed and traced back to its root, tells us its own story, and though in listening to these stories we may occasionally be deceived, that is no reason why we should not attempt to do what we can. It is no sign of scientific honesty to attempt to claim for what is in reality a branch of historical research, a character of mathematical certainty. We all know that in dealing with the earliest phases of human thought, whether in language, or religion, or mythology, our evidence is often very imperfect, and our conclusions liable therefore from time to time to considerable modifications. This is so; it cannot be otherwise; and it is only the rawest recruit who expects mathematical precision where, from the nature of the case, we must be satisfied with approximative aimings. If we cannot interpret every word, let us interpret those we can. If we cannot guard against the possibility of error, let us guard at all events against too positive assertions. No one knows better than the hardy workman, who has

whether in form or in meaning, this means no more than that in Sanskrit we cannot go beyond such roots. Thus NṚT, to dance, is certainly very far from being primitive, but if we try to go beyond, we find that NṚ is no root at all, at least in Sanskrit, and that there is no concept, either more special or more general, to which in Sanskrit that of dancing can be traced. Why will people always ask for what is impossible, namely, the discovery of Pre-Adamite roots, instead of trying with all their might and main to do what is possible, namely, to discover the real constituent elements of real language?

passed his whole life in opening a mine and digging for gold, how many dangers he has to face, and how often he may take for gold what only glitters. But though he knows the risks he runs, and the disappointments that await him, he does not therefore give up his work and throw away his tools. It is the idle lounger who thinks it folly to enter a shaft where there has ever been an accident, and who sneers at anything which, when brought to light, does not turn out to be pure gold. New facts must modify old theories. In all historical sciences—and etymology, as such, must be called an historical science—we keep a door open for the discovery of new documents and for a more accurate interpretation of old documents. A historian who claims absolute certainty for his arguments, or infallibility for his conclusions, may pose as an oracle, but his utterances will be ignored by all who know what real history is.

In the Semitic languages we are never satisfied till we have traced words back to their roots, and even though the radical meanings assigned to some nouns are very startling, the general principle that words must have had a radical predicative meaning is never doubted in Hebrew or Arabic. Why then should it be considered so incredible that the same holds good with regard to the Aryan languages? Nothing seems to have given so great offence to certain students of anthropology as what I consider one of the fundamental principles of the Science of Language, namely that everything in language had originally a meaning, or, what is the same thing, that every word is derived from a predicative root. These roots may not always give the anthropologist the answer which he expected, they may sometimes startle even unprejudiced scholars by the strangeness of their replies. But without supposing that our interpretation of the facts of language is always right, the facts themselves remain, whether they are ignored or ridiculed, and they will have to be explained, however troublesome they may appear.

Much has been written of late against my interpretation of words expressive of the different degrees of relationship in the Aryan languages, and more particularly in Sanskrit, but nothing, as far as I know, to invalidate in the least degree the lessons which I thought we ought to learn from the interpretation of these words.

What is, for instance, the meaning of the word Father? Has any more plausible interpretation been offered than that it meant feeder, protector, ruler? Pater, Sk. pitar, consists of a radical element Pa, and a derivative element tar. The root PÅ means to feed in pa-bulum, food; it means to protect in Sk. go-pa, cow-herd; and it means strong, ruler, king, in Sk. pa-ti, lord, δεσ-πό-της, lord, potis, strong. Some scholars may doubt about the connection of pa in pati with pa in pater, but the fact that father was intended by the early Aryas as a feeder, protector, and lord, would not be in the least affected by this. Which of these three meanings was present to the mind of the original framers of the word it is impossible to say. A root lives in its derivatives, and its meanings are called out and differentiated by the varying purposes which it is made to serve. But whether the Aryas, before they were broken up into Hindus, Persians, Greeks, Italians, Teutons, Slaves, and Celts, conceived the father as a feeder, or a protector, or a ruler, it is quite clear that they could not have framed such a name during the so-called metrocratic stage, when, as we are told, the mother was the feeder, protector and ruler of her young, and the father no more than a casual visitor.

Whether in unknown times the Aryas ever passed through that metrocratic stage in which the children and all family property belong to the mother, and fathers have no recognised position whatever in the family, we can neither assert nor deny. But if Aryan language makes the Aryan man, then the Aryan man had certainly emerged from that half-brutal state before he could form such a name as father, Sanskrit pitár, Armenian hayr, Greek πατήρ, Latin pater, Gothic fadar, Irish athir, whether it means nourisher, protector, or ruler. To the students of Agriology such facts are unwelcome, and they try to laugh them away. They hoped to see in the image of the earliest stage of society as reflected in the mirror of language, clear traces of metrocracy, of communal marriage, of omophagy and cannibalism, but there were none. It does by no means follow therefore that the Aryas never passed through these stages of brutality, savagery, and barbarism. They may or they may not have done so. All I maintain is that their language has preserved no traces of it, and that there is no evidence, so far as I know, more ancient and more trustworthy than language.

If Agriologists are quite convinced that all humanity must begin with metrocracy, communal marriage, omophagy, and cannibalism, there is every excuse for their declaring that the Aryan period, as reflected in the common dictionary of the Aryan languages, must be very modern and very far removed from the equivocal birth of the primitive savage. It may be so. But when I look at what is pretended to be the more ancient picture of bloody savagery, such as the students of prehistoric ages have drawn it, I find that it is mostly composed of far more modern elements, of sketches in fact taken from uncivilised races of the eighteenth and nineteenth centuries. To transfer the customs, myths, and religious beliefs of these modern savages to the end of the glacial period requires a bold flight of imagination, which we may admire, though we should not like to imitate it. One advantage, therefore, may be justly claimed for our modern narrow picture of modern Aryan life. It really rests on ancient evidence, and on evidence which can be criticised and verified by every student, without appealing to mere authority or trusting to his own fertile fancy.

We are restricted to the evidence which language, by means of a careful analysis, can be made to reveal to us. The Agriologist is under no such restraints, and he can fill his canvas with whatever suits his taste and purpose. If his work is done conscientiously, it deserves no doubt the highest credit, and may still lead to great discoveries. But there should be for the present, at least, a broad line of demarcation between his studies and our own. Our materials are different, our method is different. We cannot listen to the Agriologist when he tells us that pater may be derived from Pa, and mater from Ma, which are called sounds of nature uttered by savages all over the world. I know there are great names which may be quoted in support of such theories, but we are dealing here, not with great names, but with small facts. If pitar were derived from Pa, and mâtar from Ma, then bhrâtar, brother, ought to be derived from a natural sound BHRÂ, and duhitar from a natural sound DUH, and *sic in infinitum, et in absurdum.* Whenever language has been forced to give evidence in support of metrocratic and similar theories, the attempt has always failed. I do not for one moment deny the existence of a metrocratic stage of society in some part of the world, nor do I maintain that we find no traces of it here and there, in the customs even of certain Aryan races. All I object to is the unnatural craving of discovering such customs *à tout prix.* Because, for instance, the Hindus say mâtâ-pitarau for father and mother, not pitâ-mâtarau, it has been argued that they were still in a metrocratic stage when they formed that compound, as if the children's love and a father's inborn chivalry did not supply a far better explanation.

Another attempt to discover in the Aryan languages traces of the former prevalence of marriage between brothers and sisters, has been equally unsuccessful. Because bhartar, husband, is derived from the same root as bhrâtar, brother, it was argued that in the earliest phase of Aryan life there was no distinction between brother and husband. One might argue in the same way, as has been truly remarked by Fick, that because φαρέτρα, quiver, and φέρετρον, litter, are both derived from the same root, therefore the early Aryas used litters instead of quivers, or quivers instead of litters.

The root BHAR, to carry, assumed at a very early time the meaning of supporting or feeding. A mother supports, i. e. feeds her child with her milk. Bh*ri*ti means food and pay, bh*ri*tya, a servant. Hence bhartar meant supporter, husband, and bhâryâ, she who is to be supported, or a wife.

From the root BHAR a secondary root was formed BHRÂ[1], like MNÂ from MAN, DHMÂ from DHAM, etc. Bhrâtar therefore may at first have meant no more than carrier, helper. This may be called idyllic or pastoral, but if the ancient Aryas formed their vocabulary, such as we know it, during a half-nomadic, half-pastoral state, why should not their language show some traces of it? And if the young men in the wanderings of a family from one valley to another were called the carriers, why should not the young girls, the daughters, have been called the milk-maids? We see nothing strange in unmarried women being called *spinsters*, why should the derivation of duhitar, daughter, from DUH, to milk, be considered so incredible? That it is a dead certainty, no one in his senses would dare to assert; that it is more plausible than any other etymology hitherto proposed, no one in his senses would dare to deny. More than this we cannot and we ought not to expect.

But the words for brother have been made to yield another proof of metrocratic life, if not among all the Aryas, at least among the Greeks. If bhrâtar meant originally no more than the carriers of a family, or a clan, we can understand how in Homer φρήτρη came to be used in the sense of a company of young men, living

[1] 'Science of Thought,' pp. 375, 525.

together, working together, and fighting together, without necessarily being the sons of the same parents. And if *φράτωρ* in Greek became restricted to the meaning of a member of a *φρατρία*, a new name was wanted to express children of the same parents, brothers and sisters. We see the same process repeated in modern language where, as in Spanish, frey takes the sense of friar, and is replaced by hermano in the sense of brother, as sorella is by hermana. But the Agriologists at once smell a rat. Why, they ask, was a brother called *ἀδελφός* in Greek, which meant *ἀ-δελφός*, i.e. co-uterinus, born of the same mother? Does not that show that brotherhood was determined by the mother alone, and that the Greeks were still in a metrocratic state when they invented this new name?

I do not deny that this argument is clever, nay that it would carry a certain weight, if the historical existence of that metrocratic stage in Greece had been proved by independent evidence. But is there not a much more natural explanation? Children of the same father, but of different mothers, were allowed to marry at a time when marriages between children of the same mother were considered incestuous. Hence what could be more natural and useful than to distinguish the *ἀ-δελφός*, i.e. the co-uterinus, or, in Sanskrit, the sa-garbha, by a new name, which name in aftertimes became generalised and applicable alike to all children, to all brothers and sisters?

And if in Sanskrit bhrâtar meant originally the carrier, bhártar, husband, bhâryâ, wife, svásar, sister, also may well from the first have been intended for those who took care of the well-being of the family. Svás-ar is formed by ar (like dev-ár, nánândar) from svas, to be well. This compound root we have also in svas-ti, i.e. well-being, εὐεστώ. This may again sound very modern or sentimental, still the combination is phonetically safe, and psychologically intelligible, and more than that we cannot hope to achieve.

In *s*vá*s*uras, which stands for sva-*s*uras, I see likewise an old compound, meaning the lord of his own people or of his own estate. That sva is used in Sanskrit in the sense of die Seinigen and das Seinige we see in the Upanishads, in such passages as Kaush. Up. IV, 20, yathâ *s*resh*th*ina*m* svâ bhu*ñg*ate, 'as his people live on the master.' That it meant suum, one's own, one's property, we see in the Rig-veda, VII, 82, 6, dhruvám asya yát svám, 'safe is what is his own.'

So again in the case of devár, which I take to have meant originally a play-fellow, from DIV, to play, I do not claim absolute certainty for this etymology, though it is curious that in Sanskrit devar should be used more especially of the younger brothers of a husband[1]. All I maintain is that in an early state of society such a name would have been perfectly natural. To say that not every brother-in-law is a play-fellow, is saying no more than that not every beau-frère is beautiful. A very common name for son in later Sanskrit is nandana, which cannot mean anything but rejoicer. If then a sister-

[1] Delbrück, 'Zeitschrift für d. Phil.' i. 152.

in-law also is called nanândar, why should we not understand that name also as play-fellow, companion, friend?

When we find such a name as pa*s*u in India, Italy, and Germany, used in the sense of cattle, we know that the people who used such a word must have tethered their cattle, for pa*s*u comes from a root PA*S*, to fetter. If we find in Sanskrit vadhri, in Greek ἔθρις, castratus, we may be sure that the Aryas had made some advance in the tending of cattle. It may be said that PA*S*, to tether, does not yet mean to tame or domesticate, but it is nevertheless the first step towards it. In the Vedic and the Epic periods the difference between wild and domesticated animals is clearly established. As wild animals (âra*n*yâ*h*, Zend auruna?) the following are mentioned in the Mahâbhârata, VI, 165:—si*m*ha, lion, vyâghra, tiger, varâha, wild boar, mahisha, wild ox, vâra*n*a, wild elephant, *ri*ksha, bear, vânara, ape. As tamed animals the Atharva-veda XI, 29, mentions:—gấva*h*, cows, á*s*vâ*h*, horses, a*g*ấvaya*h*, goats and sheep; and lastly púrushâ*h*, men. In the lacustrian dwellings of the stone age remains of all these animals have been found, and those of the horse also at Viville (Van den Gheyn, p. 14). Sometimes gardabha, donkey, and a*s*vatara, mule, are added to this list of domestic animals, but, strange to say, never the dog.

The name for king, *g*anaka in Sanskrit and chuning in German, seems to me still, as it did years ago, a very strong argument in support of the patriarchal theory of government. For it could only be among people where the father (*ganaka*) wielded the highest authority that the name for father could become the name for king, as *gani*, wife, became the name for queen, Gothic quinô.

We know from archaeology that weapons were made in different countries and at different times of stone, wood, and bone, before they were made of metal. Language tells us the same lesson. We have names of weapons before the Aryan Separation which clearly point to their material having been stone, wood, or bone, but none as yet which indicate their being made of metal. Thus *ἄκων* is clearly the Sanskrit á*s*an, which means stone and stone-weapon, as Rig-veda II, 30, 4, tapushâ*s*neva vidhya, 'pierce as if with a fiery stone.'

The evidence for wooden weapons we find in *δόρυ*, corresponding to Sanskrit dâru, wood.

The use of bone is confirmed by the Zend asti, arrow, which is the Sanskrit asthí, Greek *ὀστέον*, Latin os, and still better perhaps by *πέλεκυς*, the Sanskrit para*s*ú, provided that para*s*ú is connected with pár*s*u, rib and knife, and meant originally a rib of an animal, used as a falx or a curved weapon.

These few specimens may serve to show how words, if only properly deciphered, may reflect the thoughts of the people who framed and modified them, and how wide a field is still open here for both linguistic and historical research. It is extraordinary to hear young people say that there remain no kingdoms to conquer in the Science of Language. It seems to me on the contrary that there is almost the whole world to conquer. Even in Sanskrit, Greek, and Latin, there is still plenty of work to do, and one of my chief objects in writing the following papers, the 'Biographies of Words,' for *Good Words*, was to show to younger students how many straws there are still to be gleaned, how many tracts lie uncultivated, how many mines unworked in the study of words.

But the student of language has lessons to learn, not only from the Aryan, Semitic, and Turanian languages, not only from languages which possess a literature, but also from the unnumbered dialects, generally classed as savage, though if one knows what language means, it seems almost like a *contradictio in adjecto* to call any language savage. When one looks at the work that might here be done, one feels indeed inclined to say, 'The harvest truly is plenteous, but the labourers are few.' There was a time when it was thought possible to write about savages, to explain their customs, to criticise their legends and myths, and to compare their religions with the religions of more civilised races, without a previous study of their languages. That time is past. As little as a scholar would venture to compare the religion of Homer with that of the Veda without knowing Greek and Sanskrit, would any one now consider it safe to compare the legends, say, of Mangaia with those of Rarotonga, without some previous knowledge of the grammar and dictionary of these dialects. Many revelations await us here. When we are told that the people of Mangaia look upon the universe as the hollow of a cocoa-nut shell, and that at the bottom of that shell there is a thick stem, called Te-aka-ia-Roê, we seem to move in the very thick of dense savagery. But if the student of languages analyses Te-aka-ia-Roê, and tells us that it meant originally the 'Root of all Existence[1],' our savages become suddenly metamorphosed into modern metaphysicians, and we learn that even the thoughts of a Herveyan islander may have possibly some antecedents. If those who agree with me that many customs, legends, and beliefs of civilised nations can be explained by a comparison with the customs, legends, and beliefs of less civilised tribes, would only concentrate their energies on the study of their dialects, they would find ample work to do, and they might render service of real and permanent utility. In the Science of Language, Mythology and Religion, words have their history in Zulu quite as much as in Sanskrit and Greek, and the unravelling of one cluster of Zulu words would be more really useful than the most ingenious guesses on the true character of Tsui-goab[2], or on the original purpose of the Te-pi custom[3].

I look upon the work done by such scholars as Bleek, Hahn, Gill, Callaway, Brinton, Hale, and others, as every whit as important as the labours of Grimm and Kuhn and Pott. Wherever we analyse language in a truly scholarlike spirit, whether in Iceland or in Tierra del Fuego, we shall find in it the key to some of the deepest secrets of the human mind, and the solution of problems in philosophy and religion which nothing else can supply. Each language, whether Sanskrit or

[1] W. W. Gill, 'Myths and Songs from the South Pacific,' p. 2.
[2] 'Introduction to the Science of Religion,' p. 280.
[3] 'Lectures on the Science of Language,' ii. p. 37.

Zulu, is like a palimpsest, which, if carefully handled, will disclose the original text beneath the superficial writing, and though that original text may be more difficult to recover in illiterate languages, yet it is there nevertheless. Every language, if properly summoned, will reveal to us the mind of the artist who framed it, from its earliest awakening to its latest dreams. Every one will teach us the same lesson, the lesson on which the whole Science of Thought is based, that there is no language without reason, as there is no reason without language.

F. MAX MÜLLER.

Oxford, Oct. 12, 1887.

BIOGRAPHIES OF WORDS.

I. Fors Fortuna.

If ever there was an age bent on collecting old things, it is our own. Think only of our museums, brimful of antiquities from all countries and all ages, and which, like our cemeteries, will soon become small villages, if they are to hold all that was once young and alive on earth.

Besides these vast public repositories of the old things of the world, there is hardly a house of any pretensions in which we do not meet with some collection of old coins, old gems, old books, or old pictures, to say nothing of old lace and china.

Yet such collections are expensive, and become more so with every year. Then why should not those who are unable to pay for Roman coins or Greek bronzes, for Egyptian bracelets or Babylonian cylinders, collect antiquities which will cost them nothing, and which are older than the oldest things from any part of the ancient world? The fact is that everybody possesses such a museum of antiquities. Only he does not value it. He does not take the various specimens, clean and label them as he ought, if he wishes to know their real value, and hopes to make them useful to himself and others.

That museum is our language. There is no word in English, French, or German, which is not older than the oldest of the pyramids, and yet, while we are willing to pay any sum for a scarabee containing the name of Sesostris, which after all tells us very little, we attach hardly any value to words which, if we would only trace them back to their distant source, might teach us lessons of the highest import. It does not matter what language we take or what word we choose; every one of them will carry us back to times when there were as yet no statues, no gems, no coins, no cylinders, no pyramids, not even lacustrian dwellings, stone hammers, or flint-heads. For all these are the workmanship of intelligent beings, and no being can be intelligent without language.

Here therefore is an opening for all who have a taste for collecting old things, and who are too poor to pay for what are after all, in comparison to words, very modern antiquities. But although the specimens for such a collection are cheap, the labour of collecting, of sifting and analysing them is not inconsiderable. There are some provinces in the vast realm of speech which as yet have been but very imperfectly surveyed and mapped out, and I should advise no collector to begin his museum with Patagonian, Indo-Chinese, or Abchasian words. It is best to begin with our own language, and from thence to allow our researches to radiate towards the other languages of Europe.

These have all been classified. With two exceptions, all the modern and ancient dialects of our small European continent belong to three great families, the

Aryan, the Semitic, and the Turanian. The two unclassed languages are Bask and Etruscan, which as yet stand alone without any recognised relationship, while all the rest can prove their legitimate origin and their unquestioned descent. We might in fact claim the whole of Europe for the Aryan family of speech. For modern Hebrew, as spoken by a few Jews, is really a foreign language in Europe, while Maltese is a very insignificant representative of Semitic speech. As to the offshoots of Turanian speech in Europe, we have Hungarian in the south, and Finnish, Esthonian, and Lapponian in the north. Excluding these intruders, or, it may be, these exiles, the whole of Europe is the home of Aryan speech.

Before we begin to collect, however, and before we can hope to arrange our collection systematically, we must remember that the Aryan family did not take possession of this Western peninsula of Asia as an undivided body, and at one and the same time. They had been separated for centuries, nay, more likely, for thousands of years, and to such an extent that when they poured into Europe, wave upon wave, they hardly recollected their distant relationship, and had certainly become as unintelligible to one another as if they had never had the same fathers and mothers. We must therefore keep in our collections separate departments. In well-arranged museums we do not mix Greek with Roman statues, Celtic with Slavonic and Teutonic coins. We have one room for historic, another for prehistoric antiquities. We must keep the same order in our museums of words. I do not like to repeat here what every one who takes an interest in the subject can find in my 'Lectures on the

Science of Language.' I have given there a full outline of a scientific classification of the principal languages of Europe, and according to that outline every collector can arrange his small collection of words, can trace their relationship, and follow their migrations from century to century. Though these lectures were published many years ago and may possibly themselves be counted among old things, I believe they will still answer every purpose in the hands of careful collectors of words or students of Comparative Philology. It may be that some more recent linguistic theories are not mentioned in them, but in that case, though my silence does not necessarily mean dissent, still less disapproval, it may mean that *adhuc sub judice lis est*, i. e. that these theories require more careful testing before they should be admitted into a manual of the Science of Language. It may also be that some of the theories which I still adhere to in these lectures may seem to others superseded by newer theories. But here again, though in a growing science like that of Comparative Philology we naturally have to learn and to unlearn from day to day, and from year to year, I doubt whether I have in my lectures put forward any doctrines which I should now have to surrender, or whether I ever represented arguments and conclusions as firmly established which, in the present state of our knowledge, cannot be otherwise than problematical.

I may therefore, I believe, with a good conscience refer those of my readers who really wish to arrange for themselves a small museum of words to my 'Lectures on the Science of Language' (last edition, 1885), where they will find all those rules which a librarian wants for a *catalogue raisonné* of his books, or the keeper of a collection of coins for a proper arrangement of his chests and drawers.

And as example is always better than precept, I shall select a few specimens in order to show how words should be collected, how they should be cleaned and arranged, and how their migrations should be traced from century to century, or from country to country; for words are tossed about in the world, and their fates are often very strange. Each word has its biography, beginning with its birth, or at least with its baptism. We may speak of its childhood, its youth, its manhood, and old age, nay, even of its death, and of its heirs and successors. The early chapters of these word-biographies are no doubt the most difficult and require very careful treatment; but, as in the lives of men and women, they are also the most important, and in the case of most words they often determine the whole of their subsequent career. In the earliest chapters we shall find that our authorities sometimes differ and are not always quite trustworthy; nay, there are many lives in which as yet the earliest chapters are entirely missing. But there are rich archives which have still to be ransacked, and every conscientious student, I believe, will find that, with proper care and judgment, his researches will be amply rewarded.

I shall begin with a word that seems to be very easy to place and to trace, but which, nevertheless, will prove somewhat troublesome when we try to follow it up to its first beginnings.

Fortune came into English with that large class of words which the Normans brought into England from the north of France. The Normans, being themselves of Scandinavian, that is, of Teutonic origin, adopted Northern French as their language, and had to learn a number of Latin words in that form which they had assumed in the *langue d'oïl*, or the northern dialects of Gaul. The Latin fortuna thus became the Norman fortúne, and with a change of accent the English fórtune.

These later fates of the word require indeed but few remarks. Almost every one of the meanings which fortuna has assumed in English can be traced back to French, to mediæval Latin, and finally to classical Latin.

We speak of good and evil fortune, so did the French, and so did the Romans. By itself fortuna was taken either in a good or in a bad sense, though it generally meant good fortune. It is the same in French, though in such expressions as *Dieu vous préserve de mal et de fortune* it is clear that it can only be intended for *mauvaise fortune*. Whenever there could be any doubt, the Romans defined fortuna by such adjectives as *bona*, *secunda*, *prospera*, for good; *mala* or *adversa* for bad fortune. Fortuna thus became at a very early time one of those numerous words which, when their real origin has once been forgotten, prove very troublesome to all thoughtful speakers, and as they seem to be full of contradictions, call forth numerous more or less ingenious explanations. Fortuna came to mean something like chance, and the ancient Romans accustomed themselves at a very early time to believe that certain things happened by chance (*forte quādam*), while others were ordered by a divine will (*divinitus*). Sometimes they speak doubtfully whether there is such a thing as chance, or whether there is a god who cares for what happens to us (Cic. Att. iv. 10[1]); while more philosophical minds deny altogether the possibility of any chance, if all things are held together by necessity. (Cic. Divin. ii. 7, *Si haec habent talem necessitatem, quid casû fieri aut forte fortunâ putemus? Nihil enim est tam contrarium rationi et constantiae quam fortuna: ut mihi ne in deum quidem cadere videatur ut sciat quid casu et fortuito futurum sit.*) In another place, however, he admits that, according to the judgment of all men, fortune may be asked from the gods, while wisdom is to be found within ourselves only (Nat. D. iii. 36). In this manner the word was tossed about. A distinction was sometimes attempted between fors, having the sense of chance, and Fortuna, being the name of a goddess, a distinction which is clearly artificial, and is contradicted by the old name of the goddess herself, which, as we shall see, was Fors Fortuna.

Another more definite sense which 'fortune' has assumed in English and in French, namely 'wealth,' seems at first sight unclassical, but it is not so. As we say of a young lady that she has no fortune (which is not necessarily a misfortune), *elle n'a point de fortune*, or as we speak of a man who has made or lost his fortune, the Romans used fortuna, and particularly the plural, fortunae, in the sense of riches, or what the Germans call *Glücksgüter*. Cicero himself (pro S. Rosc. Amer. 3) says, *a Chrysogono peto ut pecuniâ fortunisque nostris contentus sit.*

There are other meanings, however, which fortuna assumed in the mouths of the less classical descendants of Cicero, for which we are unable to produce

[1] Sed de ista ambulatione fors viderit, aut si qui est qui curet deus.

any warrant from classical writers, though, of course, this does not prove that fortuna, in its early youth and manhood, did not possess those meanings. In mediæval Latin fortuna means a storm, or peril of the sea, and so it does in French. Froissart (I. I. 108) writes: *Leurs vaisseaux eurent si grande fortune sur mer que plusieurs de leurs nefs furent perdues*, which leaves no doubt that *fortune* here means misfortune. Rabelais uses fortunal for tempest, and a sail which may be left during a storm is even now called voil de fortune. In Italian too fortunoso is used for a tempestuous sea, though originally it may have meant no more than perilous; peril and fortune being used almost synonymously in such expressions, for instance, as *à ses risques, perils, et fortune.*

Another curious meaning was assumed by fortuna when in mediæval law-books it occurs in the sense of *treasure trove*, i. e. *trésor trouvé.* Thus we read in the Stabilimenta St. Ludovici, lib. i, *Nus n'a fortune d'or, se il n'est rois*, i. e. no one has a right to treasure trove of gold, unless he be king.

Such are the later chapters in the history of the word fortuna, and it might seem that nothing more was wanted to make us understand the whole of its *curriculum vitae*, if only we are satisfied that from the very beginning fortuna meant chance, fortune, or misfortune, both, to our minds, very familiar ideas, and which seem to require no further justification. If an etymology was wanted, nothing seems more natural than to derive fors and fortuna from ferre, to bring, so that fors would have meant something that brings, and Fortuna a goddess that brings good or evil gifts. Why should we wish to know any more, or why should we hesitate to accept so natural a derivation?

I appeal to those who have studied the biographies of similar words in Latin whether they do not feel some misgiving about so vague and abstract a goddess as *Dea quae fert*, the goddess who brings. That Fortuna and Fors were names of goddesses cannot be doubted. The only doubt is, whether the abstract noun fortuna was raised into a goddess, like Virtus or Victoria, or whether the name of the goddess became afterwards an abstract noun, as in the case of Venus, Gratiae, Mars, &c.

When abstract nouns are changed into goddesses, they seem in most cases to represent acts or qualities of men and women, such as virtus, virtue, pudicitia, shame, victoria, victory. Fortuna, however, is of a very different character. She is something unknown or divine, supposed to bring good or evil to man. We ask, therefore, Who is she? What is her birthplace? What stuff is she made of? And here, if we inquire into the earliest traditions about the birth and the parents of Fortuna, we observe a very great difference between her and such thin and airy personifications as Fides, Spes, Virtus, Pavor, Pallor, Honor, Victoria, Concordia, Pudicitia, and all the rest. These abstract goddesses have hardly any antecedents, and even later poets have no more to say of them than what any poet might say even at present, when addressing such heavenly spirits as Virtue or Honour.

Very different are the early credentials of Fortuna. To the later Romans Fortuna may have seemed to be no more than 'one who brings,' *dea quae fert*, but Fors was one of the most ancient Italian deities, and her worship flourished in many places. One of her oldest names is Fors Primogenia, or Primigenia, the first-born of the gods, though she is represented at other times as the daughter of Jupiter. One inscription[1] is addressed to her as *Fortunai Diovos fileiai primoceniai*, others as *Fortunae Jovis puero primigeniae*. This puer (child) or filia of Jupiter held an even more exalted position in some parts of Italy, for Cicero tells us of an old sanctuary and oracle at Praeneste, where Fortuna was represented as holding Jupiter and Juno on her lap, and giving the breast to young Jupiter.

I ask, can such a goddess be explained as one of the modern abstract deities, like Fides or Spes? Do we find in Roman mythology anything analogous to a nondescript 'being who brings,' but occupying at the same time old sanctuaries, and being raised to the rank of either the mother or nurse or the child of Jupiter? It will be said, no doubt, that if we have in Greek such abstract goddesses as Moira or Aisa, we are hardly justified in objecting, on principle, to a Latin goddess, Fors, in the sense of a bringer. But, first of all, old Italian mythology is not the same as Greek; and secondly, Moira, at least in Homer, shows no traces of that truly mythological character which can be discovered in Fors Primogenia. I believe that throughout Homer we might take Moira as a simple appellative, meaning share or fate, without destroying the poetical character of any passage in

[1] See H. Jordani Symbolae ad historiam religionum Italicarum, in the Index Lectionum ex Regia Academia Albertina per aestatem anni 1885 habendarum; Regimontii, 1886.

which it occurs. I remember neither parents nor offspring of Moira and Aisa in Homer, nor do I think that, either in the Iliad or in the Odyssey, are prayers ever addressed to either of them. In later times, no doubt, they assume new names and a new character, but this seems chiefly due to their being joined or even identified with such really ancient goddesses as the Erinyes, Keres, and Charites.

Who, then, was this Fors, the first-born, who can be conceived both as the daughter and as the mother of Jupiter? According to the language of Aryan mythology, the first-born of the bright gods is the Dawn. She is called Agriyâ, the first, who comes at the head of all the other gods, who brings, indeed, precious gifts, namely, light and life, and who, therefore, is invoked first (prathamâ) at every morning prayer (pûrvahûtau). The same Dawn is also called the daughter of Dyaus (Zeus), duhitâ Diva*h*, and in other places she is, like Fors, represented as the mother of the gods (Rig-veda i. 113, 19), and as carrying her bright child, rusadvatsâ. There are, in fact, few praises bestowed in the Veda on Ushas, the Dawn, which cannot be transferred to Fortuna, thus showing her to have been originally, like Ushas, the bright light of each day, worshipped from the earliest days as the Fortuna hujusce diei. Fortuna had one temple near the Circus Maximus, another in the Campus Martius, and her own festival fell on the 30th of July. This Fortuna hujusce diei was very much what we might call Good Morning. There was likewise a Fortuna Virgo, reminding us of the Fer-onia as Juno Virgo, and her festival fell on the same day as that of the Mater Matuta. Are all these purely fortuitous coincidences, or may we not see in all these sayings the same thought which Isaiah expressed in a parallel Semitic metaphor: 'Thy light shall break forth as the morning, and thine health shall spring forth speedily?' (ch. lviii. 8.)

And if in the concept of Fors Fortuna we cannot but recognise a reflex of the goddess of the Dawn, who brings everything, who in her lap has good and evil gifts, or who, as the German proverb says, 'has gold in her mouth,' does her name resist our attempt to trace fortune back to the East and to recognise in her an old Aryan name of the Dawn? No one who is acquainted with the phonetic laws which determine the form of Aryan roots in Latin and Greek, will hesitate for one moment to see in Fors a possible and, as far as phonetic rules are concerned, a perfectly legitimate descendant of the Sanskrit root HÆ, to glow, from which many names expressive of the light of day have sprung. In Sanskrit, by the side of HÆ, we find the fuller form GHÆ, and from it we have a large family of words, such as gh*ri*n*a, heat, but also gh*ri*n*â, warmth of the heart, or pity; gh*ri*n*i, sunshine, gharma (*θερμός*), summer, but likewise a name for a warming vessel, a kettle, and for what is warmed in it, hot milk; gh*ri*ta, melted butter, fat, &c. This root is most prolific, particularly in words expressive of the affections of the heart. Thus h*ri*-*n*î-te is used in the sense of being angry, i. e. of being hot against a person, while har-yá-te means he is hot after something, i. e. he desires it. From this we have har-yata, desirable, beautiful, Lat. gratus, while in hrî, the original meaning of heat or blushing has been changed into that of shame. Many names of colour too owe their origin to this root, such as hari, harit, hari*n*a, and harita, all meaning originally bright, but afterwards specialised, so as to express the colours of red, yellow, or green. Two of these adjectives have in India become mythological names, hari and harit, both being used in the Veda as the names of the horses of the sun and of Indra.

And while harit in Sanskrit remained the name of the horses or rays of the morning, in Greek the same word Χαριτ became the name of one and afterwards of many bright and graceful goddesses of the morning, well known to all lovers of Greek poetry and art as Charis and the Charites. From the same source that yielded χαριτ we may, I believe, safely derive Fors, Fortis, taking it either as a mere contraction, or as a new derivative, corresponding to what in Sanskrit would be Har-ti, and would mean the brightness of the day, the Fortuna hujusce diei.

But it will be said, Why should the people of Italy have called her Fors, and not Hors? To answer this question fully would require a long phonetic disquisition, and I prefer therefore to appeal here to a few facts only. Latin was poor in what we call aspirated sonant consonants. Greece was entirely deficient in them. If, therefore, we have in Sanskrit words beginning with h, gh, dh, or bh, we must be prepared in Latin to find either the aspiration altogether dropped, or h and f doing service for guttural, dental, or labial aspirated sonant consonants[1]. That f and h vary in Latin we know from the statement of Latin grammarians, who mention fostis by the side

[1] See Grassmann, in Kuhn's 'Zeitschrift,' xii. 89.

of hostis, fostia by the side of hostia. Our shortest way, however, to show that Fors may stand for Hors, is the Latin word corresponding to gharma, heat, Greek θερμός, which is the same as the Latin adjective formus, a, um, hot. If gharma could become formus, harti could become forti. On phonetic grounds it is impossible to raise any objections. From a mythological point of view Fors finds its full and perfect justification as a name given originally to the bright Dawn, as the daily bringer of good or it may be evil tidings, as the unknown or uncertain goddess, as the first-born of all the bright powers of the sky, and the daughter of the sky; but likewise, from another point of view, as the mother of the daily sun, who is the bright child she carries in her arms.

It is a very common fate for etymologies of this kind to be set down as ingenious and plausible, but no more. Now I protest against this. I do not claim absolute certainty for any etymology, but I maintain that, if all phonetic rules have been carefully observed, and if all psychological difficulties have been cleared away, an etymology ought to be accepted and treated like any other historical fact. I do not claim more, but I cannot accept less. Like all historical facts, an etymology also is liable to correction by the discovery of new evidence. We accept the fact that Napoléon was born in 1769, but we do not say that it is impossible he should have been born in any other year, and if new evidence should be forthcoming to show that his birth took place in 1768, we should be perfectly ready to accept it. The same applies to the birth of words. Show that Fors could not have sprung from the root GHÆ, and that there is evidence that it sprang from the root BHÆ, and we are willing to reconsider our conclusion. But, as the case stands now, we have a right to say, that unless some analogy can be shown for an ancient Italian deity having so thin and unmeaning a name as 'she who brings or carries away,' and this, not as an epithet of another more substantial deity, but as a pure appellative, we must object to the explanation of Fors as Dea quae fert. We have likewise a right to say that Fors, as derived from GHÆ, and meaning the bright or golden, would, like *χαροπή*, *αἰγλήεσσα*, *λαμπροφαής*, *φαεννά*, be a most natural name of the brightest of all goddesses, the Dawn, the Morning, the Day. If a better etymology can be found, let it be produced, but until then let us accept our facts, as we accept all other facts, liable to correction, but, until so corrected, true. There are historians who doubt whether Napoléon ever existed, and there are philosophers who doubt whether the Dawn and other manifestations of nature had any existence in the poetry and mythology of the ancient world. With such antagonists I am too old to fight. But if any should doubt that Nature in her common and yet her grandest aspects is reflected in the myths of the most ancient poets, let them consult the myths of the most modern poets, and they will see in them too 'the calm, all-permitting, wordless spirit of Nature—the sunrise, the heaving sea, the woods and mountains, the storm and the whistling winds, the gentle summer day, the winter sights and sounds, the night, and the high dome of the stars[1],' absorbing the

[1] See 'Birds and Poets,' by John Burroughs, Edinburgh, 1887, p. 255; the Flight of the Eagle (Walt Whitman).

spirit of the beholder, and quickening and purifying the thoughts of the true poet with fresh and unbreathed morning air.

Thus our biography of Fors Fortuna ends, as the biographies of most words end, with thoughts taken from that nature by which man found himself surrounded when he formed his first concepts of words, by which he was taught his first lessons, and supplied with the first metaphors for the expression of higher and less tangible ideas. It may seem a long journey from the golden rays of the dawn, which were a fortune to our earliest ancestors, to the bright gold coins which are supposed to constitute our own fortune. But there is really no break on the road on which Fors or Fortuna travelled from East to West, if only we look carefully for the faint footprints which she has left behind.

II. Words in their Infancy.

THERE are not many words whose history, like that of Fórtuna, can be traced back without a break from their old age to their very birth, but whenever this can be done, we invariably find that, like Fors and Fortuna, every word expressed in the beginning something that could be handled or smelt or seen or heard. Every word, in fact, has had to spend some time in the cradle and in the nursery, and during that period there is little call for abstract ideas or sublime conceptions.

For some reason or other a certain class of philosophers has always protested, and is still protesting, against this view, whether it is advocated as a mere theory by sagacious thinkers like Locke, or proved as a fact by the students of language. They seem to consider it almost as an indignity that language should have started with such poor and home-spun materials, and should not from the very first have been endowed with general, abstract, spiritual, and sublime ideas—should have been earth-born, in fact, not heaven-born. But why should these idealistic philosophers feel uneasy on that score? When will people learn that in order to know what a thing is, we must always try to learn what it can become? As far as any outward signs of language and reason are concerned, no doubt a baby is no better than a puppy. But an infant, that is to say, a being that speaks *not yet*, grows into a speaker, a puppy never develops into anything but a barker. Aristotle would have said that with regard to language a baby and a puppy were alike *actually*, but not so *virtually*.

I confess I like these old scholastic terms, if only they are properly understood, and it is by no means easy to replace them by more telling words. We might say that there is virtue in the baby, but not in the puppy; and that though the infant does not speak as yet in very deed, there is in it a germ which sooner or later will unfold—will blossom and bear fruit. Aristotle, who was one of the first to struggle with these distinctions, called what we call germ or power or force *δύναμις*, which in Latin was rendered both by potentia and virtus, while what was perceptible in act or deed was said by him to exist *ἐνεργείᾳ*, which mediæval philosophers have translated by actû. When we now use these words *virtually* and *actually*, we hardly remember to whom we owe them; nay, we sometimes imagine that it was reserved to the nineteenth century to discover the constant transition of the *virtual* into the *actual*—the real essence of evolution and development—a misconception which has lately received a well-deserved castigation at the hands of Professor Huxley[1].

But it is strange that not philosophers only, but philologists also, nay, even comparative philologists, seem to have a kind of feeling that there is something disheartening in the confession that language is entirely of the earth, earthy. They would like to

[1] 'Nineteenth Century,' December, 1885, p. 854.

make an exception, if only in favour of a few words. Thus, while Cousin pleads as a philosopher for at least two words—je, I, and être, to be—as of equivocal birth, G. Curtius, whose recent death will long be felt as a real calamity by all who have the true interests of the science of language at heart, claims an exemption from the general rule for at least three pet roots of his own, viz. MAN, to think; SMÆR, to remember; and GNÂ, to know.

Cousin, in his 'Lectures on the History of Philosophy during the Eighteenth Century' (Paris, 1871, vol. ii. p. 274), writes:—

'I shall give you two words, and I shall ask you to trace them back to primitive words expressive of sensible ideas. Take the word *je*. This word, at least in all languages known to me, is not to be reduced, not to be decomposed; it is primitive, and expresses no sensible idea; it represents nothing but the meaning which the mind attaches to it; it is a pure, true sign, without any reference to any sensible idea. The word *être* is exactly in the same case; it is primitive and altogether intellectual. I know of no language in which the French verb *être* is rendered by a corresponding word that expresses a sensible idea; and therefore it is not true that *all* the roots of language in their last analysis are signs of sensible ideas!'

A 'sensible idea' is a horrible mixture, but supposing that it is meant for a sensuous percept, there is no difficulty any longer in discovering a very definite percept which is at the bottom of être. The French être has passed no doubt through many vicissitudes, and it really stands for so monstrous a grammatical blunder as essere instead of esse. It does not stand for stare, as has been sometimes supposed, though stare was used to express the concept of mere being in the French été, j'ai été, i.e. ego habeo statum. The question therefore is whether we are able to discover something earthy even in so airy a concept as être, to be. Without entering here into the whole history of that word of which I have treated elsewhere[1], I think I may safely say that AS, which is the corresponding form in Sanskrit, meant originally to breathe, just as BHÛ (fui, φύω) meant to grow, VAS (Germ. wesen, I was) to dwell, VÆRT (Germ. werden) to turn. All these are what Cousin would call very sensible ideas; and in the same way, whenever we press hard on the so-called auxiliary verbs, they will always disclose behind their faded features clear traces of an original purpose, very definite, very palpable, very sensible.

The case is somewhat different with je, ego. This pronoun does certainly not express what Cousin would call a sensible idea, but, like all pronouns, it is simply demonstrative, pointing to something in space or time, not very different originally from the Greek ὅγε or ὅδε, this man, i. e. I.

It might be said, no doubt, that Cousin produced these objections a long time ago, and at a time when the results of comparative philology had not yet become the common property of all educated people. This is true. But what shall we say then of Curtius? Though he too is sometimes represented as *passé*, I doubt whether very much that is really new and true has been added to the permanent capital of the science of language by those who are constantly telling us themselves that they have so far outstripped him. By all means let us all outstrip one another, and let us

[1] 'Lectures on the Origin of Religion,' p. 197.

readily confess that in some things the young are sure to outstrip the old. Curtius was the very last man to grudge the younger philologists their new discoveries, their more minute distinctions, their filigree-work traced on the somewhat cyclopean walls on which the founders of our science had erected their noble edifice. He did not object to being criticised; he was ready to learn even from his own pupils. But he certainly seems to have been surprised, as others have been, when those who had built some very useful attics, declared again and again that the first and second floors of the building erected by such men as Bopp, Grimm, and Pott, were no longer fit for respectable people to live in.

Well, I have often differed from Curtius, and he from me; but our differences have generally ended in a mutual understanding, for the simple reason, I believe, that we both cared for truth, and not for victory. I feel no hesitation, therefore, in expressing my dissent from him even now when he himself can no longer reply, and I deny that the three roots which he mentions[1] as exceptions to the general rule that all abstract words are derived from concrete, constitute real exceptions.

With regard to the root SMÆ, to remember, Latin memoria, I have fully shown in a chapter devoted to the root MÆ[2], a parallel form of SMÆ, that it meant to care, to love, to desire, as we see in Sanskrit smara, love, and in Greek *μερμαίρω*, *μέριμνα*, *ἰόμωρος*, etc.; and I have tried to explain by what process the concepts of caring, loving, dwelling on, could be ex-

[1] 'Grundzüge der Griechischen Etymologie,' p. 102.

[2] 'Lectures on the Science of Language,' vol. ii. p. 347.

pressed by a root which meant originally to make soft, to melt, the very concept which is assigned to the root MÆR, the sister root of SMÆR.

The root of GNÂ, to know, had no doubt reached its abstract meaning in all Aryan languages before the Aryan family was broken up, and that is a long time ago. But we can still perceive that the root GNÂ is formed from a root GAN, like MNÂ from MAN, DHMÂ from DHAM, etc. Now this root GAN meant really, I am strong, I can, and originally, I beget, as we may see in such derivatives as γονεύς, parens, Sk. *g*anitâ, γενετήρ, genitor, etc. A root which originally meant, 'I am strong,' 'I can,' and afterwards, 'I know,' may surely be said to have expressed a very sensible idea. We say in German *Ich kann Griechisch*, in the sense of 'I know Greek,' and this includes both the practical knowledge, the τέχνη, and the theoretical knowledge, the ἐπιστήμη of Greek. This ἐπιστήμη, or knowledge, is, as Aristotle tells us, the result of repeated ἐμπειρία, of practical experience, power, or skill. In Sanskrit SAK means to be strong or able, the desiderative SIKSH means to learn. We can thus understand how in an early phase of thought, I can, i. e. I have mastered, came to mean I know, while in a later phase of language I know came to mean I can, for, in Anglo-Saxon, ic can, I can, is really an old preterite of cunnan, to know[1].

There remains, therefore, out of the whole capital of language one root only, MAN, to think, of which, according to Curtius, it would be impossible to find a material origin. Let us see whether we really cannot follow up that root also a little farther, and trace it to its homely nursery. We find here again two forms of

[1] Skeat, 'Principles of English Etymology,' p. 126.

the same root, MAN and MNÂ, giving rise to such words as *μένος*, mind, Sk. manas, Lat. mens, and re-min-iscor, but also to *μνήμη*, memory. That this root MAN is the same root which we have in *μένω*, I remain, or in Latin maneo, has been admitted by Curtius and by most comparative scholars; but Curtius thinks that 'the concept of remaining and continuing was secondary, and derived from the primary concept of meditative and hesitative thought as the opposite of quick deed' (l. c. p. 103). Unnatural as this may sound, there is much to be said for it, as for most of Curtius's observations. In the growth of language and thought words do not only change their material into a spiritual, but likewise their spiritual into a material meaning. While at first the quickness of thought is likened to the quickness of lightning or of horses, after a time the quickness of horses is likened to the quickness of thought. As early as the Veda we find horses called mano*g*ava, 'quick like thought.' And as thought is not only quick, but, from another point of view, may also be said to be slow, Curtius's view is by no means unnatural, and might be supported by not a few analogies. If we ask a man whether he is coming, he might say, 'I am thinking,' i.e. 'I am hesitating.' The great Cunctator, Fabius, might really be translated as the thoughtful general if, as Curtius thinks, cunctari is connected with the Sk. SANK, to ponder, the Gothic hugjan.

But in spite of all this, everything seems to me to point in a different direction when we are looking for the true origin of MAN, to think. The fact that MAN would be the only root which started with an abstract meaning would alone be enough to make us feel very doubtful. But there is stronger evidence in support of the theory that MAN meant first to remain, or, in a causative sense, to make remain, to stop, to hold; and that it afterwards only took the meaning of holding, remembering, thinking. I am almost afraid to quote Aristotle once more, for we have of late been told so often that he is antiquated, and that in our days a knowledge of Plato and Aristotle disqualifies rather than qualifies a man for giving an opinion on any philosophical questions. However, I shall summon up courage and point out how Aristotle clearly saw in the remaining of impressions the origin of remembering and thinking. After stating that all animals possess sensation, he divides them into two classes—those whose sensations remain (*μονή*) and those whose sensations do not remain. Those whose sensations do not remain possess no knowledge (*γνῶσις*) beyond sensation, while those whose sensations do remain are again divided by him into two classes, according as they are able or not to gather the permanent sensations which remain (*λόγος*). The process, therefore, by which, according to Aristotle, thought arises is first sensation (*αἴσθησις*); then permanence (*μονή* or *μνήμη*, memory). Then from repeated acts of memory comes experience (*ἐμπειρία*); and lastly, from experience arise both art (*τέχνη*) and knowledge (*ἐπιστήμη*), which deal with the one in the many, that is with the general, and constitute in fact what we call the acts of the mind. If this should be called a very primitive analysis of our mental development it will answer our purpose all the better; for it will make it all the more plausible that what struck Aristotle as the first step leading from sensation to thought may have been in the minds of the early framers of language also, when they chose the root MAN, to remain or retain, which we have in *μονή*, to express the act of memory, *μνήμη*, and what is closely connected with memory, Sk. manas, *μένος*, mens, mind.

No doubt every one of these words took its own peculiar colouring from the atmosphere in which it was brought up. No doubt also there is still a great step from mere memory to thought. But so there is from a shepherd to a king (gopa), from a hearth to a temple (aedes); and yet the name of the one grows slowly and imperceptibly into the name of the other.

Nor is there any real weight in the objection that *μένω* and manere are intransitive verbs, meaning to remain and not to retain. Most ancient verbs can be applied both in a transitive and an intransitive sense, and language to supply her wants took as great liberties in ancient as in modern times, when, instead of *subvenit mihi aliquid*[1], 'something comes up in my mind,' we say *je m'en souviens*, 'I remember it.'

But if it should seem strange that what we call memory was expressed at first as that which remains, and that to remember should have been conceived as holding back or causing to remain, let us consider that our own word recollection comes originally from a very rough and ready word, namely from re-colligo, to bind together, while intelligo, i.e. inter-ligo, meant much the same, namely to bind or combine one thing with another, and cogito, i.e. co-agito, was originally no more than putting two and

[1] Gell. xix. 7, 2, 'Ut quaeque vox digna animadverti subvenerat, memoriae mandabamus.'

two together. Intellectnal acts which go beyond mere sensation are over and over again expressed by words which meant originally to hold back or to hold together. Thus to apprehend meant to take hold of, to comprehend to hold together, just as in German we have ergreifen, to grip, i.e. to apprehend, begreifen to comprehend. In Sanskrit upa-labh, to take hold of, is likewise used in the sense of apprehending and perceiving. Percipere from meaning to seize, came to mean to perceive (*percipere animo et memoria custodire*, Cic. de Or. i. 28, 127). Concipere, to lay hold of on all sides, was used in the same sense, though in time it took more prominently the sense of understanding, thus preparing the modern distinction between percept and concept, the one sensuous, the other intellectual. From nehmen, capere, we have not only wahrnehmen, to perceive, but likewise the German name of reason, Vernunft. Vorstellen in German means to stand or place before, and a Vorstellung was originally used in the sense of an image placed before the mind. The question whether Verstand comes from the same source, and meant originally the act of stopping, arresting, or holding sensations, is extremely difficult to answer. If it were so, this derivation would throw some light on the equally difficult word ἐπιστήμη, understanding, knowledge, which seems to be connected with ἐφίστημι, to stop, and more particularly with ἐπίστασις, which means stopping, but is often used in the sense of attention or noticing. In that case, understanding also would perhaps receive some rays of light, though, at present, its formation and first intention are still involved in much doubt.

And as the names of our intellectual faculties, which are mostly expressions for various acts performed by them, lead us back invariably to the simplest occupations of the child which stops, seizes, holds, gathers, it may be smells and tastes whatever is brought within his grasp, other names also of that which is supposed to be within us, call it mind, or spirit, or soul, or anything else, disclose much more primitive meanings, whenever we succeed in discovering their baptismal certificates. Thus spirit meant at first no more than breath, then life, then soul, then mind. Animus is connected with anima, air. I still know no better etymology of soul, though it has been much attacked, than that which connects it with the Gothic saivala, and with saivs, the sea, and traces these words back to the same root which appears in Greek σείω, I shake (Lobeck, Rhemat., 112), a root which Curtius identified with the Sanskrit root SHŪ, pre-ra*n*e, to set in motion. Though this derivation must remain somewhat uncertain, the possibility of forming a name of the emotions and passions within us from roots expressive of violent external motion is fully proved by the Greek *θυμός*, which, as even Plato knew (Crat. p. 419), is closely connected with *θύειν*, to rush, to rage, from which *θύελλα*, a gale, and similar words. I must confess that it was chiefly this remark of Plato in the Cratylus (p. 419), that *θυμός* is so called from the raging and boiling of the soul, that led me to suppose [1] that the idea of boiling might also be at the root of such words as Geist in German and ghost in English, AS. gást. To boil in Greek is *ζέω* for *ζέσω*, from which *ζέσις*, boiling, and probably also *ζῆλος*,

[1] 'Lectures on the Science of Language,' vol. i. p. 434.

ardour, zeal. In Sanskrit the same verb exists as YAS and YESH, which would account for Old High-German jes-an, to ferment, from which A.S. gyst (for geost). The representation of a Sanskrit y by a Teutonic g has been needlessly called in question. We see an analogous change in such forms as Middle High-German gise, jas, jâren, gejësen; in gist, foam, by the side of gest and jest, yeast. In Icelandic geisa means to chafe and rage, and in Swedish dialects gajst means a sharp wind. I still think, therefore, as I did in 1861, that ghost and Geist may come from the same root, and I may now refer to Grimm's Dictionary, s.v. Geist, in support of my theory, and in explanation of certain peculiar changes of the vowels of this very root. Why the name of the famous Geysir in Iceland should not come from the same root, though with a modified vowel, I cannot see; and even the name of Gas, though it is an artificial word, seems to me to have been formed under the influence of these words. It was the Belgian chemist Von Helmont (died 1644), who, as Dr. Skeat informs us, invented the two words Gas and Blas; and in inventing them he had no doubt in his mind the Dutch geest, a volatile liquid, and blazen, to blow.

If we think of other words for spirit, soul, or mind, they all tell us the same tale. As we speak of the heart and the brain, the Greeks spoke of the midrif, *φρένες*; the heart, *καρδία, κέαρ, ἦτορ*; and even of the liver, *ἧπαρ*; while *ψυχή*, which expressed in time almost everything that goes on within us, meant originally no more than spirit or breath [1].

[1] For further information on this point see 'On the Philosophy of Mythology,' in Selected Essays, vol. i. pp. 594–97.

Whatever words we take which now express the most abstract and spiritual concepts, they have all passed through their infancy and early youth, and during that time they were flesh and bone, and little else.

What was the original meaning of to consider? It meant star-gazing. In Latin it is frequently used together with contemplare, to contemplate, and that is derived from templum, a space marked out in the heavens for the observation of auguries. The Latin percontari, to interrogate, to examine, comes from contus, the Greek κοντός, a pole used for punting and for feeling the bottom of a river (Donat. ad Ter. Hec. i. 2, 2). To govern was originally guvernare, to steer, formed from the Greek κυβερνᾶν, to steer, and this from κύβερνον, guvernum, the helm, the rudder, possibly so called because it was a slightly bent pole attached to a ship, and derived from κύπτω, to bend, from which κύβδα, bent forward, etc. (See Schmidt, Vocalismus, p. 162.) When we hear of an exploded error, we are apt to think of an explosion, as if the exploded error was like an exploded bomb, burst and harmless. But to explode meant originally to clap the hands till an actor took off his mask or left the stage, as Cicero says: *E scena modo sibilis sed etiam convicio explodebantur.* We see nothing strange when we speak of weighing our arguments or pondering the etymology of a word. Why should we wonder at the French using penser, i. e. pensare, to weigh, in the sense of thinking? We speak of well-weighed statements, and in the same sense the Romans said exactus, exact, from exigere, to drive out the tongue of a balance, to weigh carefully. Such a careful weighing was called exagium, the French essai, the English Essay, which is always supposed to be a careful and exact treatment of a subject.

What is sagacity? The Romans themselves tell us that sagacitas applies primarily to the keenness of scent in dogs. They tell us of a goose being more keen-scented than dogs, *canibusve sagacior anser* (Ov. M. xi. 599), and speak of a man as an animal providum, sagax, multiplex, acutum, memor, plenum rationis et consilii (Cic. Leg. i. 7, 22). But what is the origin of the word sagax? Cicero derives săgax from sâgire. '*Sâgire*,' he says, '*sentire acute est: ex quo sâgae anus quia multa scire volunt; et săgaces dicti canes. Is igitur qui ante sâgit quam oblata res est, dicitur praesâgire, id est futura ante sentire.*' Classical scholars will probably be shocked at the idea of deriving săgax with a short a, from sâgire with a long, but nothing is more common than the change of *ă* to *â*, when there is a reason for it. In one sense, however, they are quite right. Sâgire is derived not from săgax, but from sâgus, like saevire from saevus; but for all that săgax and sâgus sprang originally from the same root.

But what is that root? I believe it was Lottner, himself a man of great sagacity, who first proposed to connect săgax and sâgus with Greek ἡγεῖσθαι. In Greek ἡγεῖσθαι means to lead and to think, just as dûcere in Latin. This ἡγεῖσθαι cannot possibly be derived from ἄγω, though not only classical scholars think so, but even Curtius (*Grundzüge*, p. 171). But it may be connected with the English to seek, the Gothic sokian, so that a dog was at first called sagax because he led well or sought well, because he was a good pointer. This implied his possessing a keen scent, and hence the applicability of the word sagacity even in the case of a Prime Minister, who must be a good leader, a good seeker, a good pointer, and, let us hope, a good retriever also.

We have thus seen how important in the biography of words must always be the chapter of their nursery recollections. We shall see hereafter how the school-days also have left their lasting impression on the character of many words.

III. Persona.

We have seen how strikingly Locke's famous aphorism, *Nihil in intellectu quod non ante fuerit in sensu*, was confirmed by the testimony of language. The whole temple of language is built of bricks, and every one of these bricks is made of clay; or, in other words, every word in our dictionary is derived from roots, and every root, as Noiré has shown, expressed a primitive act of primitive men, such as digging, platting, cutting, shaking, chewing, drinking, roaring, etc. Even Curtius's three abstract roots SMÆR, to remember, GNÂ, to know, and MAN, to think, when closely pressed, had to confess their humble origin.

But roots belong to prehistoric periods, and we have now to inquire whether the same law holds good in historic times likewise, and whether we too must be satisfied to use common clay wherewith to mould and model the most sublime, the most airy, the most abstract conceptions of our mind.

An experiment is always more convincing than mere argument. Let us take such a word as Person. Nothing can be more abstract. It is neither male nor female, neither young nor old. As a noun it is hardly more than what to be is as a verb. In French it may even come to mean nobody. For if we ask our *concièrge* at Paris whether anybody has called on us during our absence, he will reply, '*Personne, monsieur*,' which means, '*Not a soul, sir*.'

Of course person is the Lat. persona. It came to us from Rome, but the journey was long and its adventures many.

In Latin persona meant a mask, made of thin wood or clay, such as was worn by the actors at Rome. It is curious that while the Greek actors always wore these masks, the Roman actors did not adopt them at first. Thus while nearly all technical Latin terms connected with the theatre were borrowed from Greek, the name for mask, *πρόσωπον*, was never naturalised in Italy. The story goes that a famous actor, Roscius Gallus (about 100 B.C.), introduced masks, which had been unknown before on the Roman stage, because he had the misfortune to squint. This may or may not be true, but I confess it sounds to me a little like a story invented by malicious friends. Anyhow it is strange that, if Roscius had introduced masks simply in order to hide certain blemishes of his face, the name given to them in Latin, possibly by Roscius Gallus himself, should have been persona, i.e. that which causes the voice to sound. We can understand why the Greeks called their masks *πρόσωπον*, which means simply what is before the face, the mask thus worn being meant to indicate the character represented by each actor on the stage. To us it seems almost incredible that the great Greek actors should have submitted to such mummeries, and should have deprived themselves of the most powerful help in acting, the expression of the face. But so it was, and we are told that it was necessary, because without these prosôpa, which contained some acoustic apparatus to strengthen the voice of the actor, they could not have made themselves heard in the wide and open-air theatres of Greece.

Why these masks should have been called persona in Latin, i.e. through-sounder, requires no further explanation; but the story of Roscius Gallus, the squinting actor, becomes thereby all the more doubtful, particularly if we remember that Plautus already was able to use the diminutive persolla in the sense of 'You little fright!' (Plaut. Curc. i. 3. 36.)

I see no reason to doubt that persona, as a feminine, was a genuine Latin word, the name of an instrument through which the voice could be made to sound, and more particularly of the mask used by Greek actors.

Gellius (v. 7) informs us that a Latin grammarian who had written a learned work on the origin of words, Gavius Bassus by name, derived persona from personare, to sound through, because 'the head and mouth being hidden everywhere by the cover of the mask and open only through one passage for the emission of the voice, drives the voice, being no longer unsettled and diffused, into one exit only, well gathered together, and thus makes it sound more clear and melodious. And because that mask makes the voice of the mouth clear and resonant, therefore it has been called persona, the o being lengthened on account of the form of the word.'

I should have thought that with regard to the origin and the formation of a word which had become current at Rome not so very long before his time, the testimony of a scholar such as Gavius Bassus was, would have carried considerable weight. But no;

there is nothing that scholars, who can discover nothing else, like so much as to discover a false quantity. The o in the Latin adjective persŏnus, they say, is short, that in persôna is long No doubt it is, and Gavius Bassus was well aware of it, but he says the o was lengthened on account of the form of the word. Is not that clear enough for a grammarian? Are there not many words in which the vowel is lengthened or strengthened on account of the form of the word? Have we not in Sanskrit the same root, SVAN, which forms svăna, sound, but svâna, sounding?

However, before we enter on the defence of our own derivation, let us see whether our opponents can produce a more plausible one. Scaliger, the great Scaliger, in order to avoid a false quantity, went so far as to derive persona from *περὶ σῶμα*, what is round the body, or even from *περιζῶσθαι*, to gird round. Is not this straining at a gnat and swallowing a camel? We have only to consider that such an etymology was possible, and possible with a Scaliger who, taking all in all, was perhaps the greatest classical scholar that the world has ever known, in order to see how completely classical scholarship has been purified and reinvigorated by comparative philology. Would even the most insignificant of Greek professors now venture on such an etymology which, not much more than three hundred years ago, was uttered without any misgivings by the prince of classical scholars?

About a hundred years later, another great authority, Vossius, the author of an *Etymologicum Magnum*, represented persôna as a corruption of the Greek prosôpon. Now it is quite true that the Romans made sad havoc with some of the words which they adopted from Greek, but we may go through the whole *Tensaurus Italo-graecus*, lately published by Saalfeld (1884), without finding anything approaching to such violence.

However, I must confess classical scholars are not the only offenders. Professor Pott, the Nestor of comparative philologists, rather than incur the suspicion of committing a false quantity, suggests that persôna may be a corruption, if not of prosôpon, at least of a possible adjective prosopina, while the change of prosôpina into persôna might be justified by the analogous change of Persephone into Proserpina. I do not think that the equation Persephone : Proserpina=prosopina : persôna would be approved of by many mathematicians, and there remains besides the other objection that Persephone was a real Greek word, but prosopina was not.

We must try to find out, therefore, whether Latin could not have formed two words, one persŏnus, meaning resounding, and another persôna, meaning a resounding instrument. It is well known that the radical vowels i and u are constantly strengthened in certain derivatives. I still think that the best name for that change is Gu*n*a, but if it is thought better to begin with the strong vowels or rather diphthongs ai and au, and call i and u their weakened forms, I do not think that we either lose or gain much by this change of fashion. I hold that what Hindu grammarians have explained as Gu*n*a, or strengthening, accounts best for such words as dŭx, dŭcis and dûco, fĭdes and fîdus, dĭcax and dîco, etc.

Exactly the same process would account for sŏno and persŏnus by the side of persôna. We are not surprised at sŏpor and sôpio, tŏga and contâgium, săgax and sâgus, plăcidus and plâcare, even sĕdere and sêdare. We have in Sanskrit âsu, quick, in Greek ὠκύς, in Latin ôc-ius, all derived from a root AS, which preserves its short vowel in ăcus and ăcutus. We know that causative verbs in particular lengthen, if possible, their short vowel, as we see in sôpire, plâcare, sêdare[1]. If therefore our phonetic conscience pricks us, all we have to do is to admit a causative formation of sŏnare, and persôna would then mean exactly what it does mean, namely something which causes the voice to sound through. In fact persôna by the side of sŏnare is no more irregular than perjûgis, continual, by the side of jŭg, in conjux, conjŭgis.

Whoever invented or started this word, whether a squinting actor or some maker of musical instruments at Rome, had certainly no idea of what would be the fate of it. It is a very fascinating, though, no doubt, a very mischievous amusement, to roll down stones from the crest of a hill. Some start away briskly, but come to a sudden stop. Others roll down slowly, and after a time vanish from our sight. But now and then a quite insignificant pebble will strike against other stones, and they will roll down together, and loosen a large stone that was only waiting for a slight push. And down they go, like an avalanche of earth and dust, tearing up the turf, uprooting trees, jumping high into the air, and making havoc all

[1] Corssen, 'Über Aussprache des Lateinischen,' vol. i. pp. 391 seq.; Hübschmann, 'Indogermanischer Vocalismus,' p. 57.

along their course, till they settle down at last in the valley, and no one can say how these strange boulders came to be there. So it is with words. Many are started, but they will not roll. Others roll away and nothing seems to come of them. But this word persona has rolled along with wonderful bounds, striking right and left, suggesting new thoughts, stirring up clouds of controversy, and occupying to the present day a prominent place in all discussions on theology and philosophy, though few only of those who use it know how it came to be there.

Persona proved to be a very handy and useful word, and I hardly know what we should have done without it. In languages which do not possess such a word whole trains of thought are missing which we express by distinguishing between the mask and its wearer. Both came to be called persona, and hence a very important double development in the meanings of the word.

When persona was taken in its first meaning of mask, representing not the real, but the assumed character of an actor, nothing was more natural than to say, for instance, of a dishonest man that he was wearing a persona. Thus persona took the sense of false appearance, and Seneca (Ep. 24. 13) was able to say that we ought to remove the mere appearance or *persona*, not only from men, but also from things: *Non hominibus tantum, sed et rebus persona demenda est et reddenda facies sua.* Personatus was used of a man who had to appear different from what he really was, and Cicero, writing to Atticus (15. 1. 4), exclaimed, *Quid est cur ego personatus ambulem?* 'Why should I walk about in an assumed character?' We speak of personating in a slightly different sense, namely, when some one, for fraudulent purposes, tries to pass for some one else. In Latin, however, persona was not always used in the sense of a deceptive appearance, for we see Cicero remarking that 'He who teaches philosophy takes upon himself a very serious part': *Qui philosophiam profitetur, gravissimam mihi sustinere videtur personam* (Cic. in Pis. cap. 29).

But while in these cases persona is used in the sense of the mask worn, we find it in others expressing the real character represented by the actor on the stage. When we now read of Dramatis Personae, we no longer think of masks, but of the real characters appearing in a play. After all, an actor, wearing the mask of a king, was for the time being a king, and thus persona came to mean the very opposite of mask, namely a man's real nature and character. Thus Cicero, for instance, writes to Caesar that his nature and person, or what would now be called his character, might fit him for a certain work:—*Et ad eam rationem . . . existimabam satis aptam esse et naturam et personam meam, characterem dicere hodie solemus.* Nay, what is still more curious, persona slowly assumes the meaning of a great personage, or of a person of rank, and, in the end, of rank itself, as when Cicero (de Fin. I. 2) says:—*Genus hoc scribendi, etsi sit elegans, personae tamen et dignitatis esse negant*, 'Though this kind of writing be elegant, they deny that it is weighty and dignified.'

This sense of persona prevailed during the Middle Ages, and continues, as we shall see, to the present day. A man magnae personae means in mediæval Latin a man of great dignity. We read of viri nobiles et personati, also of mercatores personati, always in the sense of eminent and respected. In ecclesiastical language persona soon took a technical meaning. Personatus meant not only dignitas in general, but it was used of those who held a living or several livings, but committed the actual cure of souls to a vicar. *Personae maxime ii qui beneficia seu ecclesias per vicarios deserviri curant;* 'Persons are chiefly those who let their benefices and churches be served by others.' These so-called personae held very high rank, *Habent dignitatem cum prerogativa in choro et capitulo.* A Canonicus, we read in a charter (anno 1227, tom. 2, Hist. Eccl. Mell. p. 120), *non habebit in choro nostro staulum in ordine personarum, sed habebit primum staulum in ordine sacerdotum;* 'A canon shall not have in our choir a stall in the row of the *personae*, but shall have the first stall in the row of the priests.' No doubt, this led to many abuses. We read of a nepos, a word of peculiar meaning, which still lives in our own word nepotism, who *turpi commercio in diversis ecclesiis adeptus est personatus*, 'who by dishonourable means has obtained personatus in different churches.' As early as 1222, in a council held at Oxford, the question had to be discussed, *utrum vicarius onera ecclesiae subire debeat an persona*, 'whether a vicar should fulfil the duties of the church or a persona.' From this persona comes no doubt the modern name of parson, and it is strange that so learned a man as Blackstone should not have known this. For though he knows that parson is derived from persona, he thinks that he was called so because the church, which is an invisible body, was represented by his person.

Blackstone, as a lawyer, was evidently thinking of another technical meaning which persona had assumed from a very early time. *Omne jus*, we read in Paul. Dig. lib. i. lit. 5, leg. 1, *quo utimur vel ad personas pertinet, vel ad res, vel ad actiones.* Anybody who had rights was in legal language a person, and slaves were said to have no person by law; *nam servi personam legibus non habent* (apud Senat. lib. 6, Epist. 8), where persona may be really translated by right. This is still more clearly seen in such phrases as *habere potestatem et personam emendi et vendendi*, to possess the power and right of buying and selling. In this sense, no doubt, the parson may be said to be the persona of his church, but this was not, as we saw, the historical origin of the ecclesiastical persona, as opposed to vicarius.

Lastly, persona came to mean what we call a person, an individual. We read in mediæval writers of *universi personae qui capti sunt ex utraque parte*, all the persons who were taken on either side; and what is curious, this use of persona as a masculine continues even in modern French, where, under certain circumstances, we may treat personne as a masculine.

But even here the biography of persona is by no means ended. At one time the fate of Christianity seemed to depend on the right meaning of the word *πρόσωπον* or persona. Without entering here into all the intricacies of theological controversy, we can easily see that nothing was more natural to a Christian who spoke and thought in Greek than to apply to the three manifestations of the Godhead the name of prosôpa, or masks. In doing this the earlier writers were quite conscious of the metaphorical meaning of the word. Thus in the third century Clement (Protrepticus, x. 110, 86 P.) speaks of Christ as assuming the human mask (τὸ ἀνθρώπου προσωπεῖον) and acting the drama of human salvation (τὸ σωτήριον δρᾶμα τῆς ἀνθρωπότητος ὑπεκρίνετο). A very similar expression is found in Clement's Stromata, vii. 11 (313, S.), where we read, ἀμεμφῶς τοίνυν ὑποκρινόμενος τὸ δρᾶμα τοῦ βίου ὅπερ ἂν ὁ θεὸς ἀγωνίσασθαι παράσχῃ: 'Blamelessly acting whatever drama of life God gave him to act.' It would have been impossible to find a better metaphor for what these early Christian philosophers wished to express, namely that the substance of the Godhead was one, but that it had manifested itself to us under three aspects, or, as it were, under three masks, the Father, the Son, and the Holy Ghost. This form of thought would have satisfied the simplest peasant and the most hair-splitting philosopher, so long as they were content to see through the glass of metaphor darkly. But the Eastern and Western Churches spoke two different languages, and the Greek word prosôpon always differed somewhat from the Latin word persona, by which it was translated. Prosôpon retained more or less the meaning of mask, persona added to it the meaning of the wearer of the mask. Persona connoted what stood behind the mask, the hypostasis; prosôpon did not always.

Hence the Greek ecclesiastics after a while became afraid of πρόσωπον or mask. They thought it might seem to favour the opinion of Sabellius, who maintained that there was one ὑπόστασις, substance, in the Godhead, and that Father, Son and Holy Ghost were but three πρόσωπα, or ὀνόματα, names, or ἐνέργειαι, manifestations. But they were equally afraid that if Father, Son, and Holy Ghost were represented as too distinct from each other, there was danger of Arianism, and that instead of three *πρόσωπα* they would have three *οὐσίαι*. They therefore took refuge in saying that there was in the Godhead one *οὐσία*, essence, but three *ὑποστάσεις*, substances. Unfortunately the distinction between *οὐσία*, essentia, and *ὑπόστασις*, substantia, was not one sanctioned by philosophers at large, and even the earlier Christian writers had used *οὐσία* and *ὑπόστασις* as synonymous. Those therefore who laid the greater stress on the unity of the Godhead remonstrated against the admission of three *ὑποστάσεις* which, in spite of all declarations to the contrary, seemed to them the same as *οὐσίαι*. It was all very well to say, as Basilius did, that *οὐσία*, essence, differed from *ὑπόστασις*, substance, as the general does from the singular, as for instance 'animal' differs from 'this man.' This did not satisfy either the philosophical or the theological conscience of honest thinkers, more particularly of those who had accustomed themselves to the use of the word persona in Latin.

There is a most touching letter of St. Jerome's to Pope Damasus[1]. He had been a follower of Origen, and though he brought himself to speak of tres personae, his conscience revolted against the new formula, tres hypostases, which to his mind conveyed the meaning of three substances. 'Which apostle,' he says, 'has ever uttered this? What new Paul, or teacher of the Gentiles, taught it? I ask, What can be understood by those hypostases?

[1] Vallarsi's edition of St. Jerome, in Migne's 'Patrologia Latina,' vol. xxii, Epist. xv. 23.

They answer, Three subsisting persons. We answer that we hold that faith. But they are not satisfied with what we mean, they insist on our using the very word, because some kind of poison is supposed to be hidden in the very syllables. We cry out that if any one does not confess the three hypostases as three enhypostata, that is, as three subsisting personae, let him be anathema. But because we do not learn the (new) words, we are judged heretical. Surely, if any one who takes hypostasis for *οὐσία* (substance) says that there is not one *οὐσία* in the three personae, he is a stranger to Christ. . . . Decide, I adjure you, if you like, and I shall not be afraid to say three hypostases. If you command it, let there be a new confession after that of Nicaea, and let us orthodox Christians declare our faith in similar words with the Arians! The whole school of secular knowledge recognises hypostasis as nothing else but *οὐσία*. And will any one, I ask, proclaim with his sacrilegious mouth three substances? There is one only nature of God which exists truly. . . . God alone who is eternal, that is, who has no beginning, has really the name of substance. . . . And because that nature alone is perfect, and there subsists but one Godhead in the three persons, which exists really and is one nature only, therefore whosoever says that there are three, namely three substances, i. e. *οὐσίαι*, dares really, under the cloak of piety, to assert that there are three natures. . . . Let us, please, hear no more of three hypostases, but let us retain the one.'

In spite of these remonstrances, however, St. Jerome had to yield. He had to use the new word *ὑποστάσις*, substantia, instead of persona, whether he could connect a new meaning with it or not. The Christian Fathers ought to have been most grateful for finding in their language such a word and such a metaphor as πρόσωπον or persona, which could be honestly applied to express what they meant by the three manifestations of the Godhead. But when that metaphor was dropt, and people were asked to predicate three ὑποστάσεις or substances of one οὐσία or essence, they could hardly help either drifting into some kind of Arianism, or using words devoid of all meaning[1].

Even here the biography of persona is not yet concluded. Still greater issues sprang from that word, and they continue to agitate the minds of the most serious thinkers of our own age. Our forefathers delighted in fathoming, as they thought, the true nature of the Godhead. There was no divine abyss into which they hesitated to plunge, no mystery into which they thought they could not throw the plummet of their language. We have grown somewhat wiser, perhaps more reverent. But our philosophers have thrown themselves with all the greater zest upon a new problem, namely, the exploration of the mystery of human nature. And here also the only diving apparatus which was at hand for their hazardous enterprise was language, and again the old word persona had to be put under requisition. We are told that what distinguishes us from all other living beings is that we are personal beings. We are persons, responsible persons, and our very being, our life and immortality, are represented as depending on our

[1] See Hagenbach, 'Lehrbuch der Dogmengeschichte' (Leipzig, 1867), pp. 187–221.

personality. But if we ask what this personality means, and why we are called personae, the answers are very ambiguous. Does our personality consist in our being English or German, in our being young or old, male or female, wise or foolish? And if not, what remains when all these distinctions vanish? Is there a higher Ego of which our human ego is but the shadow? From most philosophers we get but uncertain and evasive answers to these questions, and perhaps even here, in the darkest passages of psychological and metaphysical inquiry, a true knowledge of language may prove our best guide.

Let us remember that persona had two meanings, that it meant originally a mask, but that it soon came to be used as the name of the wearer of the mask. Knowing how many ambiguities of thought arose from this, we have a right to ask, Does our personality consist in the persona we are wearing, in our body, our senses, our language and our reason, our thoughts, or does our true personality lie somewhere else? It may be that at times we so forget ourselves, our true Self, as to imagine that we are Romeo and Juliet, King Lear, or Prince Hamlet. Nor can we doubt that we are responsible each for his own *dramatis persona*, that we are hissed or applauded, punished or rewarded, according as we act the part allotted to us in this earthly drama, badly or well. But the time comes when we awake, when we feel that not only our flesh and our blood, but all that we have been made to feel, to think and to say, was outside our true self; that we were witnesses, not actors; and that before we can go home, we must take off our masks, standing like strangers on a strange stage, and wondering how for so long a time we did not perceive even within ourselves the simple distinction between *persona* and *persona*, between the mask and the wearer.

There is a Sanskrit verse which an Indian friend of mine, a famous Minister of State, sent me when retiring from the world to spend his last years in contemplation of the highest problems:—

No deho nendriyâ*n*i ksharam atik*apalam* no mano naiva buddhi*h*,
Prâ*n*o naivâham asmîty akhila*g*a*d*am ida*m* vastu*g*âta*m* katha*m* syâm;
Nâha*m* kâme na dârân g*r*ihasutasu*g*anakshetravittâdi dûram,
Sâkshî *k*itpratyagâtmâ nikhila*g*a*g*adadhish*th*ânabhûta*h* sivo 'ham.

'I am not this body, nor the senses, nor this perishable, fickle mind, not even the understanding; I am not indeed this breath; how should I be this entirely dull matter? I do not desire, no, not wife, far less houses, sons, friends, land, and wealth. I am the witness only, the perceiving inner self, the support of the whole world, and blessed.'

IV. School-day Recollections.

WHEN speaking of the traces of the nursery which without much effort can still be discovered in words now used to convey the highest abstractions in philosophy, I remarked that the school-days also had left their impression on the Aryan vocabulary, and that I hoped to point out some of them on a future occasion.

Who were our schoolmasters? I speak, of course, of European nations only, and of those who employ Aryan languages, whether Celtic, Teutonic, Romanic, Slavonic, or Greek. The ancestors of these people, nations, and languages spent their nursery-days, together with such apparently heterogeneous races as Hindus, Persians, Armenians, and others, far away from their present abodes; according to some, on the high plateau of Asia, according to others, in more northern latitudes. But wherever their cradle stood, certain it is that they all carried away from their long-forgotten home their words for father and mother, sister and brother, dog, cow, and horse, food and drink, nay, even for that unknown Being to whom they addressed their simple prayers. These words are so little changed that even now, if carefully cleaned and placed under the microscope of the scholar, they appear almost identical.

But when the time came to go to school, and to learn the A B C, and other rudiments of knowledge and faith, the Aryan people, nations, and languages had separated. Some had gone towards the south-east, the ancestors of Hindus and Persians, others had proceeded towards the north-west, and we know little about their wild school-days except what by chance has remained imbedded in some of the layers of their language.

In Europe every nation has, directly or indirectly, received its first training from the Greeks. The Greeks taught the Romans, and the Romans, alone or assisted by the Greeks, taught the rest of Europe. We know very little about the early relations between Greeks and Romans, and what the Greeks and Romans themselves have told us about the doings of their ancestors is generally very fabulous. But there are historical documents which cannot be falsified, though they may be often difficult to interpret, I mean the words of a language. If we wished to know, for instance, who has taught us the game of chess, the name of chess would tell us better than anything else that it came to the West from Persia. In spite of all that has been written to the contrary, chess was originally the game of Kings, the game of Shahs. This word Shah became in Old French eschac, It. scacco, Germ. Schach; while the Old French eschecs was further corrupted into chess. The more original form chec has likewise been preserved, though we little think of it when we draw a cheque, or when we suffer a check, or when we speak of the Chancellor of the Exchequer. The great object of the chess-player is to protect the king, and when the king is in danger, the opponent is obliged to say check, i.e. Shah, the king! In the Book of the Duchesse, 658, as quoted by Professor Skeat, we read: 'Therewith Fortune seyde, "*chek* here!" and "*mate*" in the myd point of the *chekkere*'; i.e. Thereupon Fortune said '*check* here!' and '*mate*' in the middle of the chess-board. After this the various meanings of check, cheque, or exchequer become easily intelligible, though it is quite true that if similar changes of meaning, which in our case we can watch by the light of history, had taken place in the dimness of prehistoric ages, it would be difficult to convince the sceptic that *exchequer* or *scaccarium*, the name of the chess-board, was afterwards used for the checkered cloth on which accounts were calculated by means of counters, and that a checkered career was a life with many cross-lines, which might end with check mate, literally, 'the king is dead.'

If therefore the Romans had foreign schoolmasters, if they learnt their letters from Greek pedagogues, we should expect to find traces of that early training in their language. And so we do, though not always so clearly as we should wish. The name of the alphabet is clear enough. It was the Greek ἀλφάβητος. Juvenal, xiv. 209, says, *hoc discunt omnes ante alpha et beta puellae*, 'all girls learn this before they learn the alphabet.' That word is, in fact, worth more than many chapters of Herodotus, for it teaches us that, whatever historical sceptics may say, some Phenicians, call them Cadmus or any other name, had something to do with the early civilisation of Greece; and secondly, that these Phenicians had received the first impulse that led them to invent alphabetic writing from Egypt. For, after reading all that has lately been written on the subject, I still hold to Rougé's great discovery, that the Phenician were modifications of Egyptian hieratic letters. If the idea, first put forward by Lepsius in 1835, that the Phenician are modifications of the cuneiform letters, could be strengthened by new evidence, we ought never to be so completely convinced of the truth of our own opinion as to refuse a dispassionate hearing to any new theory. The important point, however, is this, that whatever derivation of our alphabet we adopt must be applicable to the whole series, not to a few letters only. This condition seems to me as yet to be better fulfilled by the theory put forward by the late Vicomte de Rougé than by any other hypothesis.

But it is very strange that the Romans, if they learnt their letters from the Greeks, should not have called them by a Greek name. They call them literae, a word which we hardly know how to spell correctly, much less how to explain etymologically. It is possible, of course, that the Italians or the Etruscans were cognisant of writing, long before Greek writing-masters settled at Rome. In that case litera or littera may be a foreign word of utterly unknown origin. Some scholars derive it from lino, to besmear, to daub. But there is no Latin suffix tera, added to verbal roots, and if there were, it would probably leave the vowel of lino short, as in the participle litus. And lastly, lino, if applied to writing, means to rub out, not to write. Lĭtura is the recognised word for putting wax on a writing tablet in order to erase something written. It is just possible that children may have called their letters, which in their exercises had constantly to be rubbed out, lîterae, and the use of oblîterare, to obliterate, in the same sense as oblinere, would seem to point in the same direction; but there is no evidence for it.

Such has been the despair to which comparative as well as classical scholars have been driven by the word litera that a French *savant*, who better than anybody combines in himself both characters, derives it from the Greek diphthera. Professor Bréal, in the 'Mémoires de la Société Linguistique,' vol. vi, points out that a *διφθεράλοιφος*, parchment writer, was used in Cyprus as a name for schoolmaster. Diphthera, a very different word in Greek, means prepared skins, the principal writing material before papyrus came in. This diphthera, meaning skin, and skin only, M. Bréal supposes to have been changed into littera, and to have assumed the meaning of letter. The transition of meaning is violent, yet not impossible. Far more difficult is the change of an initial Greek d into a Latin l, in a word borrowed by the Romans from the Greeks. Professor Bréal appeals to *δάκρυ* and lacruma, but these are cognate, not borrowed words, and the same applies to *δάηρ* and levir. In the middle of a word, however, that change is recognised, as in 'Οδυσσεύς, Lat. Ulyxes[1], and if we could find an analogy for the change of phth into tt, Professor Bréal's conjecture might indeed claim a certain plausibility. This, however, seems hopeless. To appeal to such modern changes as baptiser, pronounced bâtiser, or the late corrupt spelling Aegytus for Aegyptus, carries no conviction, for many things are possible in one period of a language which are utterly impossible in another. All that

[1] M. M., Selected Essays, vol. i. p. 498.

remains for the present is to confess our ignorance, a very good lesson now and then, to the etymologist as well as to everybody else.

Other words, however, are more outspoken. That the Romans received their first schooling from the Greeks we may gather from the very word schooling. To the Greeks, conversations, disputations, and even lectures were a real relaxation and pleasure, and they therefore called them σχολή. The Greek word schole is connected with ἔχω, i. e. σέχω, and meant originally a halt, a pause, a rest. The Romans, when they learnt from the Greeks to have their literary conversaziones in the house of the Scipios and elsewhere, adopted the name schola, instead of otium, and soon the place where such meetings were held, soon also the people who met there, were called a school. We now have school and schools and scholar and scholarship and scholastic philosophy, and many more ideas of the same kind, all expressed by words derived from σχολή, the delightful rest at a Roman villa after the heat of the day was over. It was the elder Scipio Africanus[1] who used to say that he never was less idle (otiosus) than when he was idle, i. e. when he enjoyed his σχολή.

Besides schola, we find at Rome a number of Greek words connected with school-life, such as gymnasium, pedagogue, charta, paper or letter, epistula, bibliotheca, diptycha, a writing-tablet of two leaves, grammaticus, a scholar, grammatista, a schoolmaster, graphium, a writing-style, orthographia, macrocollum, large-sized paper, papyrus, byblos, pegma, a bookcase, philologia,

[1] Cic. de Off. iii. 1.

scheda, a leaf, Germ. Zettel, thema, a subject, tomus, a tome, and many more.

Every one of these words has a history of its own, and not a few of them are familiar to us in English, French, and German, under various disguises. From charta we have Magna Charta, charter, and chartist; from byblos, Bible; from scheda, to be scheduled, a not very pleasant recollection of the last Parliamentary election.

But without dwelling any longer on this class of words, which recall rather the outward circumstances of education than education itself, I wish to examine here some terms which form the very framework of our thoughts, and which again point to Greece as the intellectual workshop in which they were manufactured for the first time.

What should we be without grammar? I do not mean that we should make mistakes in declension and conjugation. The Hottentots speak their own language as correctly as we speak our own. But ask them what is the nominative or accusative, the active or passive, the subject and predicate, and they will simply stare at you. I went through this process with some Japanese pupils of mine who came to Oxford to learn Sanskrit. My great difficulty with them was, not to make them learn the paradigms by heart, but to teach them such simple concepts as nominative and accusative. All these pigeon-holes we find almost ready-made in our mind. They are taught us when we begin to speak and to think. They constitute part of that intellectual wealth which comes to us almost by inheritance. But such concepts and such terms as noun, adjective, verb, case, number, gender, subject, predicate, transitive, or intransitive, had all to be elaborated, and they were elaborated not without great effort by the Greeks. From the Greeks they migrated to Rome. They were translated more or less correctly by the Greek schoolmasters, with the help, it may be, of such men as the Scipios, or Cicero or Caesar, and they now form the common property of all mankind. We all speak of cases, but why the different terminations of the nominative, genitive, dative, and accusative should be called cases we never ask. They were called so because the grammatistae at Rome thought casus the nearest approach to the Greek πτῶσις, and πτῶσις, or fall, was used to express the relation in which, as we say, one word stood to another, or, as the Greeks said, one word fell on another, or leant towards another. That was why the genitive, dative, and accusative were called cases, and why most philosophers declared that the nominative should not be called a case, for the nominative stands straight out by itself, and the other cases only can properly be said to lean against it.

Sanskrit grammarians, too, distinguish the nominative and vocative from the other cases. All cases are called kâraka, lit. doing, i.e. doing the work of a sentence, or helping the verb. But nominative and vocative cannot claim that name, nor, what is curious, the genitive, namely when the genitive is used, as it generally is, as a predicate, and not as an ablative. See B. Liebich, 'Die Casuslehre der Indischen Grammatiker' (1885), p. 7.

Grammar, however, is by no means the only subject which the Romans and we, as their pupils, learnt from the Greeks. Mathematics, music, and many other arts, all draw their original terminology from the same source. Many of the terms which were originally purely technical have long ceased to be so, and are now used by many people without the least thought of their original intention, nay, very often in a sense the very opposite of that in which our ancient Greek schoolmasters used it.

We say, 'for instance.' Instance, the Latin instantia, is a translation of the Greek ἔνστασις, but ἔνστασις, so far from being an example in support of an opinion, was originally an objection to an argument, or rather a proposition opposed to another proposition (Arist. Analyt. pr. ii. 26).

We speak of a typical instance. Now what is typical? It is derived from the Greek τύπος, the name which Greek artists used of their first sketches, the abbozzi of the Italians. Pliny speaks of an artist who, by means of a light, threw the shadow of a profile on a wall, and then sketched the outlines of that shadow. That sketch, which was afterwards used for a picture or a bust, was a type, what the Romans called adumbratio. Typos, however, derived from τύπτειν, must originally have meant that which strikes or that which is struck, and before it could be applied to a mere outline it must have meant the rude figure hammered out of metal or chiselled out of stone. This was called the type of a man, before it became his likeness; it was therefore the general form of man, and thus only could type have been used afterwards for the general form or idea of a thing, and a typical instance be employed in the sense of a general example, containing all that is really essential. When we read of *τύποι*, used by the Greeks in the sense of letters, we might almost suppose that they meant the same as our types. The Greeks, however, used *τύποι γραμμάτων* in the sense of marks of letters; we use types for what produces these marks, and we distinguish between the iron punch, the poinçon, i. e. punctio, and the copper matrix, which is stamped by it, and which in turn is used for casting the leaden types.

This looking behind the back of words may not seem very amusing, but to the student of the growth of thought it is a most interesting subject. It shows us how we came into possession of the intellectual tools, the *ὄργανα*, the instruments of thought, and makes us aware of the common debt of gratitude we owe to those who first fashioned these tools.

We speak of an amusing subject, and nothing seems simpler and more natural than such an expression. We are not aware that in using it we are simply speaking Greek. I do not mean to say that amusing has anything to do with the Greek Muses, though, I confess, I am by no means certain of its real origin. But such a common expression as subject, i.e. 'thrown under,' is certainly Greek, and could have grown on Greek soil only. It is, of course, the Greek *ὑποκείμενον*, which Aristotle uses in two senses—first, as that which underlies the predicate, for instance, the horse is white; secondly, as that which in nature underlies the acts which we perceive, what we now call the substance of all things. The Romans translated this word in both senses by subjectum. Hence, in the language of mediæval philosophers the subjective was the substance, what Kant would call das Ding an sich, while the objective was the phenomenon as perceived by us. Strange to say, in modern philosophy there has been a complete revulsion, so that with Kant the subjective is the phenomenal, the objective the real, independent of the forms of thought. Even in our ordinary language this extraordinary change in the meaning of subject and object tells. We can speak in English and French of the subject of a treatise; we could never say so in German, where the subject of a treatise is called the object, never the subject.

As little as we are conscious of speaking or thinking in Greek when we call an individual a mauvais sujet, do we know that even an individual is a Greek term? It is a mere translation of an atom, i. e. that which can be no further divided and explained, though it is that which virtually contains the germs both of species and of genus, and alone is able to account for the origin of species.

But why virtually? Virtually means potentially, as, for instance, fire is contained virtually in the flint, rain in the cloud, the oak in the acorn, or, more generally, every effect in its cause. At last virtually comes to mean 'to all intents and purposes,' as when certain politicians say that Home Rule amounts virtually to political separation. Now all this is again what the Romans, when at school, learnt from the Greeks, and we from the Romans. Aristotle was the first, as we said before, to introduce the extremely useful distinction between δύναμις, potentia, and ἐνέργεια, actus, and as the Romans rendered δύναμις not only by potentia, but likewise by virtus, lit. manhood, then strength and virtue, virtually became a current coin in all the literary intercourse of Europe, and was so much depraved and discoloured that we may now use it in the sense of almost, while actually in such phrases as, 'he has actually been and done it,' has no other object than to convey an unequivocal assertion.

One more word and we shall have done with the specimens of our schoolboy vocabulary. We have only to look around, for almost every sentence contains a few of these scholastic gems, set in the motley mosaic of our modern speech. In the expression, 'an unequivocal assertion,' unequivocal is again scholastic Greek. The history of this word is much entangled, or, as Bishop Berkeley calls it, embrangled; but we must try to disembrangle it as well as we can.

Aequivocus is the translation of Aristotle's *ὁμώνυμον*, aequivocum, which he opposes to *συνώνυμον*, or univocum. In Aristotle[1] the distinction is quite clear, but it has been greatly blurred by modern logicians, who did not see that Aristotle, when using these terms, spoke of things, and not of words. Synonyma were things which shared the same name for the same reason, as, for instance, when both man and ox are called animal. Homonyma were things which shared the same name, but not for the same reason, as when in Greek both man and an image were called *ζῷον*. Lastly, certain things are called Polyonyma, when they are called by several names, as when the same god was called Phoibos and Apollon. We now speak of two words as synonyms when they have

[1] M. M., 'Lectures on the Science of Language,' vol. ii. p. 390.

the same meaning, as Phoibos and Apollon. We call words *homonyms* if they have the same sound but different meanings, as *ζῷον*, meaning man and picture, or such words also as the English *sty* and *sty*, *right* and *write*. With Aristotle the distinction of homonymous and synonymous was of great importance. He constantly warns his disciples against the dangers that lurk in synonyms—not in synonyms in our sense of the word, but in synonymous subjects which are called by the same name and for the same reason, but which nevertheless are as different as man and ox, though both are animals. Synonymous subjects, however, belong, at all events, to the same genus; not so homonymous. Hence the expression *generatio aequivoca*, applied originally to the supposed birth of an animal which does not belong to the same genus as its parents. Again, if a man used a word which could be applied to various homonymous objects, without making it quite clear to what special object he wished the word to be applied, that was *equivocation*, and was not very far from duplicity or lying. Lastly, a social position, not very well defined, liable to doubt and misgivings, was called *equivocal*, and in French *équivoque* is a lenient term for what is really improper or indelicate.

Think of old Aristotle painfully evolving his logical terminology, and defining what should be called *synonymous*, *homonymous*, *polyonymous*, in order that in the end *homonymous*, i.e. *equivocal*, should become a convenient expression to indicate rather than to define the doubtful character of a French novel!

There are many more words of the same character,

relics of our Aryan schoolboy days. They are often much disguised, and hardly to be recognised beneath their rusty vizor. But whenever the vizor can be lifted we recognise the Greek face, and we can often still catch the accents which were heard for the first time in the Lyceum or in the Stoa.

V. Weighing, Buying, and Selling.

When we have known a child in its earliest youth, carried it in our arms, played and romped with it, petted and patted it, and then meet it, or rather him, again, grey-haired and grave, a husband, a father of a family, it may be even a grandfather, we often wonder whether a being so totally changed can really be the same being.

A similar wondering comes over us whenever we meet with words in English, French, or German, which we have known in their earliest childhood, whether in Latin, Greek, or Sanskrit. We know they are the same words, but they have assumed an expression and character so totally different from that which we remember when we first met them, that with them too we can hardly believe that they are the same words, and that there is an unbroken continuity between their childhood and their old age.

Spandate in Sanskrit means he shakes, he quivers; *il pense* in French means he thinks. We know that these two words have sprung from the same root, have grown almost on the same stem; but through what ramifications they have spread in such different directions and become so widely separated is difficult to imagine. Let us try whether we can discover some of the missing links.

Spandate means he shakes, he moves, he kicks, he quivers. Any kind of spasmodic motion can be expressed by that Sanskrit verb. Corresponding to it we find in Greek σφαδάζειν, to toss the body about, to struggle, σφοδ-ρός, impetuous, and σφενδ-όνη, a sling.

Before tracing the same word in Latin, we must remember two things. First, almost every root may give rise both to a transitive and intransitive verb; spand, therefore, may be used not only in the sense of shaking, i.e. being in a state of shaking, but likewise in the sense of shaking, i.e. shaking or moving anything up and down. Secondly, the initial s before p is an uncertain consonant, and comes and goes, we cannot tell how or why. Thus we find in Sanskrit itself spas and pas, to see; stan, to sound, to thunder, and tan, to stretch; stanayitnú, thunder; tanayitnú, thundering; skar and kar, to make, &c. We may also add that the aspiration of p after s, sph for sp, is common in Greek, but in Greek only[1].

After these preliminary remarks we can rest assured that the equation between the Sanskrit spand, the Greek σφανδ, and the Latin pendo is correct. But what about the meaning? Pendo in Latin means I weigh and I pay, and the first question is how it could have assumed that meaning if it meant originally I shake? It is generally supposed that the first meaning of pendere was to fasten something to a balance and thus to weigh it. But pendere is never used in that sense in Latin. It always means either to weigh or to pay. In fact, if we wish to

[1] Kuhn's 'Zeitschrift,' xxii. p. 105.

account for the transition of meaning from shaking to weighing, we must at first forget the balance altogether. A balance, though, no doubt, a very ancient invention, is nevertheless an artificial machine, and such machines do not belong to the earliest periods in the growth of civilisation, of thought, and of language. Nor has the balance a common Aryan name, though the necessity of weighing things had probably been felt long before the Aryan separation. We must remember, however, that even at present, when we possess every kind of contrivance for weighing, we may often see a peasant, if he is asked the weight of a goose, lifting up the bird bodily by its legs and shaking it, and then putting it down and saying, 'About ten pounds, I guess.' This was the oldest balance, and it is also the most modern, for we have only to watch ourselves in order to find that we constantly lift and shake a thing in our hand in order to find out roughly how much its weight might be. Any railway-porter will guess the weight of a portmanteau by that rough-and-ready prehistoric process, while a letter-sorter will, in the same way, tell the true weight of a letter within half-an-ounce. The man with his outstretched arms, holding something in each, was the type of the balance with two scales; the man lifting and shaking something with his right hand was the type of the statera. From this point of view, too, it is true that, as Protagoras said[1], 'Man is the measure of all things,' *παντῶν μέτρον ὁ ἄνθρωπος*.

Pendo, therefore, meant really first to shake, to lift, and afterwards only to weigh. The common idea

[1] Plato, 'Krat.' 386.

that pendere meant to weigh, because originally it meant to attach something to the beam of the balance, has no foundation whatever. It is generally said that pendêre, to hang, was derived from pendere, to weigh. Correctly speaking, however, both are derived from the same root, one as an intransitive, pendêre, to swing; the other as a transitive, pendere, to swing, to shake, to lift, to weigh.

From meaning to weigh, pendere came to mean *to pay*, because one of the earliest forms of payment in Italy consisted in weighing metals. Thus, *pretium quod emptor penderet* meant originally 'the price which the buyer should weigh out on the balance,' i.e. the price which he should pay.

The transition from this to weighing in the sense of pondering, valuing, considering, thinking, is easy enough. We find magni pendere, to esteem highly, parvi pendere, to esteem lightly, or vilipendere, to consider things as vile, a word which is still used in English, to vilipend.

Pensum was originally anything weighed out, such as, for instance, a portion of wool weighed out for a day's work to the slaves of Rome. From it came a new verb, pensare, meaning again to weigh. Thus the Romans said *pensare aliquos eâdem trutinâ*, to weigh persons in one and the same balance. It was more frequently used, however, in the sense of requiting, or, as we now say, compensating, as in *beneficia beneficiis pensare*, to requite, or to recompense benefits by benefits. It also meant to make up for and to purchase. But the meaning of weighing is never entirely lost, and even in such expressions as *ex factis, non ex dictis, amicos pensare*, 'to judge one's friends, not by words, but by deeds,' we could easily substitute to weigh for to judge.

The gap between shaking (Sk. spandate) and thinking (il pense), wide as it seems, has thus been bridged over, and in reconstructing that bridge we come across many more traces of the steps by which, here as elsewhere, the human mind climbed up from the lower valleys of mere matter of fact to the commanding heights of abstract thought.

We saw that pendere and pensare, when used in the sense of paying, meant originally to weigh the rude metal, the *aes rude*, such as it was used at Rome before the adoption of coined money. It was supposed, therefore, that in aestimare, to value, to esteem, we had a similar relic of the ancient custom of weighing metal. Some scholars, like Corssen[1], saw in the second half timare the Greek *τιμα*— of *τίμημα*, valuing, but they forgot that *τιμᾶν* was a Greek word, unknown in Latin, and that such compounds of Latin and Greek words are not admissible. Others thought that the second portion had something to do with *τέμνειν*, to cut, and that cutting the metal meant fixing the proper prices. But the same objection applies to this derivation. Latin does not know *τέμνειν*, nor does it often form such hybrid compounds. The explanation of aestimare is by no means easy, and to derive it from the Sanskrit root ISH, to wish, or the Sabine aisos, prayer, or, with Bopp in his Glossary, 1867, to explain aid-tumo as adhi-tumo, is no more than to confess that its derivation is impossible. If I may venture on a new etymology, I

[1] 'Aussprache der Lateinischen Sprache,' ii. p. 527; see also Bréal et Bailly, 'Dictionnaire Etymologique Latin,' s.v. *aestimare*.

should compare Latin words formed by timus, such as mari-timus, close to the sea, fini-timus, close to the frontier. Closeness to a thing came to mean occupation with a thing, so that aedi-tumus occurs as one connected with the temple, a sacristan, and from it aeditumari, to act the part of a sacristan. Now as aeditumari presupposes aeditumus, au-tumari, to surmise, like augurari and auspicari, presupposes au-tumus. This word is lost in Latin, but its meaning could hardly have been anything but one conversant with birds and the auguries of birds. Applying this to aestumare, I should feel inclined to derive it from a lost word, aes-tumus, one conversant with aes, an aerarius, who fixes the true value of metal. This would give to aestimare the meaning which it possesses, namely to appraise, to value, to esteem.

But to return to pendo, we can trace back to it a large class of words familiar to us in Latin, French, and English.

Thus dependere, or depensare, to weigh out, to pay, accounts for the French dépenser.

Expendere, to weigh out, to pay, explains the English to expend, expenses, and expensive.

From this, or, more properly, from dispendere, comes our spending, which sounds very much like a Saxon word, particularly in such a compound as spendthrift, but is, nevertheless, borrowed from Latin. The preposition dis appears in French as dis and di in old compounds, as dis, or dés (before vowels), and dé (before consonants), in new formations. In Italian dis before consonants often dwindles down to a mere s, as in s-traziare for dis-traziare, to distract, spendere for dispendere, to spend. The same change appears already in Mediæval Latin, as in spendium, spensa, for dispensium and dispensa. So far, no doubt, as phonetic rules are concerned, Italian spendere and spendio might come from expendere and expendium, as well as from dispendere and dispendium, for ex as well as dis dwindles down to s in Italian, as we see in spandere from expandere, spedire from expedire, &c.[1] Historical tradition, however, points to dispendere, not to expendere, as the original of our spending.

Spencer, now a very aristocratic name, was originally a Dispenser, the official employed in a dispensary; nay, a spence was an old English word for buttery or cellar.

Appendere in Latin does never mean to append, but to weigh out something to a buyer, and appendix was originally what was thrown in, the same as mantissa. After a time, however, appendix came to mean any appendage or addition, and the word, or its derivative appendium, turns up again under a strange disguise, as penthouse. For penthouse, a projecting shed, is a corruption, due to a popular etymology of pentice, for appentice, and had originally nothing to do either with pent or with house.

Impendere, again, meant originally to weigh out, to expend, then to devote, to apply.

Compendere meant to weigh together, not one by one; and hence compendium, a weighing together,

[1] Professor Skeat, in his 'Etymological Dictionary,' which is a mine of useful information, gives the same derivation, but he takes *dispendere* for another form of *dispandere*, 'to spread, to expand.'

a short process, and compendious, brief. Even Compiègne, the beautiful Compiègne, where Napoléon III. used to pass the summer, was originally compendium, i.e. compendium viae, a short cut, and occurs under that name as early as the time of King Chlodwig.

Perpendere is to weigh carefully or to examine; perpensus meant deliberate, which likewise comes from libra, balance; and what we now call 'of malice prepense' was originally, I believe, 'of malice perpense,' i.e. with deliberate malice.

Rependere means to weigh back, to pay back, to repay, to requite, though also to weigh again, to ponder.

In all these compounds the original meaning of pendere, to shake, to lift, to weigh, is still clearly visible. In one compound only, in suspendere, it has almost vanished, for suspendere is always used in the sense of suspending, hanging up, stopping, supporting; never, I believe, in that of weighing.

We could collect nearly as many derivative meanings in compounds formed with pensare; such as compensare, to counterbalance, to recompense or to compensate; dispensare, to weigh out, to pay out, to distribute, to manage, to order; expensare, perpensare, repensare, &c., all showing the different ways in which language, like a good dispensatrix, managed with a very limited supply of material to satisfy every possible wish or whim of the human mind.

Nor have we mentioned yet a large number of derivatives formed directly from the root pend, such as pondus, weight, now a pound, pensio, payment, or pension, stipendium, for stipi-pendium, originally the payment of the stips, the small piece of money paid to the soldier, whom we now call soldier because he receives a sou or a sol, a solidus, a hard coin, or, what is the same, because he receives his pay, in German Sold.

The French poids, weight, was formerly written pois, which is preserved in avoirdupois, because it was derived from pensum, pesum, and not from pondus. Probably in order to distinguish pois, pea, from pois, weight, a learned printer introduced the diacritical d, which he remembered in pondus, just as an English printer introduced the s into island, because he remembered the s of isle and insula, and forgot the A.S. ígland, the M.E. iland, the German Eiland. The Middle High-German Einland, from which Kluge has again derived Eiland, as if 'land lying alone,' is entirely due to a popular etymology. The High-Germans, as land-lubbers, had forgotten the original meaning of Eiland, i.e. water-land, and therefore misinterpreted it as Einland.

We have thus seen how with such heavy words as pendere, shaking and lifting, pensare, weighing, language managed in the end to express such abstract and airy notions as recompense, dispensation, pensive, and even imponderable substances. One unbroken chain connects the two extremes, and the further we grope our way back by means of that unbroken chain, the clearer shall we see how language becomes an historical guide, and reveals to us chapters after chapters in the early history of civilisation which no other guide could have pointed out. It shows us the Aryan peasant lifting and shaking his goods, before selling or buying them. It shows us the Aryan trader weighing his rude metal in paying his customer.

It shows us the Roman soldier receiving his stips, possibly at first a mere bar of metal, as a compensation for his military service, and likewise a pension, when he had become unfit for active service. We also see the origin of the balance, originally in Greek stathmos, i.e. an upright post with a beam, representing the man standing, with his arm outstretched. The weight which made the arm or beam stand in different positions was called statêr, from which the Romans formed statera, balance, The Sanskrit name for balance is tulâ, and the verb tolayati means to lift in order to weigh. Both words seem connected with the Latin tulo, tetuli, (t)latus, also with tollo, to lift, and tolerare, to bear, and with the Greek *πολύ-τλας*, much-enduring, *τάλ-αντον,* weight and balance. From this to talent, to putting one's talent in a napkin, i.e. to talent in the sense of natural endowments, there is again a long, though a clear and intelligible transition.

Balance, It. bilancia, is of course bi-lanx, having two scales, and scales is now used in much the same sense as balance.

Were we to follow up the various derivatives of the intransitive pendêre, to swing, to hang, we should considerably increase our store of words. We should easily account for dependents, dependencies, independence; for impending dangers and for dangerous propensities, for suspended animation and suspension of judgment, for the pendulum of a clock and for all perpendicular movements.

Let us remember then that in spand and pend we had a root which from meaning to shake, to lift, came to mean to weigh and to pay, and let us now examine another root which also meant originally to shake, namely KAP or KAMP, and branched off afterwards into meanings analogous to those of pendere in its later phases.

KAMP in Sanskrit means to tremble, and to make tremble.

With the preposition anu, after, anu-kamp becomes an excellent expression for sympathy, lit. to tremble after some one else, to vibrate in sympathy with him.

Kapi, ape, has been supposed to come from the same root, meaning the climbing or swinging animal, and from it kapila, kapisa, monkey-like, i.e. brown, or reddish brown. This, however, is doubtful.

KAP or KAMP, if it existed in Latin, would be cap, and this we have in capio, cepi, captum, to take, but originally to shake and to lift, to lay hold of and capture. But while, if used by itself, capere expresses rather a violent form of taking, as in captivus, a prisoner, we find it in mancipium, expressing a recognised or legal form of taking, namely buying. Mancipium is the mode of formal sale by a symbolical taking of something in the hand and weighing out of the money. It is afterwards used for what is thus sold and acquired, particularly a slave. Mancipo and mancupo mean to capture, and likewise to dispose of or to sell, while manceps is a purchaser. The two meanings of selling and buying vary according as the act of 'hand-taking' was intended for the one or the other purpose.

If cap, as we see in mancipium, could be used in the sense of lifting, offering for sale, it becomes possible that κάπηλος and καπηλεύω may be derived from the same root. The word, however, stands too isolated in Greek to admit of any certain etymology. The same applies to Latin caupo, a huckster and innkeeper, and côpa, his female associate. Here the au and o for a admit of explanation, but the derivation is nevertheless very doubtful. What seems more certain is that Old Slavonic kupiti, to buy, and Gothic kaupôn were borrowed from the Roman caupones, who as travelling traders may have brought both drink and foreign wares to the inhabitants of Slavonic, Celtic, and Germanic provinces.

But while in the Latin capere the original meaning of shaking, lifting, has almost entirely vanished, we can discover clearer traces of it in German. The Gothic haf-jan, hôf is the same as Latin capio, cepi; so is A.S. hebban, hôf; English heave, hove; German heben, hob. They all mean to lift, to raise. Ein Hebel is a lever, Latin vectis; erheben means to lift up; heblich in erheblich means heavy, unerheblich, unimportant; erhaben and erhoben mean high. The first meaning of this root is not, therefore, as Grimm supposes, to take and then to lift, but rather to lift and then to take. In some expressions heben reminds us strongly of weighing, as in the expression Das hebt sich, literally 'it lifts itself,' it is equal, e.g. Zehn gegen zehn hebt sich, ten against ten lifts.

But to lift did not only assume the more general meaning of taking, holding, but in a parallel form, namely as Gothic haban, it came to mean to hold, to possess, to have, the Anglo-Saxon habban, Old English habbe[1].

[1] See Grimm, s. v. *haben*. The change of *f* and *b* is explained by Grimm's, some cases by Verner's law.

Derivatives with the sense of lifting are German Hebel, vectis, G. Hefe, leaven, G. Hobel, a plane; English heavy, heaven (?), and A.S. haef, sea, German Haff.

Derivatives with the sense of taking and holding are κώπη, handle, German Handhabe, capulus, halter, hilt, capax, holding, Old Saxon haft, captus, German Haft, prison, Heftel, hook, heftig, pertinax.

Professor Skeat reminds me of an interesting Shropshire word eft, which, as the initial h is never sounded there, stands really for heft. It means to lift as a verb, and a thing lifted as a substantive. Miss Jackson, in her Shropshire Glossary, p. 203, quotes the following: 'W'y, Betty, han yo' carried that basket all the way!' 'Iss, an' yo' jest 'eft it.' 'My 'eart! it is a good 'eft.'

But leaving that large family of descendants of the root KAP, we have still to deal with two waifs, namely to buy and to sell, two verbs which have hitherto yielded to no etymological analysis, but which may now possibly receive some light from the history of the words derived from pendere.

We saw that to pay was in ancient times expressed by weighing of rude metal. Now it is well known that in early days not only metal, but other articles too were used as means of exchange or money. Among them we have salt, which even at present is used as money in the interior of Africa. Suidas tells us that a slave bought for salt, ἁλώνητος, was a poor or worthless slave (not worth his salt?—hardly), and that the Thracians sold slaves for salt. Now in Old Slovenian, as Miklosich states, prasoliti means to trade, prasolŭ, a trader, both derived from solĭ, salt.

Why should not the A.S. sellan come from the same source? There is no Aryan or Teutonic root from which to sell can be derived, and there is no lack of analogies to show that words for money, for selling and buying, were derived from the name of the articles which were used at different times and in different countries as circulating media. Without mentioning the Latin pecunia, the Gothic faihu, A.S. feoh, English a fee, we may point to the Irish sed, Old Irish set, Mediæval Latin sentis, which is explained as a standard of value among the Gaedhil, by which rents, fines, stipends, and prices were determined. Every kind of property was estimated by this standard, the unit being a milch-cow, which was the prime Sed[1].

Cloth was used as money, and in the North, as Vigfusson tells us, the vádmál (cloth measure) was the standard of all valuation and payment before coined gold or silver came into use. In the Chron. Slav. Helm. lib. i. cap. 28, p. 95, we read of the inhabitants of the island of Rügen *nec est in comparandis rebus consuetudo nummorum, sed quidquid in foro mercari volueris panno lineo comparabis*[2]. 'They do not use coins in buying things, but whatever one wishes to buy in the market, one has to pay for with a piece of linen cloth.' Furs, also, were used like cloth as a means of payment, and thus we find that in Old Russian the name for money is kuna, kuni, i.e. vestis pellina,

[1] W. K. Sullivan in O'Curry's 'Manners and Customs of the Ancient Irish,' iii. 480, as quoted by O. Schrader in his excellent work, 'Linguistisch-historische Forschungen,' p. 116. He also quotes Chr. Crusius, 'Commentarius de originibus pecuniae a pecore ante nummum signatum,' Petropoli, 1748.

[2] O. Schrader, l. c., p. 119.

Med. Lat. gunna, English gown. In Finnish raha, originally fur, came to mean money. The Woguls call a Russian rouble sêt-lîn, i.e. one hundred squirrels.

I have little doubt therefore that the A.S. sellan came from the same source as the Old Slovenian pra-soliti, negotiari, particularly as salt, and the name for salt, seem to have travelled to the North from the South. Phonetically, this etymology is unobjectionable, and the growth of meaning is quite as intelligible as that which is generally admitted for the Gothic sal-jan. If sala meant originally a handful of salt, the Gothic sal-jan, the A.S. sellan (for salian), would have meant to take or to give a handful of salt, to trade, to sell. What must not be forgotten, however, is the sacred character attributed to salt by different races at a very early time, and its employment for confirming bargains and for hallowing sacrificial offerings. But though some of the intermediate steps may still be doubtful, I do not doubt that to sell sprang originally from the old name for salt, Lat. sal, Greek ἅλ-ς. To an historian this may seem bold, but the student of language knows full well that words have taken even wilder leaps in their passage from their distant sources to the wide ocean of literary speech.

My last etymology will seem bolder still. To buy, like to sell, has been an old puzzle to English scholars. In appears in earlier English as buggen, biggen, and beyen; Anglo-Saxon gives us bycgan and bicgan, and Gothic bugjan. Some people have connected this with Sanskrit bhu*g*, to enjoy, Lat. fungor. But why should the act of buying be called an enjoyment?

Others trace it to Sanskrit bhug, in the sense of bending, turning, because buying is in one sense a turning, as we see in ἀμείβεσθαι, in Lith. wertimnas, trade (Lat. verto), a change and exchange. It may be so, but is there no better way of accounting for this troublesome word? Let us remember that in Icelandic baug-r means money, but originally a ring (derived from the root biúg, baug, bog), in A.S. bêag, French bague; and let us consider what Vigfusson tells us in the Icelandic Dictionary, namely 'that in olden times, before coined gold and silver came into use, the metals were rolled up in spiral rings'; that 'in law the payment of weregild is particularly called baugr'; and that bauga-brot are cut-off pieces of baugr, bad money. In Old Saxon, too, wunden gold, wound gold, is the gold used for buying, as we might say coined gold. A mere lump of gold or any other metal would have been useless for such purpose, because it could not be divided; while, after it had been reduced to a more pliant form, it could not only more easily be carried about in the form of twisted rings or coils, armlets, bracelets, necklets, but could also more easily be bent, broken, and divided. We read in the old 'Hildebrandslied':

> Want er dô ar arme wuntane bouga
> Cheisuringu gitân, so imo sê der chuning gap,
> Hûneo truhtîn. . . .

> He wound there from the arm twisted hoops,
> Made of imperial rings (coin), as the King had given them to him,
> The Lord of the Huns[1].

This shows that these hoops or armlets were really

[1] Max Müller, 'German Classics,' vol. i. p. 8.

twisted coils of gold that might be used either for presents or for payments. If then, in Icelandic, baugr, from meaning coil, ring, came to mean money, why should not a verb, meaning to bend, to coil, have been used in the sense of buying? The formal development of the verb is seen most clearly in Gothic; there, as Grimm has shown, we have the verb biugan, baug, bugun, to bend, and by the side of it, bugjan, bauhta, bauht, to buy, just as in Anglo-Saxon we have bûgan, bêah, to bend, and bucg(i)an, bohte, to buy. If we once know that baugr in Icelandic meant money, because it meant originally bent metal or rings, and that A.S. byge meant trade[1], because it meant originally money, everything else becomes clear. We might then, as Professor Skeat[2] suggests in a letter to me, suppose that bycgan, i.e. byg-ian, was formed from byge, as sallan, i.e. sal-ian, was from sala, namely, in the sense of using rings or using salt for trade or barter. Whether the Saxons, in using bycgan in the sense of buying, were

[1] Ettmüller, in his Anglo-Saxon Dictionary (1851), p. 302, mentions *byge*, masc., meaning a bend, and *byge*, neuter, meaning commerce or trade, quoting from Schmidt, Die Gesetze der Angelsachsen, 1858, p. 108.

[2] Professor Skeat suggests the following pedigree:—

	Weak Stem.	Middle Stem.	Strong Stem.
Teutonic:	BUG	BEUG	BAUG
Gothic:	bug	biug	boug
Anglo-Saxon:	bog	bûg	bêag (bêah)
	bog	búg	bêag
			bêah, ring
a coil,	byge (by Umlaut)		bŷgan / bêgan (caused by Umlaut)
to barter with coils,	byg-ian (by deriv.) / bycgan		

still aware of the original meaning of the verb, namely, to bend or to twist or to handle a wire of gold, is a question difficult to answer. In Icelandic, where *baugr* has retained both meanings, ring and money, the reason why money was called *baugr* might have been more easily remembered. But when, as in Anglo-Saxon, such reminders were lost, the memory of *bycgan*, to buy, having meant originally to bend or to break off a piece from a coil of gold, would vanish very rapidly, as rapidly as the Romans forgot the original purport of *pensio*, and as entirely as the recollection that to pay is to pacify (*pacare*), and *quits* is connected with *quietus*, quiet, has passed away from our own memory.

VI. The Home of the Aryas.

If we find the same words with the same meanings in Sanskrit, Persian, Armenian, Greek, Latin, Celtic, Slavonic, and Teutonic, what shall we say? Either the words must have been borrowed from one language by the other, or they must have belonged to an older language, from which all these so-called Aryan languages were derived. It is not always easy to decide this question, but, generally speaking, the character of each of the Aryan dialects, as we may call them, is sufficiently marked to enable us to say at once that such and such a word in Latin is Greek, in German is Latin, in Celtic is German. With the exception of such foreign words, however, it is clear that all words, and all grammatical forms also, which the Aryan languages have in common, must have constituted the bulk of an ancient inheritance from which the principal heirs carried away whatever seemed most useful and valuable to them.

This fact being once fairly established, scholars have rushed at a number of conclusions which seemed very plausible at first, but have often turned out quite untenable after more careful consideration.

Surely, it was said, if these languages are all derived from the same source, it ought to be possible to reconstruct that primitive Aryan language. Forthwith the attempt was made, but it proved a failure. If those who began to write fables in the Proto-Aryan speech had attempted to construct, first of all, a Proto-Latin speech out of the fragments scattered in Italian, Provençal, French, Spanish, Portuguese, Roumanian, and Roumansch, they would have seen that even this task, which ought to have been much easier, was beyond our power. And why? Because it is a mistake to imagine that there ever was one uniform Proto-Aryan language—*tota, teres et rotunda*—from which Sanskrit, Greek, and Latin, and all the rest were derived, as Italian was from Latin. Ancient languages, as I have tried to point out in my 'Lectures on the Science of Language,' live, move, and have their being in dialects, and it is out of a living mass of dialectic speech that literary languages slowly emerge. Dialect has two quite distinct meanings, which ought never to be confounded. It means the ancient feeders of a literary language; but it also means the later channels branching off from a literary language. We can see literary languages emerging before our very eyes, if we watch the less civilised races whose spoken dialects have not yet been centralised by literary cultivation. In the small Island of Mangaia, as one of its first missionaries, the Rev. W. W. Gill, informed me, several slightly different dialects were spoken. After twenty years of teaching and preaching, and of washing and combing too, the dialect which he himself had learnt, with any peculiarities of grammar and pronunciation that might have been due to himself, has become the recognised language of the whole island. If there had been at the same time a French and a German missionary, we might probably have had three Mangaian grammars, and three Mangaian Catechisms and

Bibles. But would it have been possible to construct out of them a uniform Proto-Mangaian language? Certainly not. We cannot reconstruct what never existed, and we cannot, therefore, build up a uniform original Proto-Aryan speech containing the type of every word and every grammatical form that meets us in Sanskrit, Zend, Armenian, Greek, Latin, Celtic, Slavonic, and Teutonic.

The second equally thoughtless endeavour was to fix the date at which the Aryan separation took place. How, in the world, was that to be done? It was thought that, as in geology we can count the years in which certain deposits have taken place within historical times, and argue from that to the years required for the formation of more ancient deposits, we might apply the same test to the growth of language. We see how many centuries it has taken for Anglo-Saxon to become English, for Latin to become French, for Zend to become Persian. Why should we not be able to discover, without minding a century or two, how long it would have taken for Sanskrit, Greek, and Latin to branch off from a common stem and accumulate that amount of difference which separates them from each other? The answer is simple enough. There are two kinds of change in language—the one produced by internal, the other by external causes. The internal changes are due chiefly to economy of muscular energy, to the working of analogy, and similar causes; the external changes, and these are the most palpable, are generally the result of political and social revolution, or foreign conquest. Anglo-Saxon would never have become what it has become in English, but for the ill-treatment it received from the Normans. Latin would never have become French, but for the brutality with which it was mangled by Franks and other barbarians. Persian is only the wreck of Zend, and bears clear traces of all the persecutions which Persia underwent from its Mohammedan conquerors. No one can measure the bearings of such events, any more than a geologist, in his calculations of the progress of stratification, can make accurate allowance for earthquakes, volcanic eruptions, or cataclysmal floods.

We do not even know how long Sanskrit had been Sanskrit, and Greek Greek before the time when we become aware of their existence. Literature, or, at all events, written literature, is a very late invention in most countries. In India we have no trace of the existence of books before the fifth century B.C. Are we to say then that Sanskrit began in the fifth century B.C.? But it would be much truer to say that Sanskrit ended at that time, because at that time, and even before that time, Sanskrit was degenerating into Prâkrit, and the first written documents of Sanskrit which we still possess are really the inscriptions of Asoka in the third century B.C., all written in what may be called Prâkrit, or modern dialects of Sanskrit. Are we to say then that Sanskrit began with the hymns of the Veda, say 1000–1500 B.C.? But in these hymns Sanskrit appears as a thoroughly elaborated language, with ever so many traditional irregularities, with ever so much detritus of earlier periods. Sanskrit, as it appears in the Veda, is not the Proto-Aryan language, whatever that may be. Even if we trace it back to the period of its unity with Zend, it is Sanskrit already, or at least perfectly different from Greek and

Latin and all the other Aryan dialects by very marked phonetic and grammatical tendencies. Thus Sanskrit and Zend alone possess a developed system of palatals, and such forms as *k*akrire in Sanskrit, *k*âkhrare in Zend, prove that when these forms arose both Sanskrit and Zend possessed a palatalised a, which changed the reduplicated k into *k*. Sanskrit had other phonetic and grammatical peculiarities, such as its aversion to double final consonants, its dislike of hiatus, its sensitiveness to consonantal incongruities, etc. Sanskrit therefore was Sanskrit long before the Aryas migrated towards the Seven Rivers; it was Sanskrit long before the hymns of the Veda were composed; it was Sanskrit long before one line of it was reduced to writing.

In Greece we know indeed of inscriptions several centuries earlier than the inscription of Asoka; but of written books, in our sense of the word, I still doubt the existence before the seventh century B.C. It is true that oral tradition, before the invention of writing and printing, has proved itself a very safe guardian of poetry, and few would doubt that the earliest poetry which we know in Greece goes back at least to 1000 B.C. But it may go back, for all we know, to 2000 or 3000 B.C., and even at that time people who spoke Greek and Sanskrit would have been as unintelligible to each other as a Bengali and a modern Greek are at present.

When the attempt at fixing the date of the first Aryan separation was given up as hopeless, much time and ingenuity were wasted on the question whether we might not be able to find out how that separation took place, which races started first, and which remained together for some time after they had broken away from the rest. It is easy to start such problems, but it is far wiser to look before we leap. I was not aware, till I saw it stated by Professor Schrader, in his excellent book called 'Sprachvergleichung und Urgeschichte' (p. 70), that I was myself responsible for the first step in that direction, having been the first to point out that, at some time or other, the Aryan family separated and became divided into two distinct branches, the *South-Eastern*, comprising the languages of India and Persia, and the *North-Western*, comprising Greek, Latin, Celtic, Slavonic, and Teutonic. I do not mean, however, to shirk that amount of responsibility. When we find, as we do, in the most ancient languages of India and Persia, in the Vedic Sanskrit and in Zend, identical words of decidedly secondary character, technical terms even, connected with a peculiar system of religion and sacrifice, and such words not borrowed, but modified according to the phonetic system of either Sanskrit or Zend, we are safe. These two languages must have continued together, after they had separated from the rest, in which no traces of these words occur. Thus we find in Sanskrit hotar, the name of a special priest, in Zend regularly changed into zaotar. We find another name for priest in Sanskrit, atharvan, in Zend, âtharvan. The sacrificial plant, which in the Veda is called soma, occurs in Zend as haoma. While other Aryan languages have common numerals up to one hundred only, Sanskrit and Zend have the same word for thousand also, viz. sahasra in Sanskrit, changed regularly in Zend into hazańra. Such evidence is sufficient to prove that the people who spoke Sanskrit and Zend must have remaïned united for some time after they had left the common Aryan home, and after they had become separated from the speakers of the other Aryan dialects. Beyond this, however, all is uncertain and mere guesswork. It was my chief object in the inaugural lecture which I delivered at Strassburg, in 1872[1], to warn scholars against wasting their time on an impossible problem. I pointed out how certain peculiar similarities had been discovered:

1. Between Slavonic and German, by Bopp, Zeuss, Grimm, and Schleicher;

2. Between German and Celtic, by Ebel and Lottner;

3. Between Celtic and Latin, by Newman and Schleicher;

4. Between Latin and Greek, by Mommsen and Curtius;

5. Between Greek and Sanskrit, by Grassmann, Sonne, and Kern.

What does all this prove? It proves no more than that all the Aryan languages are cognate dialects. If some of them agree on certain points on which they differ from all the rest, this is no more than we should expect; if they differ, this is again exactly what we are prepared for. Nothing but coincidences in late, secondary, or technical terms, such as we find between Sanskrit and Zend, for instance, but certainly not between Greek and Latin, or German and Slavonic, ought in any way to disturb our equanimity. Such coincidences, however, as could in the least compare with the coincidences between San-

[1] Selected Essays, vol. i. p. 174.

skrit and Zend, we find nowhere else, not even in Greek and Latin, and therefore the problem of the gradual separation of the Aryan languages, beyond the great split into a North-Western and a South-Eastern branch, is, from the nature of the case, insoluble, and must be abandoned. I do not deny that the ancestors of Greeks and Romans, of Romans and Celts, of Celts and Germans, of Germans and Slavs, may have remained together for some time, before they became finally separated; all I maintain is that the linguistic evidence is too weak to support such conclusions. It may seem a kind of intellectual cowardice to withdraw from an undertaking which appeared so promising, but if there is no evidence for solving a problem, the true scholar ought surely to have the courage to say so, and not to waste valuable time on mere guesswork which simply cumbereth the ground. About the same time, when I had published my Strassburg lecture, Professor Schmidt made a bold attempt to save what could be saved of the shipwreck; but in the end his researches led to much the same conclusion. We both admit that there was from the beginning dialectic variety within certain spheres, but no sphere was entirely excluded from contact with the other spheres, till the great split between the North-West and the South-East took place. The cherished idea of a real pedigree of all the Aryan languages has to be surrendered once for all. Let any Romanic scholar attempt to fix the time when Italian, Provençal, Spanish, Portuguese, French, Roumanian and Roumansch branched off respectively from Latin, or how long some of them remained united before assuming an independent existence, and he will be less surprised at the failure of all attempts to restore the *stemma genealogicum* of the ancient Aryan languages.

And now we come to the last question. Is it possible to fix the original home of Aryan speech, and to determine the migrations of the races who spoke Sanskrit, Persian, Greek, Latin, Celtic, Slavonic, and Teutonic, in their progress from their original historical head-quarters?

Before we attempt to answer this question, we must first try to clear our ideas of what we mean by the Aryan race. It is generally taken for granted that in the beginning, whenever that may have been, there was an immense Aryan population somewhere, and that large swarms issued from a central bee-hive which contained untold millions of human beings. This may or may not have been so. But first of all we ought to remember that a common language is by no means a certain proof of a common bee-hive. We know from history how families, clans, and whole nations were conquered and led into captivity, and had to learn the language of their conquerors; how tribes were exterminated, women and children carried off; and how even conquerors had sometimes to adopt the language of the country which they had subdued. All this does not destroy the continuity of language, but it breaks the continuity of blood. If a black man marries a white woman, or a black woman a white man, their offspring is either white, or black, or mixed. It is easy to say that the stronger race always prevails; the question is, which is the stronger race except that which prevails? Besides, it is a well-known fact that a race-type, which disappeared in the children, often breaks out again in the grandchildren. But if a Frenchman marries an Englishwoman, their children speak either French or English or both, they never speak a mixed language. In fact, in spite of all that has been said to the contrary, there is no really mixed language, while there is at present no race that can safely be called unmixed. Languages may adopt ever so many foreign words, foreign idioms, even foreign grammatical forms, and in that sense every language may be called mixed. But these adopted elements always remain foreign elements. They are like adopted children in a family. They may have the same name, but they have not the same blood. There is a continuous growth in every language, which enables us to say, even in the case of so motley a language as English, that it is Low-German, whether it be spoken by Celts, Saxons, Danes, Normans, or by Zulus, Malays or Chinamen. If the indigenous races of India learnt Sanskrit and dialects derived from Sanskrit, they became *ipso facto* representatives of Aryan speech, whatever their blood may have been. Have not the Jews forgotten Hebrew, and learnt English, German, and French? Have not the Beauchamps and St. Legers broken their tongues to Saxon idiom and Saxon grammar in England? How then shall we tell from language what races had to learn the language of their Aryan conquerors or their Aryan slaves? There is no Aryan race in blood, but whoever, through the imposition of hands, whether of his parents or his foreign masters, has received the Aryan blessing, belongs to that unbroken spiritual succession which began with the first apostles of that noble speech, and continues to the present day in every part of the globe. Aryan, in scientific language, is utterly inapplicable to race. It means language and nothing but language; and if we speak of Aryan race at all, we should know that it means no more than x+ Aryan speech.

And why should there have been in the beginning a vast number of that Aryan race? Let us remember that one couple, having two children, would, if every successive marriage was blest with two children only, produce a population of 274,877,906,944 human beings in about 1200 years[1]. Now the population of the whole earth at the present moment is vaguely estimated at 1500 millions. We are not driven, therefore, particularly if the first Aryan separation may be placed at least 3000 years B.C., to the admission of a vast Aryan stock which was broken up into seven or more nationalities. That may be the more natural hypothesis, but whether more natural or not, it is not the only possible hypothesis. Granted two Aryan couples, each with seven children, and everything that has to be explained may be explained quite as well with this as with the bee-hive theory. Each of the seven children, by marrying children of the other family, might become, particularly if they settled in different forests or valleys, founders of dialects; and each of these dialects might, in twenty generations, or six hundred years, be spoken by more than two millions of human beings. Two millions of human beings, however, are much more difficult to move from one country to another than two hundred; and it is, at all events, quite open to us to imagine that the Aryan migra-

[1] Gustav Mosen, 'Was ein Morgensonnenstrahl hervogerufen hat,' p. 46.

tions took place by tens or hundreds instead of by millions. If one missionary is able, in twenty years, to impose his peculiar, and perhaps not quite grammatical, dialect on the population of a whole island, why should not one shepherd, with his servants and flocks, have transferred his peculiar Aryan dialect from one part of Asia or Europe to another? This may seem a very humble and modest view of what was formerly represented as the irresistible stream of mighty waves rolling forth from the Aryan centre and gradually overflowing the mountains and valleys of Asia and Europe, but it is, at all events, a possible view; nay, I should say a view far more in keeping with what we know of recent colonisation.

But the old question returns, Can we not discover the cradle of our race? I say, decidedly we cannot. We may guess, with more or less probability, but if our guesses are to be submitted to the test of mathematical certainty, not one of them will stand that test. This ought to be understood; and is, in fact, understood among most scholars. Many opinions held with regard to periods of history which are beyond the reach of historical evidence can never be more than possible or plausible. To demand for them a different character does not show any critical sagacity, but rather ignorance of the limits of our knowledge. Thus, when we see the Celts driven to the western parts of Europe, pushed forward by Teutonic tribes, and these again pressed hard by Slavonic neighbours, we naturally conclude that the Celts were the first to arrive in Europe, the Germans the second, the Slavs the third. But there is no mathematical certainty for this. It is nothing but the result of an historical combination, and can never be more. Again, if we see Hellenic civilisation extending from Asia Minor to Greece, and from Greece to Italy, and if we find the Italians pressed by successive inroads from the north, we are inclined here too to admit a progress of Aryan speech and thought from the east to the west, and from the north to the south. If, on the contrary, we consider that the Aryan conquerors of India came clearly from the north along the rivers of the Panjâb, while before that time they

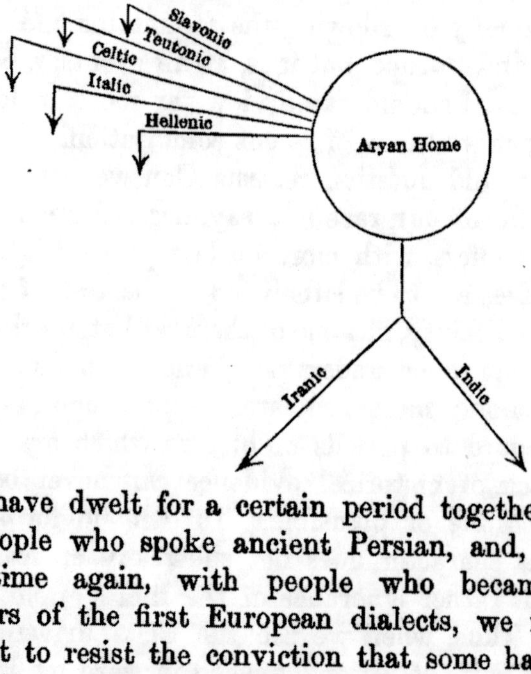

must have dwelt for a certain period together with the people who spoke ancient Persian, and, before that time again, with people who became the founders of the first European dialects, we find it difficult to resist the conviction that some half-way point from which the North-Western and South-Eastern tribes could have diverged may mark the original home of the Aryans. This may be roughly represented by the sketch above.

But if we proceed to ask in what exact spot the

Aryan centre has to be placed geographically, the answers will vary very considerably. 'Somewhere in Asia,' used to be the recognised answer, and I do not mean to say that it was far wrong; only we must not expect, in a subject like this, our much-vaunted mathematical certainty. The reasoning which we have to adopt is one that Mill recommends for other complicated and, at first sight, confused sets of appearances[1]. We have to begin by making any supposition, even a false one, to see what consequences will follow from it, and by observing how these differ from the real phenomena. The simplest supposition which accords with the more obvious facts is the best to begin with, because its consequences are the most easily traced. This rude hypothesis is then rudely corrected, and the operation repeated, and the comparison of the consequences deducible from the corrected hypothesis with the observed facts suggests still further correction, until the deductive results are at last made to tally with the phenomena.

Now the first rough hypothesis was that the cradle of the Aryans may have been somewhere in Asia.

There may have been a time when scholars were so much impressed with the primitiveness of Sanskrit that they would have preferred India as the cradle of the Aryas, and Sanskrit as the mother of Greek, Latin, and the other Aryan dialects. But that time, if it ever existed, is long past. We know that the Aryas were originally strangers in India, and that, if primitiveness of language could settle the home of those who speak it, Iceland would be the original home of the Scandinavians, and the Danube that of all the Germans.

[1] Logic, iv. 14, 5.

But though conclusions like these, to be drawn from the primitiveness of Sanskrit, have been surrendered, the fact that Sanskrit is the most primitive language of the Aryan family is as true to-day as it was fifty years ago. Though it has been clearly shown that Greek, Latin, Teutonic, Slavonic, and Celtic cannot be derived from Sanskrit, as little as French can be derived from Italian, no grammarian in his senses would listen to the idea that Sanskrit could be derived from Greek, Latin, Celtic, Slavonic, or Teutonic, least of all from Scandinavian.

Yet that extraordinary theory has lately been started by certain ethnologists, who maintain for various reasons that Scandinavia was the fatherland of all the Aryas, and that Scandinavian, or Lituanian, or all the European Aryan languages together, are more primitive than Sanskrit.

It is really difficult to know how to treat such arguments, for even when we have shown that on almost every point Sanskrit is more primitive than Scandinavian or Teutonic, we have only wasted our time, because our very opponents turn round and reject as no argument the argument which they tried to support by facts which are no facts.

But in order to show what is possible in mere assertion, let us see what it really means when we are told by ethnologists, nay even by certain students of language, that 'instead of being the most faithful representative of the parent-speech, Sanskrit is in many respects far less so than are its sister-languages of Europe. Its vocabulary, for instance, has been thrown into confusion by the coalescence of the three primitive vowel-sounds of ă, ĕ, ŏ into the single monotonous ă. Greek, or even Lituanian, has preserved more faithfully than the Sanskrit of India the features of the parent Aryan. If the faithfulness of the record is any proof of the geographical proximity of one of the Indo-European languages to this common mother, it is in the neighbourhood of Lituania, rather than in the neighbourhood of India, that we ought to look for the first home of the Aryan family.' And again: 'It will be in the neighbourhood of that starting-point and in northern Europe that we shall expect to find the largest number of undiluted Aryan languages and the purest example of Aryan blood. In Greece and Armenia, in Persia and India, we must look for mixture and decay.'

What is the meaning of all this? First of all, if all that is here asserted were true, nothing would follow from it, because, as we have been told again and again, the primitiveness of language is no proof whatever of the primitiveness of the geographical habitat of its speakers. It would be a mere revival of the exploded argument that all the Aryas must have come from the Sarasvatî. So much for the argument which is no argument. Now for the facts which are no facts? Where is there any confusion in the Sanskrit vocabulary? Such confusion may arise from two causes, from a too great and from a too small variety of phonetic and alphabetic representation. In our case we are told that it arose from the latter cause, from the coalescence of the three primitive vowels ă, ĕ, ŏ into the monotonous Sanskrit a.

But in fact there has been neither coalescence nor confusion. There has been differentiation of a common vowel, and all we want to know at present is the *vera causa* of the differentiation, called *Ablaut*. In Sanskrit, even supposing that short a was always pronounced alike, the people distinguished such words as *φέρω* and *φόρος* quite as well as the Greeks, by saying bhárami, but bhârás[1].

We must remember that short a is never written in Sanskrit. It is pronounced where no other vowel is written. Even initially अ marks really the spiritus lenis, as in ऋ, ओ, औ, while in आ the long vowel has been added. It is quite possible, therefore, that the ă, which Pâ*n*ini (viii. 4, 68) describes as different from all other vowels, namely, as sa*m*v*ri*ta, closed, may have varied in its pronunciation in different parts of ancient India as it does to the present day. Nor is this mere surmise. For, first of all, it is a mistake to say that Sanskrit does not tolerate the sounds of ĕ and ŏ. This is true for Pâ*n*inean Sanskrit only, but in the Vedic Sanskrit we have ĕ and ŏ[2], and in Pâli and Prâkrit again it is well known that every final a and o can be treated as either long or short[3].

Secondly, the change of k into *k* in such forms as *k*akâra can be explained on one supposition only, namely, that the a in the reduplicated syllable was the palatalised a, that is, ĕ, and thus caused the change of the guttural into a palatal consonant. Nor can this change be ascribed to some not yet Sanskritic period, for it is in Sanskrit and Zend only that we have this peculiar change of k into *k*; it is in the South-Western branch only that the palatal series has been so fully developed. We may really say that what in

[1] For the vowel-changes by which the *Ablaut* was rendered in Sanskrit, see Hübschmann, *Vocalsystem*, 1885.

[2] M. M., Translation of Rig-veda-sa*m*hitâ, vol. i. p. lxxxiii.

[3] Lassen, 'Inst. Linguae Pracriticae,' pp. 145, 147, 151; Cowell, 'Vararu*k*i,' Introduction, p. xvii.

the N.W. branch was phonetically represented by kĕ was in the S.E. branch represented by *kă*, the intention being the same in both cases.

And if we look at this matter historically, how can we call the ă, ĕ, ŏ series the most primitive in Scandinavian or Teutonic in general, if in the oldest representative of Teutonic, in Gothic, we find as yet no trace of it? We look in vain in Gothic for written exponents of ĕ and ŏ, and yet there is in Gothic no more difficulty than in Sanskrit in representing the changes of Ablaut. Gothic, the most primitive representative of the Teutonic class—more primitive, therefore, than Scandinavian, and, as we are told, infinitely more primitive than Sanskrit—has no ĕ and ŏ, so that in writing Greek words ε and ο have to be represented by ai and au. And in addition to this, Gothic has not even a long â, nor a long î, while the degenerate Sanskrit possesses not only a, i, u, â, î, û, ê, ô, âi and âu, but *ri*, *rî*, and *li*.

I ask then, what is the meaning of saying that Sanskrit, phonetically at least, is less primitive than Scandinavian, or Greek, or Latin, or Lituanian? In Lituanian too we find that in several instances a is written, but, as in Sanskrit, the pronunciation is e[1].

And when from the vowels we turn to the consonants, where do we find the most perfect system? Five modifications of each check, guttural, dental, labial; a whole palatal series, and a lingual series, which is not by any means restricted to non-Sanskritic words; five modifications of the nasal, and five modifications of the Visarga;—is not this a set-off against

[1] Schleicher, 'Litauische Grammatik,' p. 27; and on the non-primitive character of the Lituanian vowel-system, p. 62.

the loss of ŏ and ĕ, supposing that these sounds were really unknown in Sanskrit?

I do not mean to say that for representing the changes which are comprehended under the name of Ablaut, the three vowels ă, ĕ, ŏ are not very convenient in Greek and in the later Teutonic languages. But by means of a, i, â, and by dropping of the vowel, Sanskrit obtains exactly the same results which other languages obtain by ă, ĕ, ŏ, and there is, at all events, no confusion of any kind. And when we come to declension and conjugation, a mere look at an Icelandic or Lituanian grammar is enough to make us see the utter romance of saying that these languages are more primitive than Sanskrit. Lituanian has preserved some precious relics of Aryan grammar, but as a whole it is not even the most primitive representative of the Balto-Slavonic branch [1], and Balto-Slavonic is certainly not the most primitive representative of the Aryan family. I can here give a few specimens only.

	Sanskrit.	Lituanian.	Greek.
Sing.	dádâmi, I give.	dũ(d)mi	δίδωμι.
	dádâsi	dũdi	δίδως.
	dádâti	dũsti	δίδωσι.
Dual	dadvás	dũ(d)va.	
	datthás	dũsta	δίδοτον.
	dattás	dũsti	δίδοτον.
Plural	dadmás	dũ(d)me	δίδομεν.
	datthá	dũste	δίδοτε.
	dádati	dũsti	διδοῦσι.

Gothic has nothing to put by the side of these primitive forms, and I have therefore added Greek.

[1] Schleicher, 'Litauische Grammatik,' p. 2. 'In grammar, at least in the conjugation, Slavonic comes before Lituanian.'

A look at these three paradigms will show that, though we may speak in very high terms of Lituanian as having preserved to the present day faint traces of a reduplicated present and a dual, yet by the side of Sanskrit its vaunted primitiveness assumes a very different character from what is commonly supposed.

	Sanskrit.	Lituanian.	Gothic.
Nom.	v*ri*kas	vìlkas	vulfs.
Acc.	v*ri*kam	vìlką	vulf.
Abl.	v*ri*kât.		
Gen.	v*ri*kasya	vìlko	vulfis.
Loc.	v*ri*ke	vilkè,	
Dat.	v*ri*kâya	(vìlkui)	vulfa.
Instr.	v*ri*kâ, v*ri*ke*n*a	vilkù.	
Voc.	v*ri*ka	vilkè	vulf.
Nom.	v*ri*kâs	vilkaí	vulfôs.
Acc.	v*ri*kân(s)	vilkùs	vulfans.
Gen.	v*ri*kâ*n*âm	vilkú	vulfê.
Loc.	v*ri*keshu	vilkůsù.	
Dat. & Abl.	v*ri*kebhyas	vilkáms	vulfam.
Instr.	v*ri*kais	vilkaís.	

I do not mean to say that it is not quite delightful to find in Lituanian a locative plural such as vilkůsù, or in Gothic an acc. plur. such as vulfans. But these are a few gems, while Sanskrit offers a complete diadem. That Lituanian has a dual in declension places it above Gothic, but here again it is no match for Sanskrit.

I repeat, therefore, without fear of contradiction, that although no historical conclusions may be drawn from the primitiveness of Sanskrit, that primitiveness itself remains the same as ever, whether we follow Bopp's, Schleicher's, or Brugmann's Comparative Grammar.

We now return to the question, Do we know of any facts which make that rough hypothesis of an Asiatic home of the Aryas untenable? If we do, then it is worth while to reopen the question, and no one would be more willing than I am to shift the Aryan home to any quarter of the globe, from the Arctic to the Antarctic regions, if only there were an atom of new tangible evidence forthcoming.

The first fact that was supposed to militate against the Aryan home being somewhere in Asia was the absence of common Aryan names for animals which, we were told, ought to have been known to dwellers in Asia, such as the *lion*, the *elephant*, the *ape*, the *tiger*, and the *camel*. The dog, it was said, must have been known to the Aryas before their separation, because it has the same name in Sanskrit, *s*van, in Zend, span, in Greek, *κύων*, in Latin, canis, in Irish, kú, in Lituanian, szů, in Gothic, hund. These are all dialectic modifications of one typical form kuan. But there are no common Aryan names for *lion*, *elephant*, *ape*, *tiger*, and *camel*, and therefore, it is concluded, the Aryas could not, before their separation, have known these animals or lived in a country where they were known.

This argument is *ben trovato*, but no more. First of all there are parts of Asia where none of these wild animals are known, and where the Aryas might have had their earliest seats. M. de Ujfalvy, in a classical passage, quoted by M. J. Van den Gheyn[1], says: '*Les vallées qui avoisinent le Pamir, le Darwâz, le Karategine et le Kohistan satisfont à toutes les données de la paléontologie linguistique. Il y a là*

[1] 'L'origine Européenne des Aryas,' 1885, p. 43.

un pays froid, de la glace et de la neige en hiver; l'été est court. Les plantes alimentaires et les animaux domestiques sont bien ceux que signale le vocabulaire aryaque. On trouve le pin, le bouleau et le chêne. Les grands fauves n'y vivent pas. Les montagnards de l'Oxus sont de rudes piétons, adonnés dès les temps les plus reculés aux pratiques mazdéennes. Pasteurs et agriculteurs, ils irriguent leurs champs et se servent de la charrue la plus primitive.'

Secondly, if some obstinate critic were to say that the Aryas may have possessed common names for these wild animals, but lost them all, we might indeed shrug our shoulders, but we could not prove the contrary. Ever so many Aryan words exist in one or two branches of that family only, and if they disappeared in some, they might have disappeared in all.

Lastly, we find that the animals which have common Aryan names are mostly such as had become familiar and useful by being domesticated. The fact that cow, goat, sheep, dog and horse have common names in all Aryan languages seems to me a strong proof that they had been tamed and domesticated. Tigers and lions were simply wild beasts, and there was no necessity for distinguishing and naming them beyond classing them as fera or *θήρ*, the objects of the chase (*θήρα*). And suppose that the elephant and the camel had really been known and utilised as beasts of burden by the united Aryas, when living in Asia, would it not have been most natural that, when transplanted to more northern regions, their children, who had never seen a camel or elephant, should have lost the names of them? We have no longer any doits, and the word would have been altogether lost but for such familiar phrases as 'I care not a doit.' The Americans have no *pence*, and in America *penny* is no longer an American, but only a foreign word. Sometimes, as in the case of ush*t*ra, we see that the Aryas both in Persia and India possessed it; but the Iranians used it for a camel, the Vedic Indians for the humped ox, while in later Sanskrit it again means camel. Ush*t*ar, nom. *t*â, in the Veda means ox only[1].

The negative argument, therefore, which, from the absence of common Aryan words, tries to establish the absence of their objects during the Aryan period, breaks down. It is plausible, and combined with other arguments it appeals to scholars and historians, but it cannot by itself stand a cross-examination in a court of law.

Much stronger, however, is the positive argument. If the North-Western and South-Eastern Aryas have the same word for bear, for instance, they must, unless it can be proved that one language borrowed the word from another, have known the bear before they separated, and have lived in a country where that animal was well known. The bear is no doubt a wild beast, but he is not so ferocious, and has never been so dreaded as the tiger and lion. He was often considered as a friend and patron of a village, and at an early time became quite a character in local traditions. Many families and tribes, such as the Arcadians and

[1] Similar uncertainties in the meaning of words ought to make us very careful in drawing conclusions. We know that φηγός means oak in Greek, while fagus in Latin means beech. Ulbandus in Gothic means camel, though the name is clearly derived from elephant. In Mod. Greek τζακάλης is a badger, though it seems connected with jackal, the Persian shaghâl, Sk. *s*rigâla. (See Kuhn's 'Zeitschrift,' i. p. 501.) Hence, even though the names may be the same, the animals or trees intended need not always have been the same.

even the Arsacidae, were proud of their descent from the bear, and we need not be surprised, therefore, to find his name as *r*iksha in Sanskrit, as ἄρκτος in Greek, and as ursus in Latin.

But because the Aryas, before they branched off into North-Westerns and South-Easterns, knew the bear, it does not follow that we must push their original home away from Central Asia to the extreme Arctic regions, and still less to Europe. Even the north of India may be called arctic in one sense, for the Great Bear is visible there; nor need we go to Arcady or Germany in order to meet with real bears. That the Aryas did not come from a very southern climate has long been known, for they possessed common names for winter, such as Sanskrit himâ, Greek χειμών, Latin hiems, Old Slav. zima, Irish gam. Ice, too, is represented by îs in Teutonic, by isi or isu in Iranic; snow by nix in Latin, νίφα (acc.) in Greek, snaiv-s in Gothic, sněgŭ in Old Slavonic, snigi in Old Irish, and snizh, to snow, in Zend. There being a common name for the birch-tree, bhûr*g*a in Sanskrit, bereza in Russian, birke in German, likewise points to a more temperate climate[1]. But none of these climatic indications drives us as yet out of Asia, as may be seen from the description quoted above from M. de Ujfalvy. The birch (*Birke*), which, being mistaken for the beech (*Buche*), has lately been said to be confined in Europe to countries westward of a line drawn from Königsberg to the Crimea, flourishes and abounds in the North of India. I possess Sanskrit MSS. from Kashmir, written on birch-bark. The roofs of houses are thatched there

[1] Klaproth, 'Nouveau Journal Asiatique,' v. p. 112; *anno* 1830.

with birch-bark, and boats even are made there of the same material, without any necessity as yet for importing it from Russia. In Kâlidâsa's Urvasî and elsewhere the bhûrga-patra is mentioned as a common writing material. And I now see, from a letter dated Sept. 2, 1887, signed Geo. B., and published in the *Times*, that birchworts are found all over Northern Europe, Northern Asia, Northern America, and on the Himalayas and the mountains of Peru and Columbia, and in the Antarctic regions [1].

However, taking the bear and the birch together, I confess I was at one time inclined ('Selected Essays,' i. 187) to follow Benfey, when, on the strength of this and similar linguistic facts, he proposed, in the preface to Fick's *Wurzellexicon*, 1868, and in his *Geschichte der Sprachwissenschaft*, 1869 (p. 600), to fix the original home of the Aryas on the very frontiers of Asia, 'north of the Black Sea, from the mouth of the Danube to the Caspian Sea.' But Benfey himself perceived that he had been too rash in trying to fix the home of the Aryas so definitely, and in 1875 he speaks with far more caution on that subject [2]. Any-

[1] Sir George Birdwood adds: 'Moreover, the common birch (*Betula alba*) is not restricted to the parts of the Euro-Asiatic continent westward of the line drawn by Professor Sayce, but is a native of all the colder regions of Europe and Asia. It is found everywhere throughout the Russian Empire, and the oil extracted from it is used in the preparation of Russia leather. Two species are common to the Himalayas—viz. *Betula acuminata*, found in Tibet and Nepaul and the outer ranges of the Himalayas generally; *B. Bhojpattra*, called *bhûrja* (i.e. birch) in Sanskrit, and *bhûjpattra* in the North-West Provinces, a native of Ladak, Lahoul, Cashmere, Spiti, Kunawar, Sikkim, and Bhutan. The inner back of the *bhûrja*, which is closely allied to *B. papyracea* of North America, has been used by the Hindus as paper from the beginning of the Christian era.'

[2] 'Allgemeine Zeitung,' 1875, No. 208, Beilage, p. 3270; Schrader, 'Sprachvergleichung,' p. 127.

how, the arguments which he promised have never been forthcoming, while the arguments which other scholars have produced, and by which they have tried to push the frontiers of the Aryan home as far as Germany, Scandinavia, and Siberia, seem to me to have rather weakened than strengthened their case. The reasons which induced Geiger[1] to proclaim Germany as the original home of the Aryas, have not stood the criticism of unprejudiced scholars, though the evidence with which we have to deal is so pliant that it is possible to make out a more or less plausible case, as M. Piètrement has done for Siberia, and Dr. Penka for Scandinavia, as the true *officina gentium Aricarum*. Dr. Penka's arguments are in themselves extremely interesting[2]. He tries to show that the picture which linguistic palæontology has drawn of Aryan life previous to the separation, coincides with the picture which archæological palæontology constructs from the neolithic remains discovered in Scandinavia. But how would this prove that the Aryas were autochthonous in Scandinavia or in Switzerland or along the Po? Even the identity of the flora and fauna of Scandinavia with the fauna and flora attested by the common Aryan language would in no way decide the question, unless we could prove that no other country could put forward a similar claim.

Dr. Schrader has likewise collected a considerable amount of evidence to show that the civilisation, if so we may call it, revealed to us in the common vocabu-

[1] 'Zur Entwickelungsgeschichte der Menschheit,' 1871. See also Cuno, 'Forschungen im Gebiete der alten Völkerkunde,' 1 Theil, Die Scythen, 1871.

[2] 'Origines Aricae,' 1883; 'Herkunft der Arier,' 1886.

lary of the Aryas, corresponds in several details[1] with the civilisation attested by the remains of the lacustrian dwellings of the stone period. But he does not lay it down therefore as an established truth that the Aryas had their original home in Switzerland; he only doubts whether their Asiatic origin is quite as certain as was formerly supposed. I may quote his own words: 'If we survey these certain and, as it seems to me, well-established points, I urge once more that I do not believe they suffice in order to solve at present the question whether the origin of the Indo-Germans is to be looked for in Asia or in Europe, in a final and decisive way. But, in conclusion, I should not like to conceal the fact that, contrary to my former belief, the European hypothesis, i.e. the view that the origin of the Indo-Germanic peoples is to be looked for in the West rather than in the East, seems to me far better to agree with facts.'

We ought to be extremely grateful to M. Van den Gheyn, who, in his recent essay, *L'Origine Européenne des Aryas*, Anvers, 1885, has taken the trouble to subject all these theories recently put forward by Cuno, Poesche, von Löher, Schrader, and Penka, to a minute examination. It is often far easier to start a theory than to refute it, the domain of the possible being so much larger than that of the impossible. We have had similar theories before. Goropius tried to prove that Dutch was the language of Paradise; Kempe preferred Swedish; Erro, Bask[2]. M. Van den Gheyn treats the views of Schrader and

[1] M. Van den Gheyn shows that the sheep is not found in the terramares of the Po, which are later than the stone age, while the horse has been found at Viville.

[2] See M. M., 'Lectures on the Science of Language,' vol. i. p. 149.

von Löher with the respect which they deserve. Neither of them goes beyond asserting that the Asiatic origin of the Aryas has not yet been placed beyond the reach of doubt, and should not be treated as an established fact, like, for instance, the continental origin of the Saxons in England. But M. Van den Gheyn is justly impatient with the theories of Cuno, Poesche, Tomaschek, and Penka, because their conclusions, advanced with so much assurance, rest on arguments which crumble at the very first touch. Tomaschek is satisfied with claiming Eastern Europe as the home of the Aryas, Poesche restricts their home to the sources of the Danube, Cuno relegates them to the centre of Germany, Penka to Central Europe (p. 91), and then to Scandinavia. Not one of these theories, as Van den Gheyn shows, reaches even the lowest level of probability, while in every one of them facts or arguments are simply ignored, which strongly point in a different direction.

Much stress has been laid by Penka and others on the physical characteristics of the Aryan race, as pointing to Scandinavia as our original home. No one can deny the fact that the people who speak Aryan languages are partly dark and brachycephalic, partly fair and dolichocephalic, and partly mixed. The majority, however, even at the present day, is with the dark and brachycephalic tribes. Nevertheless, we are asked to believe that our earliest forefathers were dolichocephalic, had blue eyes and blond hair, though nothing is said as to how they became brachycephalic, and how their eyes became brown and their hair black. Poesche, in his book *Die Arier*, 1878, tells us indeed of a place in the Rokitno swamps of

Russia, near the river Prypet, a branch of the Dniepr (the old Borysthenes), where depigmentation takes place very rapidly, not only among plants and animals, but also among men, and where in consequence he places an important station of the Aryas. But if the dark Aryas might possibly have been bleached there, we know as yet of no place where the fair Aryas could have been blackened.

The whole idea of depigmentation is purely gratuitous. If the people who speak Aryan languages are partly dark and partly fair, simple conquest would explain all that has to be explained. Some of the blackest inhabitants of India now speak Sanskritic dialects, Franks speak a Romanic, Celts in England a Teutonic language. Historical conquests explain all these facts, and pre-historic conquests would explain many more. But, apart from all that, when will people learn at last that blood has nothing to do with language, and that all we can do as philologists is to classify languages, taking it for granted that they were spoken by somebody, but leaving those somebodies to the tender mercies of the ethnologist?

M. Van den Gheyn has performed his task of critic with great patience, moderation, and skill; and if the theory of a European origin of the Aryas is to be taken up again, it is to be hoped that its advocates may first of all take to heart the lessons which M. Van den Gheyn has taught them.

Let us examine now the purely linguistic arguments. On no subject have positive assertions been made with such assurance as on the character of the people who spoke the original Aryan language. If it is difficult to prove, it is equally difficult to disprove anything with regard to such distant times, and scientific imagination has therefore free scope to roam. Scholars, however, who know how thin the ice really is on which they have to skate, are not inclined to go beyond mere conjecture, and they tremble whenever they see their own fragile arguments handled so daringly by their muscular colleagues, the palæontologists and cranioscopists.

Dr. Penka, for instance, tells us with great assurance that the Aryas had a common name for the sea, but he must know that this is one of the most contested points among scholars. I hold that ἅλς (fem.) meant, first, sea, afterwards, as a masc., salt. Others take the opposite view. I connect ἅλ-ς and sal with salila, water, in Sanskrit. Curtius objects to that derivation. I think that Benfey was right in assigning to Sanskrit sará the meaning of salt (see his last article in *Sitzungsberichte der Göttinger anthropologischen Gesellschaft*, 15 July, 1876), but I still doubt whether this proves that sea-salt was known to the Aryas before they separated. Though ἅλς meant salt, because it first meant the sea, no one can prove that sará in Sanskrit meant first the sea, and afterwards salt[1]. The Aryas have no common name for the sea, for even if mîra did mean sea in Sanskrit, that word could never be identified with mare, Goth. marei, Irish muir, Old Slav. morje. I do not say that therefore the sea must have been unknown to the united Aryas; I only say, we cannot prove by linguistic evidence they had reached the sea before they separated.

Over and over again we see palæontologists, in their eagerness to prove their point, taking for granted

[1] Schrader, l. c. p. 374.

what scholars would either decline to grant, or grant only with every kind of caution. Dr. Penka tells us, for instance (p. 45), that the beech was known to the Aryas before they separated. But that is not so. There is no word in Sanskrit or Zend corresponding to *φηγός*, and *φηγός* in Greek is still the oak, not yet the beech. If we are told that the original Aryas must have lived in Europe west of a line drawn from Königsberg to the Crimea, because the beech does not overstep that line, we must observe, first, that Grisebach, on whose authority this statement rests, allows the growth of the beech along the Caucasus, and, secondly, that the whole nerve of the argument is cut by the fact that no word corresponding to fagus occurs in Sanskrit. One more instance of Dr. Penka's courage and we have done. Dr. Penka (p. 23) is bold enough to say that we have evidence of Aryas in the names of the Chatu-arii, Attu-arii, Ansu-arii, Ripu-arii, Chasu-arii, Boructu-arii, Cantu-arii, Vectu-arii, Teutono-aroi, and Boio-arii. This is really unpardonable. So long as we deal with names of which the historical antecedents are unknown, a mere guess that they may have meant this or that is pardonable. But in Cantuarii we have the Anglo-Saxon Cant-ware, men of Kent, as in Rôm-ware, the men of Rome; and who would venture to see in ware a representative of Arya?

Let us now see what has more recently been said in support of an Asiatic home. Nothing, I know, is so dangerous as when we find our own opinions suddenly supported by quite unexpected evidence. It seems almost ungracious to examine our new ally too closely, and we generally succumb to his friendly pleadings. Thus when in 1879 Dr. Hommel of Munich showed in a very learned paper, *Die Arier und Semiten*, that the Aryan and Semitic nations possessed in common a number of names connected with early civilisation, and that therefore they must have lived in very ancient times, previous in fact to the Aryan Separation, in very close proximity, I felt sorely tempted. I thought at first that this would settle once and for all the Asiatic home of the Aryas. No one has yet doubted that the Semitic nations were of Asiatic origin[1], and if we could prove that the Aryas had borrowed from the Semites words which are found both in the North-Western and South-Eastern branches of the Aryan family, no one could question again the Eastern origin of the Aryas. The principal words which Dr. Hommel mentions as ancient Semitic loan-words are the names for *bull*, *horn*, *lion*, *gold*, *silver*, and *vine*.

Though I am arguing against my own interests, I must say that in most cases his etymologies seem to me doubtful, the words lending themselves as well to an Aryan as to a Semitic etymology.

Secondly, supposing the words to be Semitic, far too much laxity is allowed in the changes which such words are supposed to have undergone in migrating from a Semitic into an Aryan language. It is quite true that foreign words undergo strange corruptions, even between languages so closely allied as Greek and Latin, yet when all depends on mere similarity of sound, some attempt should surely be made by the advocates of Semitic loans, to show how the phonetic changes could have arisen. Thus, to give a favourite

[1] By a sentence in Dr. Penka's last book, 'Die Herkunft der Arier,' p. ix, I see that he is bold enough to doubt that 'inner Asia is the home of the Semites.' What do Babylonian scholars say to this?

instance, when ὄνος, donkey, is derived from âton, we want to know why the Semitic âton, female donkey, should have become ὄνος in Greek, asinus in Latin[1]. The Aryan etymology of ὄνος is much less objectionable, if objectionable at all. If ὄνος stands for ὄσνος[2], then asinus and ὄνος point to a base as. From the same base we have Sk. as-ita[3], as-iknî, etc., expressing a dark or greyish colour. Why should not the donkey have been called the grey animal? This is at all events a possible etymology; and a passage quoted by Professor A. Weber[4] from the *S*atapatha-Brâhma*n*a throws some curious light on it. There we read, átha yád ắsâ*h* pâ*m*sáva*h* paryá*s*ishyanta táto gardabhá*h* sámabhavat, 'then from the ash-dust that was left, the donkey arose.'

Thirdly, before we admit that the Aryas borrowed some of their common words from their Semitic neighbours, we must not entirely neglect the possibility of accidental coincidences. We know as a fact that in several cases the same objects have received very similar names in languages unconnected by any ties of relationship[5].

If we examine, for instance, the name for gold, it seems now to be taken almost for granted that the Greeks borrowed their name for gold, chrysos, from their Semitic neighbours[6]. But chârûz in Hebrew is only a poetic name for gold, the ordinary name being zâhâb, presupposing a primitive Semitic

[1] Schrader, 'Sprachvergleichung,' p. 346; Curtius, p. 402.
[2] G. Meyer, 'Griech. Grammatik,' p. 249.
[3] See Boehtlingk-Roth, s.v.
[4] Kuhn's 'Zeitschrift,' x. p. 400.
[5] See Garnett, 'Philological Essays,' pp. 79, 85; M. M., 'Letter on the Turanian Languages,' pp. 95–96.
[6] Schrader, 'Sprachvergleichung,' p. 149.

*d*ahabu. As to *h*ura*s*u, which is said to be a name for gold in Assyria, I cannot tell whether it is a common name. But whatever it be, why should the Greeks have rendered the sound of chârûz or *h*ura*s*u or harûdu by chrysos? We might as well identify harûdu with gâru*d*a, a name of gold in Sanskrit. I have tried to prove elsewhere that the Greek chrysos, gold, is an Aryan word, and that it meant the yellow metal, and I do not think the similarity in sound, such as it is, between the Aryan word chrysos and the Semitic word chârûz at all surprising.

With regard to the Greek name for lion, which is likewise supposed to have been borrowed from a Semitic source, I can understand how Greek lis might have been borrowed from Hebrew laish, but how léôn could be called an adaptation of laish, or even of lâbi, or old Semitic labi'atu, I confess I cannot see. I do not maintain that we have a quite satisfactory etymology of leôn in Greek; far from it. But Lefmann's derivation from ravant (lavant), roarer, seems at all events more plausible than a corruption of the Semitic labi'atu.

Again, we are told that the Aryas borrowed their word for bull from their Semitic neighbours. But why? If the Aryas knew cows, and no one denies that, is it likely that they should have been unacquainted with bulls, or have had to borrow their name for them from the Semites? The Greek tauros, Lat. taurus, Gothic stiur, needs no foreign etymology. It is simply the Sanskrit sthûra, which means strong, like sthavira and sthira, and is actually given as a name for bull by native lexicographers.

If the Semitic name for bull is tauru or thauru, that would never account for Gothic stiur, or for Sk. sthûra or sthûla. I look upon this coincidence too as purely accidental.

Aryan scholars seem to me as a rule far too yielding towards etymologies of Sanskrit words taken from Semitic sources. Why should we derive the Aryan word for vine from Hebrew jain or Arabic wain? Neither form can be derived from any Semitic root, and, as even Schrader[1], who often favours Semitic loan-words, has pointed out, jain could never have become *οἶνος* in Greek. I doubt whether vînum in Latin is borrowed from Greek[2], though the German and Celtic names were certainly borrowed from the Romans. I have always held that vînum cannot be separated from vîtis, vîmen, etc., and that it meant originally a creeping or twining plant, from root VÎ, VYÂ, to twine, to embrace. From the same root *οἶνος* can be derived without the slightest difficulty; and if we find corresponding words in Armenian gini, Georgian ghwino, and Albanian vene, are we not justified in saying that the vine was first known to the Aryas in its natural home, the neighbourhood of Pontus and the Caspian Sea[3]?

If one considers all the historical consequences which would flow from a borrowing of Semitic words on the part of the Aryas, one cannot be too cautious. In our case Dr. Hommel's identification, if proved to be tenable, would settle once for all the original home

[1] l. c. p. 377.

[2] Traces of wine were found in the lacustrian dwellings of the Aemilia; see Helbig, 'Die Italiker in der Poebene,' 1879, vol. i. p. 62; Schrader, l. c. p. 83.

[3] See Schrader, l. c. p. 377; also 'Gedanken,' by the same, p. 7.

of the Aryas, as close neighbours of the early Semites; but decisive as no doubt it would be in support of a theory which I myself hold to be true, I do not consider the argument, as such, admissible, or capable of supporting the conclusion which is to rest on it, namely a close neighbourhood between Aryas and Semites, before the breaking up of the Aryas into a North-Western and South-Eastern branch.

I cannot even admit an intercourse between the Semitic inhabitants of Babylonia and the Aryas of India in later, though still in pre-Vedic times, such as has been asserted by several scholars on the slenderest evidence. Dr. Schrader, for instance, repeats the statement that the Accadian word mana, which Herodotus mentions as *μνᾶ*, the Latin mina, Hebrew maneh, Egyptian mn, is found in the Veda. Far-reaching speculations as to a very ancient commercial intercourse between India and the great Assyrian and Babylonian Empires have been based on this isolated fact, for if a road was once open for minas to travel from the Euphrates to the Indus, the same road would admit everything else in India for which a foreign origin was desired. But manā̃, where it occurs in the Veda, cannot possibly mean mina; it cannot even be an instrumental case, as it was supposed to be. If we must conjecture, manâ in the Veda may possibly be connected with ma*n*i, Zend minu, necklet, Greek *μάννος*, and Latin monile, a precious ornament. The lingual *n* in ma*n*i is irregular, but so is likewise the *n* of ve*n*i. Anyhow, an intercourse between Babylonia and Vedic India, whether commercial, astronomical, or religious, is as yet a mere postulate.

I may mention here another assertion which has

likewise served as the foundation for several historical theories. Because the art of riding on horseback was unknown, as Schrader[1] says, to the Vedic Indians as well as to the early Greeks, we are asked to believe that the Iranians of the Avesta had learnt that art from their nomadic neighbours of Turco-tataric origin[2], and if they had learnt that, they might have learnt many other things, no doubt, from the same masters. But the art of riding on horseback and sitting astride is several times alluded to in the Veda. In Rv. v. 61, 2, we read of the Maruts:—

> Where are your horses, where the bridle? How could you, how did you come?—the seat on the back, the rein in the nostrils?
>
> Their goad is behind, the heroes stretched their legs apart, putrakrithé ná ganáyah.

Can anything be clearer than this?

It is difficult to stop a ball after it has once been set rolling, and therefore we cannot be too cautious in starting a ball. The question as to the original home of those who spoke an Aryan language, before the Aryas separated, was a very natural question, and among scholars who bear in mind the natural limitations under which such questions can be answered, I do not say that to place that home provisionally somewhere in Asia was likely to lead to grave misunderstandings. The *prima facie* evidence points certainly to the East, and more than that no one, cognisant of these matters, would expect. We have two streams of language, one tending South-East to India, the other North-West to Europe. The point where these two streams naturally intersect, points to Asia.

[1] Schrader, 'Sprachvergleichung,' p. 344.
[2] W. Geiger, 'Osteranische Cultur,' p. 354.

Secondly, the earliest centres of civilised life were in Asia. We have evidence of oral literature in India, when there is as yet no trace of it among any of the nations of Europe, least of all in Scandinavia. It was natural therefore, though I say no more, to look to the East as the home of the Aryas.

Thirdly, we see in later times large ethnic waves rising from Central Asia and overwhelming Europe, such as the Huns in the fourth, and the Mongols in the thirteenth century.

Fourthly, if the migration had taken place from Europe to Asia, particularly from Scandinavia, we should naturally look in the common Aryan language for a number of words connected with maritime life. There is, however, no name for the sea shared by the North-Western and South-Eastern branches; while the principal members of the North-Western branch share in common, as we should expect, a name for sea; Lat. mare, Old Gaulish more, Old Slav. morje, Goth. marei, and mari-saiv, λίμνη.

We know that the people in the North of Europe, and particularly in Scandinavia, depended from the earliest times on fish for their food. The Kjökken-moeddings are there to prove it. But while we find common Aryan names, not only for special domestic animals and birds, but also for animals (pasu) and birds (vi) in general, we look in vain in the ancient Aryan Dictionary, not only for names for any special fishes, but even for a general word for fish[1]. In the Vedic hymns there is no mention of fishes being eaten, nor, as yet, in the Homeric poems.

But though most of the animals which have common

[1] Schrader, p. 171.

names occur in Europe as well as in Asia, I doubt whether, if the Aryas had lived at first in Scandinavia, they would have brought from thence a common name for serpents. Curiously enough, however, while we have no common Aryan name for fish, we have two for serpent. We have Sanskrit áhis, reproduced in Greek as ἔχις, in Latin as anguis, in Old High-German as unc. I know that those who cannot account for serpents in Germany or Scandinavia look upon ahis as a name for dragon rather than serpent, and explain it as a half-mythological recollection of prehistoric times. But there remains Sk. sarpás, corresponding closely to Lat. serpens, and even to Greek ἑρπετόν, creeping things, which cannot well be relegated to geological periods likewise. Besides, whereas ahis means large serpents in Sanskrit, Greek, and Latin, which may therefore be supposed to have been familiar to the Aryas before they separated, another animal, namely the eel, which, so far as I can ascertain, has no name in Sanskrit, was called by the Aryas, when settled in Europe, the little serpent, anguilla in Latin, ungurýs in Lituanian, ἔγχελυς in Greek. How are we to account for this, if the Aryas were first settled in Scandinavia, where they knew eels and no serpents, and afterwards migrated to India where they knew plenty of serpents, but no eels, at least not for culinary purposes. I see, however, that some of the vernacular names for eel in India may be derived from ahi.

It seems almost impossible to discover any animal or any plant that is peculiar to the North of Europe, and is not found sporadically in Asia also. However, in the case of the *crane* we may say at least this, that the bird seems to have excited no interest among the speakers of the South-Eastern languages, and that they never used its name metaphorically as the name of an engine. Sârasa, crane, in Sanskrit means no more than a lacustrian bird. In the North-Western languages, on the contrary, the crane was evidently an old friend. It is *γέρανος* in Greek, grûs in Latin, cran in A. S., žeravĭ in Old Slavonic, garan in Cornish, and kroünkn in Armenian; and the use of the same word as a name for a crane shows how familiar the bird must have become to the speakers of the North-Western dialects, after they had separated from their companions in the South-East.

However, I claim no irresistible force for any of these arguments. All I say is, that whereas such evidence as is attainable points Eastward, I know of none that points decidedly Westward, to Germany or Scandinavia.

If it can be shown by linguistic evidence that the occupations of the united Aryas were on the whole like those of the people of the kitchen-middens or of the lacustrian dwellers in Switzerland, why should not some of the early Aryas have been so far advanced as the inhabitants of those marine villages or of the Pfaalbauten? But here again we must be careful. Lacustrian dwellings determine the life and language of lacustrian dwellers. Hence if at Moosseedorf no remains of the horse have been found, that would not necessitate our denying to the united Aryas a knowledge of the horse as a tamed and useful animal. It was not wanted in lacustrian dwellings. But the name for horse exists in all the

Aryan languages, and, as I said before, people generally name only what they care for, and they do care most for what is useful. Besides, we should bear in mind that if linguistic science is still in its infancy, lacustrian science may be called almost embryonic. With every year new finds are made, and, in the case of the horse, its bones have lately been discovered at Viville[1].

I have declared again and again that if I say Aryas, I mean neither blood nor bones, nor hair nor skull; I mean simply those who speak an Aryan language. The same applies to Hindus, Greeks, Romans, Germans, Celts, and Slaves. When I speak of them I commit myself to no anatomical characteristics[2]. The blue-eyed and fair-haired Scandinavians may have been conquerors or conquered, they may have adopted the language of their darker lords or their subjects, or *vice versâ*. I assert nothing beyond their language when I call them Hindus, Greeks, Romans, Germans, Celts, and Slaves; and in that sense, and in that sense only, do I say that even the blackest Hindus represent an earlier stage of Aryan speech and thought than the fairest Scandinavians. This may seem strong language, but in matters of such importance we cannot be too decided in our language. To me an ethnologist who speaks of Aryan race, Aryan blood, Aryan eyes and hair, is as great a sinner as a linguist who speaks of a dolichocephalic dictionary or a brachycephalic grammar. It is worse than a Babylonian confusion of tongues—it is downright theft. We have

[1] See Van den Gheyn, l. c. p. 7.

[2] See my letter to H. H. Risley, Esq., dated Oxford, 20th July, 1886, published by Government.

made our own terminology for the classification of languages; let ethnologists make their own for the classification of skulls, and hair, and blood.

If it can be proved that the people who brought Sanskrit into India came from Scandinavia, let it be so by all means. But to say that the ancient language of India, that Sanskrit, can be derived from Scandinavian, even from the oldest Norse, is simply a blunder. Let anybody compare Sanskrit with Gothic or Icelandic, and he will not hesitate long as to which of the two represents a more original character. What should we make of the Norse god Týr, and Týs-dagr, his day, Tuesday, unless we had the Sk. Dyu, nom. Dyaus, and its clear connection with deva, bright? In Sanskrit all is clear and coherent, in Icelandic words and their meanings have grown hard and become purely traditional. Are the people who say tíu for ten to be considered as representing an earlier stratum of language than the Hindus who say dáśan? Is fjórdi, the fourth, a witness to greater antiquity than *k*aturthá? I know quite well it is possible to wriggle out of everything, and say that the language of Scandinavia was once, before we know it, more primitive than that of the Aryas in India. This applies to all languages, if only we go back to the Tower of Babel. But where is there an atom of evidence for saying that the nearer to Scandinavia a people lived, the purer would be its Aryan race and speech, while in Greece and Armenia, Persia and India, we should find mixture and decay? Is not this not only different from the truth, but the very opposite of it?

We ought to see clearly that the question as to the original home of those who spoke Aryan, before the Aryas separated, will never admit of a positive answer, unless some quite unexpected evidence or some very ingenious combination shall be forthcoming.

In spite of all the eloquence of the advocates of various theories, in spite of the reckless assertions made by ethnologists in their attempts to convert the linguists, and the imprudent statements made by linguists in their attempts to convert the ethnologists, the real state of the problem has during the last forty years lost none of its inherent difficulties.

To sum up,—We have proved that the South-Eastern and North-Western branches of the Aryan family lived together somewhere, before their final separation. If therefore we want to prove that the quarters of the united Aryas were somewhere in Asia, we must prove two things—

(1) That the South-Eastern and North-Western branches possess words in common which refer to objects found in that neighbourhood;

(2) That the South-Eastern and North-Western branches are deficient in common words which refer to objects not found in that neighbourhood.

With reference to (1) our case is easy. Many such words, as the names for winter, snow, ice, cow, sheep, goat, dog, birch, etc., are common to the South-Eastern and North-Western branches,—so many that with them we can compose a more or less complete picture of the early life of the united Aryas. But unfortunately the same objection applies to all of them: they are all found, whether indigenous or naturalised, not only in Asia, but in Europe also and in other parts of the world. With reference to (2) our case is stronger. We ask, What would follow if the Aryas separated in Asia, some migrating to Persia, India, others to Europe? and if we find that what we expected would follow, has followed, we have a certain right to trust our argument. Now one thing which we expect would follow is that the two branches, starting, say, from the neighbourhood of Samarcand, would not have a common word for sea. And so it is. They have no common word for sea. But more than that. We should expect the various members of the North-Western branch to have the same word for sea, and so again it is. We have in Latin mare, in Gothic marei, in Lituanian máré, in Irish muir. Greek only is wanting, unless we appeal with Curtius to a son of Poseidon, called Amphi-maros. Again, people starting from that central home in Asia ought to have little knowledge of fishes. Fish is matsya in Sanskrit, masya in Zend, but in Latin piscis, in Gothic fisk, in Irish iasc.

In Greek, as we saw before, we have ἔγχελυς, eel, by the side of ἔχις, in Latin anguilla by the side of anguis, in Lituanian ungurýs by the side of angìs. In the South-Eastern branch on the contrary we find no such names, and it seems not unreasonable to conclude that this was owing to the fact that the South-Eastern Aryas did not fall in with the eel, or at all events, did not eat it[1].

Such fulfilments of expectations, I know, are dangerous, but they must be allowed to carry some weight, even with those to whom they are unwelcome. And we may test them once more. Suppose, as we are

[1] The eel is absent in the Black Sea and the Caspian with their tributary rivers. Brehm, 'Thierleben,' viii. p. 326; Penka, p. 46.

told, that the South-Eastern Aryas came from Scandinavia, and that the ancestors of the Aryas were the very people whose remains we can examine in the Scandinavian kitchen-middens. Well, these kitchen-middens are full—I quote from Professor Prestwich—not only of periwinkles, mussels, oysters, and three or four other species of shells, but of herrings and four or five species of fishes. These Scandinavian Aryas therefore depended on maritime food, and yet there is not a single trace of that maritime food in the common vocabulary of the Aryas.

I say so with trembling; for the assertions of the ethnologists on these points are really startling. Dr. Penka, in his *Herkunft der Arier*, p. 39, states that the name of the oyster is urarisch. But the fact is that it occurs in the North-Western branch only, and that even there it is simply a Greek word, ὄστρεον (cf. ὄστρακον, shell), borrowed by the Romans from the Greeks, ostrea, and then sent on to Anglo-Saxon as ostra, to Welsh as oestren, to Slavonic as ostreĭ, to Modern Greek as ὀστρίδι, from whence it found its way to Turkish as istridia, to Persian as istiridiya, etc. Pictet, who is generally responsible for these incorrect statements, is blameless in this case. He says, indeed, '*L'accord général des langues européennes entre elles ne saurait faire douter de l'existence d'un ancien nom arien* (*urarisch?*)[1].' But he adds very ingeniously, '*Si l'on pouvait conclure quelque chose d'un fait isolé, on serait tenté de croire que ce nom de l'huître, commun à tous les peuples européens, mais étranger aux Aryas orientaux, a pris naissance à l'époque où la race arienne commençait à se diviser en deux branches par suite de son extension graduelle vers la mer*

[1] 'Les Origines Indo-Européennes,' i. p. 515.

caspienne, dont les riverains apprirent seulement alors à connaître et à utiliser ce mollusque.'

Where is there any excuse, then, for calling *ὄστρεον* urarisch, and for extending the same denomination to numbers of other animals, all of which have common names in the North-Western branch only, but not in both branches of the Aryan family? Of course we may say that the members of the South-Eastern branch possessed all these words and lost them afterwards, but in that case it is, to say the least, extremely misleading to call them urarisch.

As the case stands at present, we may say therefore that there are no facts, whether positive or negative, which make the hypothesis of an Aryan home in Asia untenable; but we ought not to say more.

Let us now apply exactly the same tests to the Scandinavian theory. If the South-Eastern branch separated from the North-Western branch in Scandinavia, then—

(1) The two branches ought to possess words in common which refer to objects found in Scandinavia;

(2) The two branches ought to be deficient in common words which refer to objects not found in Scandinavia.

With regard to (1) there is naturally here, as before, a considerable number of words referring to objects found in Scandinavia, but elsewhere also. Still it ought to be remembered that maritime terms do not answer our expectation, and that there is not a single common word expressive of anything that is found in Scandinavia only. With regard to (2) I do not know whether the snake, ahi, may be called un-Scandinavian; if so, it would at once render the Scandinavian theory impossible, and would still further confirm the formation of the name for *eel*, as explained before.

Dr. Penka[1] gives a long list of names of animals which he declares to be urarisch. If by urarisch he means what exists in all the languages of the North-Western branch, it is simply a misnomer, and in that case nothing can be proved by these words. If he means by urarisch what is common to the North-Western and South-Eastern branches, then his facts are wrong or doubtful so far as the following animals and trees are concerned: *fox*, *lynx*, *otter* (udra is very doubtful), *hedgehog*, *beaver* (babhru is not beaver, and fiber may be, like fībra, from findo) *hart*, *roe* (not *ris*ya), *squirrel*, *marten*, *seal*, *wild cat*, *eel*, *starling*, *crane*, *quail*, *beech*, *oak*, *fir*, *horse*, *elm*, *alder*, *asp*, *ash*, *maple*, *yew*. All these names belong to the North-Western branch only. If they were common to the North-Western and South-Eastern branches, they would indeed be of great interest; but as they are not, how can any one say that the *fauna* and *flora* of the united Aryas, as represented by these words, agree with the *fauna* and *flora* of Scandinavia?

All this may sound very disheartening, but we must learn to bear with our horizons. It is wonderful enough that we should have discovered that our own language, that Greek and Latin, that Slavonic and Celtic, are closely connected with the languages now spoken in Armenia, Persia, and India. It is wonderful enough that out of the words which all these languages, or, at all events, some members of its two primitive branches, the North-Western and South-Eastern, share in common, we should have been able to construct

[1] 'Herkunft,' p. 37.

a kind of mosaic picture of the fauna and flora of the original home of the Aryas, of their cattle, their agriculture, their food and drink, their family life, their ideas of right and wrong, their political organisation, their arts, their religion, and their mythology. The actual site of the Aryan paradise, however, will probably never be discovered, partly because it left no traces in the memory of the children of the Aryan emigrants, partly because imagination would readily supply whatever the memory had lost. Nor is the actual site a matter of great importance. Most of the Aryan nations in later times were proud to call themselves children of the soil, children of their mother earth, autochthones. Some thought of the East, others of the North, as the home of their fathers; none of them, so far as I know, of the South or the West. New theories, however, have their attractions, and I do not wonder that some patriotic scholars should have been smitten with the idea of a German, Scandinavian, or Siberian cradle of Aryan life. I cannot bring myself to say more than *Non liquet.* But if an answer must be given as to the place where our Aryan ancestors dwelt before their separation, whether in large swarms of millions, or in a few scattered tents and huts, I should still say, as I said forty years ago, 'Somewhere in Asia,' and no more.

VII. The Earliest Aryan Civilisation.

THAT the words which all the Aryan languages share in common must have existed before the Aryas separated, and that they may be used therefore as evidence of what was seen and heard and known and thought and done by the Aryas at that early time, is a thought so natural that we need not wonder at its having occurred independently to various scholars.

The earliest list of common Aryan words seems to have been that of Colebrooke, made in 1801, and published by me in the fourth volume of my 'Chips from a German Workshop,' p. 418.

In 1820 J. Crawfurd, in his 'History of the Indian Archipelago,' drew up on the same principle a sketch of Polynesian civilisation, previous to the dispersion of the Polynesian race.

In 1836 F. G. Eichhoff, in his *Parallèle des langues de l'Europe et de l'Inde*, made a new attempt at a rough sketch of Aryan civilisation, which was afterwards more carefully carried out by Winning in his 'Manual of Comparative Philology,' 1838[1].

In 1845 the subject was taken up independently by A. Kuhn, in a small pamphlet, *Zur ältesten Geschichte der indogermanischen Völker, Oster-programm des*

[1] I find that it was Mr. Winning, and not, as I imagined, I myself, who first spoke of the *Lautverschiebungs-gesetz* as Grimm's Law. Mr. Winning's Manual has been strangely neglected both in England and in Germany. Considering its date, it was a very meritorious work.

Berliner Real-Gymnasiums[1]. Though it fills a few pages only, it differs from its predecessors by a far more critical sifting of the evidence, and likewise by the pronounced intention of the author to write a chapter of history based on linguistic documents.

In 1848 appeared Grimm's *Geschichte der Deutschen Sprache*, which contained a large collection of material principally intended to elucidate the earliest history of the Germans, but throwing many side-lights also on their relations with the Slavonic, Celtic, Greek, and Italic races of Europe and the ancient inhabitants of Persia and India.

During the following years a reaction set in, and many of the results that had been at first readily accepted, had to be subjected to a renewed criticism. Kuhn himself, in his *Zeitschrift*, pointed out the dangers which beset the study of linguistic palaeontology. Mommsen warned against the admission of a too far advanced state of civilisation before the Aryas migrated to Europe; others pointed out the danger of trusting to mere identity of roots without an identity in the derivative elements also.

In the year 1849 I presented to the *Académie des Inscriptions* at Paris an essay on the Early Civilisation of the Aryas, which received the *Prix Volney*. I was unable at the time to find a publisher for this work, but the MS. is in the archives of the French Institute, where any one may see and consult it. It was not till the year 1856 that I published the principal results of it in the *Oxford Essays*, in a paper entitled *Comparative Mythology*. I state these facts, not in order to establish any claims of priority, which I hate, but

[1] Republished in 'Indische Studien,' vol. i. pp. 321–363.

simply in order to correct a mistake into which Dr. Schrader has fallen in his *Sprachvergleichung und Urgeschichte* (1883). Here, in giving a history of the successive works devoted to linguistic palaeontology, he places my Essay in 1867, that is eight years after Pictet's work, whereas it was really published three years before it, and written nearly ten years earlier [1].

Pictet's work, in two large volumes, *Les origines Indo-européennes ou les Aryas primitifs*, Paris, 1859–63, second edition, 1877, excited, no doubt, much wider attention than any of the works which had preceded it. But I believe that among scholars there is but one opinion, namely that it marked no real progress. Pictet accumulated an immense material, but he was not scholar enough to sift it critically. Many of his etymologies and equations are simply impossible, and it will take a long time before all the erroneous statements which pass under his honoured name can be dislodged again. I do not mean to say that in the lists of common Aryan words collected by Kuhn, Grimm, and others, no mistakes whatever have been discovered during the thirty years that they have been before the world; that would be strange indeed in so progressive a science as Comparative Philology. What I maintain is, that after what had been published before, Pictet, in spite of his undoubted industry and in-

[1] This explains what seems inexplicable to Dr. Schrader, namely that in my Essay, i. 348 (1856), I considered *iron* as a metal known to the Aryas, while in my 'Lectures on the Science of Language,' ii. 258 (1864), I expressed the conviction, at which I had arrived in the mean time, that iron (as such) was unknown, that is unnamed, before the Aryan Separation, and that all which we can safely assert of this third metal is that it was neither gold nor silver. Dr. Schrader, by assigning the year 1867 to my Essay, and 1864 to my Lectures, is naturally puzzled by this contradiction.

genuity, has really retarded the advance of these archaeological researches by re-introducing principles of comparison which had long been discarded. After the publication of my own paper in 1856, the most important contributions to linguistic palaeontology were Justi's article in Raumer's *Histor. Taschenbuch*, 1862, and Schleicher's article in Hildebrand's *Jahrbücher für Nationalökonomie*, 1863. There were besides many contributions on special points, such as Förstemann's early papers on the names of animals in Kuhn's *Zeitschrift*, vols. i. and iii; and several articles by Pott in the same journal.

A more comprehensive treatment of the whole subject was attempted once more by Dr. Fick in his *Vergleichendes Wörterbuch der Indogermanischen Sprachen*, 1868; a book which may still be consulted with great advantage by students of linguistic palaeontology.

After this there followed another reaction, which found its most eloquent expression in Hehn's *Culturpflanzen und Hausthiere in ihrem Übergang von Asien nach Griechenland und Italien*, 1870, fourth ed. 1883. Dr. Hehn is first of all an historian, and as an historian he objects to a number of conclusions which, according to him, have been less accurately formulated by students of language than students of history would allow. In this he seems to me partly right, partly wrong. He thinks that the picture of early Aryan civilisation has been painted in too glowing colours, and that we ought to moderate our affections towards our Aryan ancestors. This is perfectly true, but I think he often exaggerates this danger. All scholars, in speaking of what may have been the state of civilisation four thousand years ago, take it for granted that those whom they address know the limitations inherent in the subject. Thus, to take an instance: Dr. Hehn lays great stress on the fact that, though the name of horse was a common Aryan word, it does not prove that the horse was tamed or domesticated before the Aryas broke up their common home. It certainly does not; and the same remark applies to several other animals. There may have been wild horses, but there may also have been tamed horses. Some tribes may have excelled in horsemanship; others, in mountainous regions or in lacustrian dwellings, may have found the breeding of horses an unprofitable occupation. But the very fact that the horse was called the 'quick,' suggests that it was quick, and useful as quick, to those who tamed and named it. The equation of vádhri = ἔθρις is very significant, while that between Sk. khalîna, bit, and χαλῑνός seems almost too good to be true. Still to say that khalîna in Sanskrit was borrowed from Greek, is as yet a mere assertion, and the occurrence of the word in the Ga*n*a arddhar*k*âdi deserves more consideration than it has hitherto received[1].

If Dr. Hehn remarks that Sk. a*g*a, Greek *αἴξ*, *αἰγός*, which we translate by goat, may have meant any 'jumping deer,' it is difficult to know what to say. It may have meant that, no doubt; it also may have meant any animal that is driven, from a*g*, a*g*ra, etc.[2] But the fact that it means goat in Sanskrit, Greek, and Lituanian is surely of some weight, to say nothing

[1] Kremer (*Ausland*, 1875, Nos. 1, 2, 4, 5) derives the Semitic sus from asva, the Arabic faras from Pâras, Persia. Hommel denies this; see Schrader, l. c., p. 60.

[2] Mr. Whitley Stokes derives ag in ag allaid (lit. wild ox) from the root a*g*, to drive.

of ag*í*na and αἰγίς, and Old Slav. azno, meaning originally goat-skin, then skin, then leather.

When we compare purî and Greek πόλις, and translate it town, we do not mean therefore a town like London. The most primitive place of safety might have been called purî, yet that such places should have been called by the same name in Sanskrit and Greek shows a significant continuity in the growth of towns from their first primitive beginnings to their latest developments.

Dr. Hehn often complains that those who connect concepts of modern civilised life with old words have no difficulty in finding our modern life in the period of the earliest beginnings[1]. But is that a fair representation of what Kuhn and others have done?

We have never held that such words as μύλη in Greek, mola in Latin, muli in German, prove that regular mills were known before the European nations became separated. What would Dr. Hehn call a regular mill? No one thought that the Aryas had large water-mills, or wind-mills, or steam-mills. Their mills were probably nothing but hand-mills, or two stones between which grain was crushed, such as have been found in neolithic strata[2]. Still, here again we see the same curious historical continuity, which shows that, though the process of grinding was constantly improved, there was no break between the first idea of a mill which sprang up in the earliest Aryan times and our present mills. Nor do I think it at all likely that, if the idea of grinding corn had been started in-

[1] 'Culturpflanzen,' p. 476.

[2] Ymer, 'Tidskrift utgiven af Svenska Sällskapet för antropologi och geografi,' iv. Förhandlingar xxx; Penka, 'Herkunft,' p. 36.

dependently by each Aryan tribe, the Greeks would have called a mill μύλη, the Romans mola, the Germans muli. It is true they all had a right to the common Aryan root MÆR; but they might have derived their names for mill from different roots also, and formed them by means of different suffixes. In Sanskrit, for instance, they did not derive the name for mill from MÆR or MAL, to crush, but took PISH, to form pish*t*a, flour, pesha*n*a, hand-mill, pesha*n*i, grind-stone; or *K*ARV, from which *k*ûr*n*a, meal, etc. There was a third root *G*Æ, to crush, from which we have grânum, Old Irish grán, possibly borrowed, Goth. kaúrn, Old Slav. zrŭno, Greek γῦρις, flour, possibly γρῦ in οὐδὲ γρῦ[1]. This also might have yielded a name for mill, and it has done so to a certain extent, when we consider the Old Slav. žrĭny, mill, the Lit. gìrnos, plural, mill-stones, Goth. asilu-qaírnus, Gk. μύλος ὀνικός, mill-stone, and the English quern. The fact, therefore, that Greeks, Romans, Germans, Slaves, and Celts, that is, all the members of the South-Western branch, have a common word for mill, derived from the root MÆR or MAL, which in Sanskrit means to pound, possesses in my eyes some historical importance, which need not be exaggerated, but which ought neither to be unnecessarily minimised.

When we say that the Aryas, before their separation, were agricultural, we mean no more than that they did not depend for their food on mere chance, but cultivated the soil and grew some kind of corn. The root ÆR tells its own story. It meant originally no more than 'to stir.' As applied to the stirring of the water by means of oars, it came to mean

[1] Clemm, 'Studien,' iii. 294; Curtius, p. 176.

to row, as we see in Sk. arítras, oar, ἀλιήρης, sea-stirring, and ἐρετμός, rudder, in Greek, rêmus in Latin, ruodar in OHG., irklas in Lituanian, rám in Irish. As applied to the stirring of the soil by means of a stick or a plough, we see it in ἀρόω, arare, Goth. arjan, Lit. árti, but ìrti, to row, Irish arathar[1]. In Sanskrit, it is true, this root is not used with the meaning of ploughing. In that sense, the South-Eastern Aryas used KÆRSH, to draw lines or furrows, which is never used in that sense in the North-Western branch. The root ÆR may, however, have left some very old derivatives there also, viz. in i*d*, i*d*â, and irâ, earth, Gk. ἔρα in ἔραζε; and in urvárâ, field, for ar-varâ=ἄρουρα. In Zend[2] urvara means what is grown, the produce of the field, rather than the field itself. If therefore Dr. Hehn admits a half-nomadic agriculture among the early Aryas, he will find this is all that we contended for ourselves.

And what applies to the oldest art, the ars *par excellence*, the art of ploughing, applies naturally to all the other arts which we ascribe to the ancient Aryas, such as platting, sewing, spinning, weaving, and all the rest. They must all be conceived as most simple and primitive, and it would be difficult in many cases to say where platting ends and weaving begins.

All this, I thought, was understood, and it seems to me really as if our critics often called up a ghost in order to lay it. In drawing the outline of so very distant a landscape as that of the common home of the Aryas we must be satisfied with broad, often with

[1] See an interesting paper by E. B. Tylor, 'On the Origin of the Plough,' in the 'Journal of the Anthropological Institute,' August 1880; and G. A. Grierson, 'Bihar Peasant Life,' 1885, pp. 1–9.

[2] Spiegel, 'Die Arische Periode,' p. 43.

faint outlines. We must neither be too confiding, as Professor Fick is sometimes in his *Spracheinheit der Indogermanen Europas* (1873), nor too sceptical, like Dr. Hehn, lest we offend against those very canons of historical criticism for which he pleads.

The best we can do under present circumstances is to let facts speak for themselves. I thought so in 1856 when I drew up a number of lists containing the words which the Aryan languages have in common, and which I accompanied with a very short commentary. I shall content myself at present with printing these *pièces justificatives*, leaving it to others to complement them and to draw from them such conclusions as they seem to warrant. I have divided them, as well as I could, according to subjects.

I.	Family-relations.	IX.	Seasons.
II.	Domestic Animals.	X.	Weapons.
III.	Wild Animals.	XI.	Metals.
IV.	Birds.	XII.	Government.
V.	House and Home.	XIII.	Body.
VI.	Home-occupations.	XIV.	Mind.
VII.	Trees and Plants.	XV.	Religion and Myth.
VIII.	Agriculture.		

Though I quite admit that the most satisfactory coincidences are those in which not only the roots, but the derivative suffixes also, agree, yet I have not excluded such equations as Sk. sûnú, son (not sűnu, as Curtius writes and many after him), and Greek *υἱός*, son, because both words seem to me to express the same concept, namely a male child, v*ri*shan, *ἄρσην*. The suffixes vary even in Greek, where we have *ὑ-ι*, *ὑ-ιο*, and *ὑ-ιυ*[1]; the Sanskrit sû-nu is therefore a

[1] See Curtius, p. 395.

fourth variety only. It is different with Sanskrit sutá, son; there the suffix has a passive meaning, and expresses one who has been begotten, corresponding to Old Irish suth, fetus, and therefore conveying a totally different concept.

When the same word has assumed various meanings in different languages, I have generally noted them. Thus Greek φράτηρ must have conveyed originally the same concept as Sk. bhrấtar, but it came to mean member of a clan, and thus ceased to be the recognised term for brother.

In Latin and Greek I have as a rule given the nom. sing., while in Sanskrit and in Teutonic, Slavonic, and Celtic words I have preferred the mere base. In cases where there could be any uncertainty I have added in Sanskrit the nom. sing.; while in some cases, when the nom. sing. or the nom. plur. seemed preferable, they have been inserted, but so that the terminations could be clearly distinguished.

I have not added references, because the words given in my statistical lists can easily be traced in the ordinary books of reference, such as Pott's *Etymologische Forschungen*, second ed., Fick's *Wörterbuch der Indo-germanischen Sprachen*, Curtius' *Grundzüge der Griechischen Etymologie.* With regard to Celtic only I felt sometimes at a loss, and had to consult Mr. Whitley Stokes, who has carefully examined the Irish words which occur in my lists. Several of the Celtic, Slavonic, and Teutonic words are clearly borrowed, but I have left them as likely to be useful.

I have still to say a few words about the sharp line of demarcation which I have always traced between words belonging to the S.E. and the N.W.

branches, i.e. between Sanskrit and Persian, old and modern, on one side, and Greek, Latin, Teutonic, Slavonic, and Celtic words on the other. The soundness of all the historical conclusions to be derived from my lists of common Aryan words, depends on that line of demarcation. I still hold as strongly as ever that the first division of the Aryan race was into two branches, the North-Western or European, and the South-Eastern or Asiatic. After they became once separated, these two branches never met again. Every word, therefore, shared in common by the South-Eastern branch and any single member of the North-Western branch is a real historical document which may safely be used to elucidate the life of the Aryas before their separation. I know that I stand almost alone in this opinion, but I also know that no real argument has ever been advanced against it [1].

Whether it will ever be possible with the linguistic materials at our disposal to draw a picture of North-Western civilisation in general, or of any subdivision of it, such as Greek, Italic, Teutonic, Slavonic, and Celtic, I am not prepared to say. But judging from what has hitherto been achieved in this line, I should think it was almost *ultra vires*. Whatever the North-Western and South-Eastern languages share in common, must have existed before the two became permanently separated. But what the North-Western and the South-Eastern possess separately, may or may not

[1] Spiegel, in his 'Arische Periode,' just published, agrees with me. 'If the Arians,' he writes, p. 20, and by Arians he means Hindus and Persians, 'share an expression with only one single branch of the European Indo-Kelts (by which he means the whole of the North-Western branch), this suffices to stamp that expression as Indo-Keltic (i. e. Indo-European) in general.'

be older than their separation. One language may have preserved what the others lost, and, once arrived in Europe, one language may have borrowed from another.

And if we attempt to draw smaller pictures of civilisation from the materials supplied by the languages of certain groups, such as the Greco-Italic, Germano-Slavonic, Latino-Celtic, etc., the chances of error are almost as numerous as the chances of truth. The very existence of such groups is extremely doubtful, for their coincidences are often outweighed by their divergences, while there is no proof that their coincidences may not go back to dialectic peculiarities, preceding even the first beginnings of national separation.

Thus with regard to mere pronunciation, Greek, Italian, Old Irish, and Teutonic are closely allied in resisting the assibilation of palato-gutturals, while Sanskrit, Zend, and Slavonic, with Armenian and Albanian, give way to one and the same assibilating tendency. While we have *ἑκατόν*, centum (i.e. kentum), Irish cêt, Gothic hund on one side, we have the assibilated Sk. *s*atám, Zend sata, Slav. sŭto on the other.

The same group of languages, Greek, Latin, Irish, and Teutonic, which is united in resisting the assibilation of palato-gutturals, is equally united in succumbing to the peculiar infection of the labio-gutturals, which in turn is successfully resisted by the other class, Sanskrit, Zend, and Slavonic, with Armenian and Albanian. Thus while we have as the base of the interrogative pronoun Sk. ka, Zend ka, Slav. kŭ-to, we have Greek *κο* and *πο*, Lat. qui,

Goth. hva, Irish cia, and Welsh pwy (for *kvey)[1]. But this coincidence in pronunciation carries no historical weight. Palatalisation, produced by i-contact, and labialisation, produced by u-contact, may have set in at different times, in different places, and among different classes. They are natural processes, perfectly intelligible from a phonetic point of view, and therefore, if possible once, possible twice and thrice.

I should say the same even with regard to the aspiration of the mediae in Sanskrit, and of the tenues in Greek, which is ignored in Teutonic (Gothic), Slavonic, and Celtic, and imperfectly observed in Latin. This too does not seem to me to prove a closer historical relationship between Sanskrit and Greek, for, after all, they differ in the character of their aspirates. Nor does it necessitate the admission of a continued association between the speakers of Gothic, Slavonic, and Celtic, for here too the phonetic peculiarity may have arisen under different circumstances. And unless we looked upon the corresponding High-German modification, namely the tenues, as a secondary and later development, a view which is, no doubt, the generally received one, though it has never been proved[2], we should be driven to admit that the Low Germans had been more widely or for a longer time separated from their High-German brethren than from the Celts and Slaves.

When we observe such partial coincidences, we must not forget the differences which separate the same

[1] See Ascoli, 'Fonologia Comparata,' 1870; Fick, 'Die ehemalige Spracheinheit,' 1873; Brugmann, 'Vergleichende Grammatik,' § 380 seq. Brugmann calls the palato-gutturals, Palatal, the labio-gutturals, Velar.

[2] 'Lectures on the Science of Language,' i. p. 216.

languages. Students of Comparative Philology are naturally far more ready to see similarities than dissimilarities, and classical scholars also find it far more difficult to perceive what distinguishes Greek from Latin than what they have in common. And yet, if we only glance at the Latin alphabet, where are the Greek aspirates, χ, θ, φ, in Latin, and where on the contrary the Latin semivowels, y and v, in Greek? If to this we add that n is often vocalised in Greek, but not in Latin, that in Latin every s between vowels becomes r, while in Greek it disappears, that in Greek every final consonant except ν, ρ, ς (κ) must be modified, while Latin is most tolerant in that respect, we begin to perceive that we are dealing indeed with languages wide apart from each other. As to grammar, Latin has no article, no dual, no comparatives in *τερος*, no futures in s, no aorists in *θην*; while Greek has no ablatives, except sporadically, no imperfects in b, no passives in r, etc. In fact Latin and Greek are quite as far apart from each other as German, Celtic, or Slavonic.

With all this, however, I do not wish to discourage all attempts at reconstructing separate pictures of the civilisation reached by those who, after they had separated from the rest, spoke Teutonic, Slavonic, or Celtic languages, or even, if such fancies are still allowable, of those who spoke a language that was not yet either Slavonic or Teutonic, or not yet either Latin or Greek. Only we must remember the many dangers which beset them. We can never tell what words one language may once have possessed and have lost, and we often find the greatest difficulty in determining which words may have been borrowed at a later time. No doubt this latter difficulty is gradually being lessened by the establishment of phonetic laws which will enable us to say that such and such a word could not have been Latin, but must have been borrowed from Greek, or must have been Celtic, and could not have been borrowed from Latin. Caduceus, for instance, must have been borrowed from the Greek κηρύκειον (Dor. καρύκιον), because, if it were a common Aryan word, the r in Greek would not have been represented by d in Latin. Sarff in Welsh must have been borrowed from serpens, because in a straight line the p would have been lost in Celtic and the s become h. But the cases are not always so clear. The Welsh arădyr, plough, was formerly supposed to be borrowed from Lat. arâtrum. We are now told that the short a in arădyr is sufficient to show that it is a common Aryan word, like ἄροτρον, and not borrowed from Latin.

Celtic scholars tell us that the common Aryan word áyas, the third metal, was changed by the Celts into *ais, *eis, and *îs, to which the Celts, and the Celts only, added their peculiar derivative arn, thus forming aisarn, îsarn. When the intermediate s, according to a Celtic phonetic rule, had to vanish, the Irish word became iarn, iarunn, Welsh haiarn, haearn. Now, as we find in Gothic eisarn, AS. îsern, iron, ON. isarn, jarn, OHG. îsarn, we are asked to believe that the Teutonic tribes borrowed this name for iron from their Celtic neighbours, who alone had the suffix arn, but that they borrowed it before the s had disappeared. If all this is true, it shows how careful we ought to be before we use such words as historical documents. We should here have a common Aryan word, borrowed by the Germans after it had been appropriated, and, as it were, stamped with a purely Celtic die, and we should be driven to admit that the Germans owed their first knowledge of iron, or, at all events, of the smelting and working of iron, to their Celtic neighbours.

All these difficulties vanish when we compare the dictionaries of the North-Western and South-Eastern branches of the Aryan family. When that family was once broken up, no historical contact and no borrowing of words was possible, till we come to clearly historical times, the times of Darius or Alexander. There are words in Sanskrit which may or may not have been borrowed from Greek, but they are seldom of any importance for periods of history, such as we are concerned with at present. We may lay it down therefore as a general rule that whatever words are shared in common by Sanskrit and Zend on one side, and any one of the Aryan languages on the other, existed before the great Aryan Separation took place, and may be used as throwing light on Aryan civilisation, such as it was at that distant time.

It has been objected in answer to this theory that, after the first separation of the South-Eastern and North-Western branches, the Greeks must have remained some time in contact with the ancestors of the Indian Aryas, because Greek shares so many words in common with Sanskrit, which we find nowhere else. Such words are:—

Sanskrit.	Greek.
ísbu	ἰός, arrow.
gyâ	βιός, bowstring.
purí	πόλις, town.
pátnî	πότνια, mistress, venerable.

Sanskrit.	Greek.
Váru*n*a	οὐρανός, sky.
vástu	ἄστυ, town.
vádhri	ἔθρις, castrated.
urvárâ	ἄρουρα, field.
*k*i	τίνομαι, to take vengeance.
tarkú	ἄτρακτος, spindle.
sahásra	χίλιοι, thousand.
dáru, tree	δόρυ, shaft.
ásan	ἄκων, stone weapon.
parasú	πέλεκυς, axe.
kshurá	ξυρός, razor.
dâtáro vásûnâm, Z. dâta vaṅhvâm	δωτῆρες ἑάων.

Words like these are no doubt very interesting, and they may be noted as indicating a closer proximity between the earliest ancestors of Greeks and Hindus at a time when the waves of the Aryan language were still running high, and each stream had not yet been confined within its own national channel. But they cannot be made to prove more, or be used for reconstructing a picture of an imaginary Indo-Greek civilisation, apart from all the rest. If my premisses are right, we may safely use these words, like any other words common to Sanskrit and one of the North-Western languages, as evidence of what the Aryas knew before their separation, for they could not possibly have been formed after the Greeks had once gone north and the Hindus had migrated to the Panjâb. Granting, for instance, that the occurrence of such a word as kshurá and ξυρός, scraper or razor, would strictly prove the existence of the habit of shaving among a segment of the Aryan family only, the Greeks and Hindus, it would prove it there at a time when the general national differentiation had not yet taken place. Even now, when we say that the nations of Europe know the art of shaving the beard or the head, we do not assert that that custom is universal. And with the same reservation, it seems to me that we are perfectly justified in claiming the razor as an achievement of ancient Aryan civilisation in general, though fully admitting that some Aryas may have strongly objected to shaving their locks or beards. The Aryan razor may have been a mere scraper of the most primitive kind, possibly made of stone, like the obsidian razors found at Mycenae. All this I readily grant to those who are afraid of our painting the Aryan Paradise in too brilliant colours. But the fact remains that the ancestors of Greeks and Hindus had a common word for razor before they separated. While they improved the instrument, they retained the old name, and that old name they gave and retained, because shaving of the beard[1] had become to them at that early time a matter of social interest[2].

I consider it therefore as a well-established principle that any word which occurs in Sanskrit or Zend, and at the same time in any one of the North-Western languages, may be used as a fossil belonging to a stratum previous to the Aryan Separation. If we find asi in Sanskrit and ensis in Latin, we may safely place that name in the list of the oldest Aryan weapons. If we find *sasa* for hare in Sanskrit, and haso for hare in OHG.[3], we need not hesitate to claim for the

[1] Barba, Lit. brazdà, ON. bardhr, beard.

[2] See Benfey, *Rasiermesser in Indogermanischer Zeit*, in 'Allgemeine Zeitung,' 1875, Beilage, 6 März and 6 April; Schrader, l. c. p. 52.

[3] In Old Prussian too the hare is called sasins, for szasins, and Mr. Whitley Stokes suggests an original *casinacca for Welsh ceinach.

united Aryas an acquaintance with that animal. I claim a right to treat Varuna as a common Aryan god, though of the other branches of the Aryan family Greek alone has preserved his memory in Οὐρανός. But if the ancestors of Greeks and Hindus worshipped Varuna, that is enough to stamp him as an Aryan god, known before the Greeks crossed the Bosphorus or the Hindus set eyes on the Seven Rivers.

We must except from this rule such words only as could have been formed by each nation out of the resources of its own language. While the Romans had no living root from which to form ensis, or the Greeks to form Οὐρανός, it is possible that the Gothic fravauhrt, sin, may have been formed independently of Zend fravarshta, and Gothic usvauhrt, righteousness, independently of Zend uzvareza, penance. We often see the same concepts expressed in the same manner by different languages. Thus the Greek προσφερής corresponds to German zuträglich; Greek ἐκφέρω to Latin effero, to bury; Sanskrit anusaya to German Anlage; Sanskrit udvâhayati to German ausführen. It is quite intelligible therefore that the idea of crime as something that is badly done may have been expressed independently by fra-vauhrt in Gothic, and by fra-varshta in Zend. With these exceptions, however, every word common to one of the South-Eastern and any one of the North-Western languages may be accepted as a trustworthy witness of the life and the thoughts of the Aryas, before they had been broken up into these two great streams.

We have only to examine the words which are

peculiar to Sanskrit and Zend a little more carefully in order to see that they confirm this view, and at the same time convey an important historical lesson. They show that no two Aryan languages are so closely united as Sanskrit and Zend, and they also teach us that the vocabulary of the two languages together marks a decided historical progress on the part of the South-Eastern as compared with the North-Western branch.

If we want to see how closely Sanskrit and Zend must have remained united after they separated from the rest, and before they separated from one another, we have only to look at the names of the deities, known to the Veda and Avesta, but quite unknown to the North-Western Aryas. Whether the change in the meaning of deva, which means bright and god in Sanskrit, but an evil demon (daeva) in Zend, is due to a real schism between the Aryas who remained in Persia and those who migrated to the Seven Rivers, is a question which has not yet been settled. My own impression is that such a change of meaning, accompanied as it is by similar changes in the character of certain Vedic gods, such as the Nâsatyas and Indra, who have become evil spirits in the Avesta (Nâoṅhaitya, Iñdra or Añdra), points to a religious schism; but I am quite willing to accept it as the result of a natural religious development, if that can be proved. What is important for our purposes is that such names as Indra, Nâsatya, Apâ*m* Napât, Aramati, Gandharva, Druh, Yama, etc. are utterly unknown to the other Aryas, and must owe their origin to a period following the Aryan Separation, during which the ancestors of the Iranians and Hindus were not yet definitely divided.

But besides these names there are many others which at once betray their later origin, and yet are preserved both in Sanskrit and Zend. Such are, for instance:—

Sanskrit.	Zend.
asvatara, mule	astar.
advesha, not hating	advaẽsha, without torture.
anrita, unrighteous	anarata.
anartha, useless.	anaretha, wrong.
anârya, not Aryan	anairya, lawless.
syena, hawk	saêna, eagle.
mriga, bird of prey	meregha, Mod. Pers. murgh; cf. Sîmurgh, i.e. sînamrû.
kasyapa, turtle	kasyapa.
matsya, fish	masya.
setu, bridge	haetu.
senâ, army	haena.

This list might be enlarged to any extent, as a look at Justi's Zend Glossary will show. But although Zend and Sanskrit may be treated almost as twins, they have each a character of their own. Sanskrit has many words which it shares with Greek, Latin, Teutonic, Slavonic, and Celtic, and of which no trace exists in Zend. This, no doubt, might be accounted for by the extreme scantiness of Zend literature. But Zend, in spite of its literary poverty, possesses also a number of words which exist in the North-Western Aryan branch and are absent in Sanskrit. As this seemed to me an important point to establish, particularly in order to rectify the false impression produced by lists of common words such as those in Greek and Sanskrit (p. 143), I collected a list of Aryan words occurring in Zend, but not in Sanskrit, which will show how far a certain degree of independence is compatible even with such very close relationship as that between Sanskrit and Zend[1].

Another very useful list might be made of words absent in the South-Eastern but present in the North-Western branch, or present in the South-Eastern but absent in the North-Western branch, provided that such words are connected with the progress of civilised life and intellectual endeavour.

The closeness of the relationship of the whole Aryan family is, of course, best shown by its different members sharing in common a grammatical articulation which can only be the result of a long previous growth, which has ceased to be alive and intelligible, and has become purely traditional and formal. The real meaning of the growth of what we call grammar has never been fathomed as yet. One single grammatical form opens vistas which far transcend our ordinary chronology. Even a single particle, such as *k*a, and, in Sanskrit, *k*a in Zend, τέ in Greek, que in Latin, h in Gothic, ch in Celtic, all placed after the word, shows a continuity of growth and opens strata of thought which lie deeper than the deepest strata of our globe. A look at the numerals from one to ten tells us more of forgotten intellectual labour than all the pyramids of Egypt and the palaces of Babylon.

But while we admire these remnants of common Aryan work, we may also learn some lessons, though referring to a later period, from differences which divide the two great branches of the Aryan family. I shall give a few specimens only. When we find

[1] Selected Essays, i. p. 225.

that the common Aryan root ÆR, which meant 'to stir,' whether the soil or the sea, was retained in the North-Western branch to express anything connected with ploughing, while in the South-Eastern branch it was replaced by KÆRSH, which means to draw, we may conclude, not indeed with the vaunted assurance of the mathematician, but with the sober reasonableness of the historian, that the habit of ploughing by having a sharp instrument drawn across the field, whether by men or by beasts, dates from a time later than the Aryan Separation. The root KÆRSH, to plough, of which we have no trace in the North-Western, is so firmly established in Sanskrit that it has yielded not only such words as k*ri*shí, ploughing, k*ri*shi-valá, plougher, but also k*ri*sh*t*í, originally plougher, which, like arya, has become in the Veda already a name for man in general. When we find that the South-Eastern has its own name for bridge, setu, Zend haetu, we may, unless there is evidence to the contrary, assume that before their final separation the Aryas crossed rivers by fords and not yet by bridges.

It has been accepted by most comparative scholars that the common Aryan name for daughter, Sk. duhitar, meant originally milkmaid, and was derived from a root DUH, to milk. Some people may call this too pastoral, others too idyllic, a name. The fact remains that nothing better has as yet been suggested. But this root DUH means 'to milk' in the South-East only, while in the North-West 'to milk' is expressed by MÆRG, 'to stroke,' i.e. ἀμέλγω in Greek, mulgeo in Latin, milchu in OHG., mlŭza in Slavonic, bligim in Irish. I do not mean to say therefore, as others might, that duhitar, milkmaid, as a name for daughter could have been formed in Sanskrit only. But I do mean to say that it was formed before the Aryan Separation, and that the South-Eastern branch only retained the root DUH in its original special meaning of milking, while the root MÆRG marks a new start in the history of the North-Western branch.

Again and again when we find these marked differences between the North-West and the South-East, we feel that they cannot be purely accidental, but that they convey some kind of historical lesson. The Aryan names for gold are all derived from the same root: but Sanskrit and Zend alone agree in their derivatives also, Sk. hira*n*ya, Zend zaranya. The names for silver too point all to the same root, but no two names for silver are so close to each other as ra*g*ata in Sanskrit and erezata in Zend. The root MÆRD and MAL, to grind, may be common Aryan property, but the actual name for mill, *μύλη*, mola, muli, is restricted to the North-West.

Among animals the donkey and the mule have their own names in the South-East on one side, khara, gardabha, a*s*vatara, and in the North-West on the other, *ὄνος*, asinus, *ἡμίονος*, mulus.

Among trees the beech is known in the North-West only. Flax has its own name in the North-West, *λῖνον*, Lat. lînum, while in Sanskrit it is úmâ and kshumâ. There is no ancient word for wine in the South-East, no word for Soma in the North-West.

Many more words might be added, all teaching us the same lesson, that the break between the South-Eastern and North-Western branches was an historical event, and that, not only the coincidences, but the differences also, between the two, are full of historical import. We find here too what we expect, and this, as I said before, is really the highest confirmation for our theories which we have any right to anticipate in this field of research.

Let us remember that we expected that the North-Western branch, if it separated from the South-Eastern branch, in Asia, should not have the same name for the sea which we find in Sanskrit and Zend. We expected it, and we found it was so. But let us now go a step further. If the Aryas of India separated from the Iranians, before they had reached the mouth of the Indus, the names for sea in Sanskrit and Persian too ought to be different. And so they are. We find sindhu and samudra, sâgara and ar*n*ava for sea in Sanskrit, but in Zend zrayaṅh, Mod. Pers. daryâ (sea and stream). This zrayaṅh may correspond to Sk. *g*ráyas, which in the Veda means tract or expanse (Rv. X, 75, 7), quite applicable to such vast expanses of water as the Iranians would be familiar with, before having seen the real sea.

And now I venture on a last step, which may seem very bold, but which certainly is not half so bold as the combinations by which Germany or Scandinavia or the North Pole has been claimed as the cradle of all the Aryas.

It is well known that there are some striking coincidences between the names of certain rivers in the Avesta and the Veda. We find—

Sarasvatî, the Sursuti in India = Haraqaîti, the Arachotus;
Sarayû, the Goggra in India = Haraeva or Haroyu, the Heri-rud;

Rasâ, a northern river	= Rangha, the Araxes;
Sapta sindhavah, the seven rivers of the Panjâb	= Hapta hindu, India.

These names, to which some others might be added, are not borrowed from Sanskrit into Persian, nor from Persian into Sanskrit. They must have existed therefore before these languages became permanently distinct. They may for a time have retained their appellative power, and been given independently to rivers known to the Aryas in Persia and India. This is possible, though it is not probable, for the coincidences are almost as strong as between Bŏston in England and Bôston in America. And with regard to one of them, that of the 'Seven Rivers,' we can hardly escape from the conclusion that it was given by the united Indo-Iranians to the Seven Rivers of the Panjâb, and not, as Spiegel thinks, to some imaginary country of Seven Rivers.

I shall not open the question here once more as to the northern Airyanem vaegânh[1], and the other countries mentioned in the first chapter of the Vendîdâd. Airyanem vaegânh, 'the Aryan Power,' need not be a country near the Belurtâgh or Mustâgh, as Lassen supposed. It may be a mere traditional name of a hyperborean home, like the Uttara-kurus in India. But the fact remains—at least I see no escape from it—that the ancestors of the Indian and Persian Aryas had reached the land of the Seven Rivers, namely the north of the Panjâb, before they became permanently separated.

Here, therefore, within sight of the Indus and its tributaries, the undivided South-Eastern Aryas spoke

[1] See Spiegel, 'Die Arische Periode,' p. 122.

a language more primitive than Sanskrit and Zend. What that language was we can to a certain extent discover by selecting words common to Sanskrit and Zend. The date of that language, at the very lowest estimate, must have been about 2000 B.C.

And now I ask my Scandinavian friends, Can they prove, or in any way make it plausible, that the people who spoke an Aryan language near the northern course of the Indus, and at least 2000 B.C., were emigrants from Scandinavia? and, is there anything in any of the Teutonic or European languages in general, which could have arisen in Europe only, and which is the necessary antecedent of any Sanskrit word or any grammatical form in Sanskrit or Zend? If there is, let them produce their facts.

I shall be as proud as anybody to look upon Germany as the cradle of all Aryan life, and upon Teutonic speech as the fountain of all Aryan thought. But if, on the contrary, no new facts have been discovered to disturb a theory which is the result of the combined labours of the most competent scholars during the last fifty years, let us not waste our time on building castles in the air, but let us be satisfied with the humbler task of testing, strengthening, and completing the noble building which has been planned by bold but trustworthy architects, and carried out by many humble but honest labourers.

The following lists of words may now speak for themselves. I have on former occasions endeavoured to interpret some of them, and to work them up into an Aryan idyll. I shall on the present occasion be content with placing before my readers the broken fragments, collected from the dictionaries of the seven principal languages of Aryan descent—though by no means a complete collection—and leave them at liberty to people the most ancient Aryan Herculanum and Pompeii with such men and women as they consider might have given expression to their thoughts and feelings with the scant vocabulary recovered from beneath the accumulations of many centuries. Some will do it with the vivacity and imagination which we admire in Fick and Schrader, others with the sobriety and care which we honour in Hehn; none, I hope, with that mere love of paradox against which I have had to protest, in common with all true scholars who care for the sure and steady progress of knowledge far more than for startling, brilliant, but too often untenable theories.

I.

FAMILY.

Note.—Under Teutonic the words, unless otherwise marked, are Gothic. Under Slavonic the words, unless otherwise marked, are Old or Ecclesiastic Slavonic. Under Celtic the words, unless otherwise marked, are Irish.

Father.

Sk. pitár, nom. pitā́. **Zend** pitar, nom. pitâ.

Greek *πατήρ*. **Lat.** pater. **Teut.** fadar. **Slav.** deest. **Celt.** athir, gen. athar.

Hypokoristic.

Child to parent and parent to child.

Sk. tâta, father, son.

Greek *τάτα, τέττα*; *ἄττα, ἄππα*. **Lat.** tata, atta. **Teut.** attan, nom. atta, father. **Slav.** otĭcĭ; *Boh.* táta, father. **Celt.** ate aite, foster-father; *Corn.* tat.

Mother.

Sk. mâtár, nom. mâtā́. **Zend** mâtar, nom. mâtâ.

Greek *μήτηρ*. **Lat.** mater. **Teut.** *OHG.* muotar. **Slav.** mater, nom. mati. **Celt.** máthir.

Hypokoristic.

Sk. attâ, mother.

Teut. aithei, mother.

Son.

Sk. sûnú. **Zend** hunu.

Greek *υἱός*. **Teut.** sunu. **Slav.** synŭ.

Daughter.

Sk. duhitár, nom. duhitá́. **Zend** dughdhar.

Greek *θυγάτηρ*. **Teut.** daúhtar; *OHG.* tohtar. **Slav.** dŭšter, nom. dŭšti; *Lit.* dukter, nom. duktĕ.

Brother.

Sk. bhrá́tar, nom. bhrá́tâ. **Zend** brâtar.

Greek *φράτηρ*, member of a *φρατρία*. **Lat.** frâter. **Teut.** brôthar. **Slav.** bratrŭ. **Celt.** bráthir.

Sister.

Sk. svásar, nom. svásâ. **Zend** hvañhar.

Lat. soror. **Teut.** svistar. **Slav.** sestra. **Celt.** siur, gen. sethar; *Welsh* chwaer.

Uncle.

Sk. pítrivya.

Greek *πάτρως*. **Lat.** patruus. **Teut.** *OHG.* fataro; *AS.* fadhu, father's sister.

Father-in-law.

Sk. svásura, for svásura. **Zend** hvasura.

Greek *ἑκυρός*. **Lat.** socer. **Teut.** svaihran, nom. svaihra; *AS.* sveor. **Slav.** svekrŭ; *Lit.* szészura. **Celt.** *Corn.* hvigeren.

Mother-in-law.

Sk. *svasrû́*, for svasrû́.

Greek *ἑκυρά*. **Lat.** socrus (also masc.) **Teut.** svaihrô. **Slav.** svekrŭvĭ. **Celt.** *Corn.* hveger.

Son-in-law.

Sk. *ğấmâtar*, nom. -tâ; also sister's husband; *ğâmí*, consanguineus. **Zend** zâmâtar, son-in-law only; zâmi, birth, breed.

Greek *γαμβρός*. **Lat.** gener. **Slav.** zętĭ, gener; *Lit.* gentì, consanguineus. **Celt.** *Węlsh* dawf.

Daughter-in-law.

Sk. snushấ (also *ğâmâ*); *Mod. Pers.* sunhâr.

Greek *νυός*. **Lat.** nurus. **Teut.** *OHG.* snur. **Slav.** snŭcha, bride.

Brother-in-law, Frater Mariti.

Sk. devár, nom. devấ; also *svasuryá*; *Mod. Pers.* khosra, frater uxoris.

Greek *δαήρ*, also *ἀνδράδελφος*. **Lat.** lêvir. **Teut.** *AS.* tâcor; *OHG.* zeihhur; *AS.* gesvirja, sister-son. **Slav.** děverĭ.

Sister-in-law.

Sk. nánândar, nom. -dâ.

Greek *γάλως*, viri soror, fratris uxor. **Lat.** glos, viri soror, fratris uxor. **Slav.** zlŭva.

Husband, Lord.

Sk. páti. **Zend** paiti.

Greek *πόσις*. **Lat.** (potis). **Teut.** fath, in brûth-fath-s, bridegroom. **Slav.** *Lit.* pàt-s.

Wife, Lady.

Sk. pátnî. **Zend** pathni.

Greek *πότνια*. **Slav.** *Lit.* patì.

Blood-relations: Grandson, etc.

Sk. nápât, náptar, nom. náptâ. **Zend** napat, naptar.

Greek *νέποδες*, lost, but reintroduced by Alexandrian poets; *ἀ-νεψιός*, i.e. connepotius; cf. consobrini, i.e. consororini, cousins; cousin or nephew. **Lat.** nepos; cf. *It.* nipote, *Fr.* neveu, nephew. **Teut.** nithji, cognatus; *ON.* nefi, brother; *OHG.* nefo, grandson, relative. **Slav.** netij, nephew. **Celt.** niae, gen. niath, filius sororis; *Welsh* nai, nephew.

Blood-relations: Granddaughter, etc.

Sk. naptí. **Zend** napti, relationship.

Lat. neptis; cf. neptia, *OF.* niepce, niece. **Teut.** nithjô, cognata; *OHG.* niftila, neptis; *ON.* nift, sister, bride, maid; *AS.* nëfe, niece, granddaughter. **Slav.** *Boh.* neter, nom. neti, niece. **Celt.** necht; *Welsh* nith.

Wives of Husband's Brothers.

Sk. yắtaras, nom. plur.

Greek *εἰνάτερες*. **Lat.** janitrices. **Slav.** jętry, *σύννυμφος*.

Wife's Brother.

Sk. syâlá.

Greek *ἀέλιοι, ἀδελφὰς γήμαντες*, i.e. *sasyalyâs, having syâlîs in common; cf. *εἰλιόνες*, husbands of sisters.

CONNECTIONS.

Sk. bándhu.

Greek *πενθερός*, father, brother, son-in-law; *πενθερά*, mother-in-law.

WIDOW.

Sk. vidhávâ. **Zend,** *Mod. Pers.* béva.

Greek *ἠίθεος*, bachelor. **Lat.** vidua. **Teut.** viduvô; viduvaírna, orphan. **Slav.** vidova. **Celt.** fedb; *Welsh* gweddw.

ORPHAN.

Sk. arbhaká, young.

Greek *ὀρφανός*. **Lat.** orbus. **Teut.** arbi, inheritance; *OHG.* arbja, heir. **Celt.** arbe, inheritance; com-arbe, heir, successor.

FAMILY.

Sk. *g*ánas, *g*anús.

Greek *γένος*. **Lat.** genus. **Teut.** kuni.

II.

DOMESTIC ANIMALS.

CATTLE.

Sk. pasú. **Zend** pasu.

Lat. pecus. **Teut.** faíhu. **Slav.** *Old Pruss.* peku.

SHEPHERD.

Sk. pâyú. **Zend** pâyu.

Greek ποι-μήν (πῶυ, cattle). **Slav.** *Lit.* pëmŭ.

OX AND COW.

Sk. go, nom. gaus, m. f.; gavyûti, cattle-field. **Zend** gâo, nom. gâus; gaoyaoiti, cattle-field; *Mod. Pers.* gâu.

Greek βοῦς. **Lat.** bôs. **Teut.** *OHG.* chuo. **Slav.** *Lit.* gow. **Celt.** bó.

BULL.

1. **Sk.** ukshán, nom. ukshấ. **Zend** ukhshan.

Teut. auhsa; *OHG.* ohso. **Celt.** *Welsh* ych, pl. ychain.

2. **Sk.** sthûrá, strong; sthaurin, ox. **Zend** staora, beast of burden; *Mod. Pers.* sutûr and ustûr.

Greek ταῦρος. **Lat.** taurus. **Teut.** stiur. **Slav.** turŭ. **Celt.** tarb.

CALF.

Sk. vatsá, yearling; cf. vatsá, year.

Greek ἰταλός. **Lat.** vitulus. **Slav.** telę. **Celt.** fithal?

HEIFER.

Sk. starí.

Greek στεῖρα. **Lat.** sterilis. **Teut.** staírô; die Stärke.

Male.

Sk. vríshan, nom. vríshâ. **Zend** arshan.

Greek *ἄρσην*.

Castratus.

Sk. vádhri.

Greek *ἔθρις*.

Sheep.

Sk. ávi.

Greek *ὄϊς*. **Lat.** ovis. **Teut.** avi-str, sheep-stable; *OHG.* auwi, young sheep. **Slav.** ovĭca; *Lit.* avì. **Celt.** ói.

He-Goat.

Sk. agá.

Slav. *Lit.* ožỹ.

She-Goat.

Sk. agâ; agína, n. goat-skin.

Greek *αἴξ*; *αἰγίς*, goat-skin. **Slav.** *Lit.* ožkà.

---

1. Swine.

Sk. sû-kará. **Zend** hu.

Greek *ὗς*. **Lat.** sûs. **Teut.** sv-ein; *OHG.* sû. **Slav.** svinija. **Celt.** *Welsh* hwch, hog.

---

2. Swine.

Sk. ghríshvi, ghrishti.

Greek *χοῖρος*. **Teut.** *ON.* grîs.

Dog.

Sk. *svan*, nom. *svá*. **Zend** span, nom. spâ (spaka, Herod. I. 110).

Greek κύων. **Lat.** canis. **Teut.** hund. **Slav.** *Lit.* szun, nom. szũ. **Celt.** cú, gen. con.; *Welsh* ci, pl. cwn.

Horse.

Sk. á*s*va. **Zend** aspa.

Greek ἵππος (ἴκκος). **Lat.** equus, Epona. **Teut.** *Old Sax.* ĕhu. **Slav.** *Lit.* aszvà. **Celt.** ech; *Gaul.* epo-s.

Foal.

Sk. pu-trá, son; pó-ta, young. **Zend** puthra.

Greek πῶλος. **Lat.** pullus; *Osc.* pu-klo. **Teut.** fula; *OHG.* folo.

III.

WILD ANIMALS.

Bear.

Sk. *r*/ksha.

Greek ἄρκτος. **Lat.** ursus. **Celt.** *Welsh* arth.

Wolf.

Sk. v*r*ka. **Zend** vehrka; *Mod. Pers.* gurg.

Greek λύκος. **Lat.** lupus; *Sab.* irpus. **Teut.** vulf-s. **Slav.** vlŭkŭ. **Celt.** fael.

HARE.

Sk. *sasa*, for *sasa*.

Teut. *OHG.* haso. **Slav.** *Old Pruss.* sasin-s, for szasin-s. **Celt.** *Welsh* ceinach, for *casinacca.

MOUSE.

Sk. mûsh; mûsha.

Greek *μῦς*. **Lat.** mus. **Teut.** *OHG.* mûs. **Slav.** myšĭ.

WORM.

Sk. k*r*imi. **Zend** kerema; *Mod. Pers.* kirm.

Slav. črŭvĭ; *Lit.* kìrmi. **Celt.** cruim; *Welsh* pryf. Not *Lat.* vermis, *Goth.* vaúrm, or *Greek* ἕλμις.

---

1. SERPENT.

Sk. áhi. **Zend** azhi.

---

a. **Greek** *ἔχις*. **Lat.** anguis. **Teut.** *OHG.* unc. **Slav.** *Lit.* angì-s.

β. **Greek** *ἔγχελυς*, eel. **Lat.** anguilla, eel. **Slav.** *Lit.* ungurý-s, eel. **Celt.** esc-uing, lit. water-snake, i.e. eel.

---

2. SERPENT.

Sk. sarpá.

Greek *ἑρπετόν*. **Lat.** serpens. **Celt.** *Welsh* sarff, from Lat.

---

3. SNAKE, OTTER.

Sk. udrá, an aquatic animal.

Greek *ὕδρα*, snake. **Teut.** *OHG.* otter. **Slav.** vydra, otter.

IV.

BIRDS.

Sk. vi, m. **Zend** vi, m.

---

a. **Greek** *οἰ-ωνός*. **Lat.** avis.

β. **Greek** *ᾠόν*, egg. **Lat.** ovum. **Teut.** *OHG.* ei, pl. eigir. **Slav.** aje, jaje. **Celt.** og, gen. uige.

Goose.

Sk. hamsá.

Greek *χήν*. **Lat.** anser. **Teut.** *OHG.* kans. **Slav.** gąsi; *Boh.* hus. **Celt.** géiss, swan.

Duck.

Sk. âti.

Greek *νῆσσα*. **Lat.** ana(t)s. **Teut.** *OHG.* anut. **Slav.** *Lit.* anti-s.

Cuckoo.

Sk. kokilá.

Greek *κόκκυξ*. **Lat.** cuculus. **Teut.** *MHG.* kuckuk and gouch. **Slav.** kukavica. **Celt.** cuach, coi.

Raven.

Sk. kârava.

Greek *κόραξ*, *κορώνη*, crow. **Lat.** corvus, cornix, crow. **Teut.** *OHG.* hraban, hruoh. **Slav.** *Pol.* kruk. **Celt.** crú.

Quail.

Sk. vártikâ.

Greek *ὄρτυξ*. **Teut.** (*OHG.* wahtala?); *Dutch* kwartel.

CRANE.

Zend, *Arm.* **kroŭnkn.**

Greek *γέρανος*. **Lat. grûs. Teut.** *OHG.* **chranuh;** *AS.* **cran. Slav. žeravĭ. Celt.** *Corn.* **garan.**

OWL.

Sk. ulûka.

Greek *ὀλολυγαία*, **adj. Lat. ulûcus.**

V.

HOUSE AND HOME.

1. HOUSE.

Sk. damá.

Greek *δόμος*. **Lat. domus. Teut. timrjan, to build. Slav.** domŭ. **Celt. dam.**

---

2. HOUSE.

Sk. vi*s*, ve*s*á. Zend vîs.

Greek *οἶκος*. **Lat. vicus. Teut. veih-s. Slav. vĭsĭ. Celt.** fîch, from Lat.

---

3. HOUSE, DWELLING.

Sk. vástu, m. n. Zend va*n*h, to dwell.

Greek *ἄστυ* (town). **Teut.** *OHG.* **wist, mansio. Celt. aross,** i. e. ar-foss, residence.

Settlement.

Sk. dhấman, n. **Zend** dâman.

Lat. familia; *Osc.* faama, house; famel, famulus.

Stronghold, Town.

Sk. pur, nom. pûḥ; and purí.

Greek πόλις.

Door.

Sk. dvar, dur. **Zend** dvara.

Greek θύρα. **Lat.** fores. **Teut.** daúr. **Slav.** dvĭrĭ. **Celt.** doru-s.

Bed.

Sk. stara. **Zend** stairis.

Greek στρῶμα; στρατός, camp. **Lat.** torus. **Teut.** *OHG.* strâo, straw. **Slav.** *Lit.* strajè. **Celt.** srath; *Welsh* ystrad.

Door-posts.

Sk. ấtâ. **Zend** äithya?

Lat. antae. **Teut.** *ON.* önd, gen. andar, porch.

Wall.

Sk. dehí.

Greek τεῖχος. **Lat.** *Osc.* feihuss, acc. plur.

Road.

Sk. pathás. **Zend** path.

Greek πάτος. **Lat.** pons. **Teut.** fad. **Slav.** pątĭ.

Ship.

Sk. naus. **Zend,** *Old Pers.* nâvi.

Greek ναῦς. **Lat.** nâvis. **Teut.** *OHG.* nacho. **Celt.** nau.

Rudder.

Sk. arítras.

Greek ἐρετμός. **Lat.** remus. **Teut.** *OHG.* ruodar. **Slav.** *Lit.* ìrkla-s. **Celt.** rám.

VI.

HOME OCCUPATIONS.

Carpenter, etc.

Sk. tákshan, nom. â. **Zend** tashan, creator.

Greek τέκτων.

Beam.

Sk. dru, m. tree; dấru, n. wood. **Zend** dru, spear; drvaena, wooden; dâuru, tree.

Greek δρῦς, tree, oak; δόρυ, spear. **Teut.** triu. **Slav.** drěvo, tree. **Celt.** daur, oak.

To cook, to bake.

Sk. pa*k*. **Zend** pa*k*.

Greek πέσσω. **Lat.** coquo. **Slav.** peką. **Celt.** *Welsh* pobi.

To roast.

Sk. bhra*gg*. **Zend,** *Mod. Pers.* birishtan.

Greek *φρύγω*. **Lat.** frîgo. **Celt.** bairgen, bread.

Raw Flesh.

Sk. kravís, n. **Zend** krvî-dru, with bloody spear.

Greek *κρέας*. **Lat.** caro. **Teut.** *OHG.* hrêo. **Slav.** krŭvĭ, cruor. **Celt.** crúu, blood; *Welsh* crau.

Meat.

Sk. mâ*m*sá; *Arm.* mis.

Teut. mimz. **Slav.** męso; *Lit.* mièsà. **Celt.** mír.

Bone.

Sk. asthí, n.; asthán. **Zend** asti, astan.

Greek *ὀστέον*. **Lat.** os. **Celt.** *Welsh* asgwrn.

Marrow.

Sk. ma*gg*an, nom. *g*â. **Zend** mazga.

Teut. *OHG.* marg. **Slav.** mozgŭ.

Juice.

Sk. yûsha, m. n. **Zend,** *Mod. Pers.* yoshîdan, bullire.

Greek *ζωμός*. **Lat.** jûs. **Slav.** jucha; *Lit.* júszè; *Pol.* jucha.

Honey, Mead.

Sk. mádhu. **Zend** madhu, honey?; *Mod. Pers.* may, wine.

Greek *μέθυ*, mead. **Teut.** *OHG.* metu. **Slav.** medŭ; *Lit.* medus, honey; middus, mead. **Celt.** mid.

To cut.

Sk. k*r*i, k*r*it; kartanî, scissors. **Zend** kar; kareta, knife.

Greek *κείρω*, to shear. **Lat.** curtus; culter, knife. **Teut.** haíru, knife.

Bark, Skin.

Sk. k*r*itti, skin, bark.

Lat. cortex. **Slav.** *Lit.* karné, bark.

Goat-skin, Skin.

Sk. a*g*ína, n.

Greek *αἰγίς*. **Slav.** jazno, skin, leather.

Wool.

Sk. ura-bhra, wether; úrâ, sheep; ûr*n*â, wool.

Greek *εἶρος*, *ἔριον*. **Lat.** vellus, villus. **Teut.** vulla. **Slav.** vlŭna. **Celt.** *Welsh* gwlan.

To stretch.

Sk. tan; tanti, string; tanu, thin. **Zend** tan.

Greek *τείνω*, *τανύ*. **Lat.** tendo; tenus, string; tenuis, thin. **Teut.** thanja; *OHG.* dunni, thin. **Slav.** teneto, string; tĭnĭkŭ. **Celt.** tana; tét, string.

To plat.

Sk. p*r*ik, to mix, to plat. **Zend,** *Mod. Pers.* péchîdan.

Greek *πλέκω*, *πλόκαμος*. **Lat.** plico, plecto, Parca. **Teut.** flahta or flahto, *πλέγμα*; falthan, *πτύσσειν*; *OHG.* flahs, flax. **Slav.** pletą.

To SPIN.

Sk. tarku, spindle; tarka, revolving, thought.

Greek ἄτρακτος, spindle; (ἄτροπος). **Lat.** torques.

---

1. To WEAVE.

Sk. ve, váyâmi; úmâ, flax; ûrna-vâbhi, spider. **Zend** vap; ubdaena, woven; ufyemi, I weave praises; *Mod. Pers.* bâftan.

Greek ἤτριον, ὑφαίνω, ὕμνος? **Lat.** vieo. **Teut.** *OHG.* wëban. **Slav.** viti. **Celt.** feith, fibra.

---

2. To WEAVE.

Sk. sthavi, weaver.

Greek ἱστός, στήμων. **Lat.** stamen. **Slav.** stakli.

---

1. To SEW, TO JOIN.

Sk. nah; ûrna-nâbhi, spider.

Greek νέω, νήθω. **Lat.** neo. **Teut.** *OHG.* nâan; nâdala, needle. **Celt.** snáthe, thread; snáthat, needle.

---

2. To SEW.

Sk. siv; syûtá.

Greek κασ-σύω. **Lat.** suo. **Teut.** siuja. **Slav.** šiją.

To DYE.

Sk. rag; rakta.

Greek ῥέζω; ῥέγος.

To dress.

Sk. vas; vástra, n. **Zend** vaṅh; vastra.

Greek *ἕννυμι*; *ἐσθής*; *ἑανός*. **Lat.** vestis. **Teut.** vas-ti; gavasjan. **Celt.** *Welsh* gwisg, garment.

To pound.

Sk. pish. **Zend** pish.

Lat. pinso, pistor. **Slav.** pišeno.

To knead, to form.

Sk. dih. **Zend** diz.

Greek *θιγγάνω*. **Lat.** fingo; figulus. **Teut.** deiga.

To stitch, to paint, to adorn.

Sk. pis; pésas; pesalá. **Zend** paesaṅh.

Greek *ποικίλος*. **Lat.** pingo, pictor. **Teut.** filu-faih-s, *πολυποίκιλος*.

To heal.

Zend madh; mad?

Lat. mederi; medicus; remedium.

Poison.

Sk. vishá, n. **Zend** visha.

Greek *ἰός*. **Lat.** vîrus. **Celt.** fí.

VII.

TREES AND PLANTS.

Birch.

Sk. bhûr*g*a.

Teut. *OHG.* bircha. **Slav.** brĕza.

Beech and Oak.

Sk. deest. **Zend,** *Mod. Pers.* bûk, wood, oak ?

Greek *φηγός*, oak. **Lat.** fagus, beech. **Teut.** *OHG.* buohha; *Engl.* buck-mast.

---

1. Fir and Oak.

Sk. dru, m. n. wood; dấru, m. n. wood, tree; devadâru, pine. **Zend** dru, shaft; drvaena, wooden; dâuru, tree.

Greek δρῦς, tree, oak. **Lat.** larix, larch ? **Teut.** triu. **Slav.** drĕvo, tree; *Lit.* dervà, fir. **Celt.** daur, oak.

---

2. Fir and Oak.

Sk. deest.

Lat. quercus, oak. **Teut.** *OHG.* foraha, pinus; *Lomb.* fereha, oak; *AS.* furh, fir. **Celt.** crann.

Withy.

Sk. vetasá, reed. **Zend** vaeti; *Mod. Pers.* béd.

Greek *ἰτέα, οἶσος, οἰσύα.* **Lat.** vîtis. **Teut.** *OHG.* wîda. **Slav.** *Lit.* vyti. **Celt.** *Welsh* gwden.

Vine and Wine.

Arm. gini; *Georg.* ghwino.

Greek *οἶνος.* **Lat.** vinum. **Teut.** *OHG.* vein. **Slav.** vino. **Celt.** fín, from Lat.

Reed.

Sk. kaláma. **Zend,** *Mod. Pers.* qalam.

Greek *κάλαμος*. **Lat.** culmus. **Teut.** *OHG.* halm. **Celt.** *Welsh* kalaf.

Hemp.

Sk. *saná*, m.? **Zend,** *Mod. Pers.* kanaw; *Arm.* kanep.

Greek *κάνναβις*. **Lat.** cannabis. **Teut.** *OHG.* hanaf. **Slav.** konep. **Celt.** canaib.

Flax.

Sk. (kshumâ and úmâ).

Greek λίνον. **Lat.** lînum. **Teut.** lein, linen; *OHG.* lîn, flax. **Slav.** lĭnŭ. **Celt.** lin, flax, from Lat.

VIII.

AGRICULTURE.

To plough, to stir.

Sk. árya, landholder. **Zend** airya.

Greek *ἀρόω, ἄροτρον*. **Lat.** arare, arâtrum. **Teut.** arjan; *ON.* ardhr, aratrum. **Slav.** orati, to plough; oralo, plough; *Lit.* arkla. **Celt.** arăthar; *Welsh* aradr.

Ploughed Earth.

Sk. i*d*, irâ, urvarâ. **Zend** urvara, produce.

Greek *ἔρα, ἄρουρα*. **Lat.** arvum. **Teut.** airtha; *OHG.* ëro.

To sow.

Sk. sítâ, furrow, from a root sâ, sî, connected with as, (a)syati, to scatter; see sasya.

Greek σάω, to strew. **Lat.** sero for seso, sevi, satum; semen. **Teut.** saian; *OHG.* samo. **Slav.** sějati, sěmę. **Celt.** síl, semen.

To plough, to draw.

Sk. k*r*ish, k*r*ish*t*i. **Zend** karsh, karshti.

Deest in *S. E.*

Plough.

Sk. koka, wolf (cf. v*r*ika, wolf and plough).

Teut. ḥôha, *occa.*

---

1. Field.

Sk. *á*gra. **Zend** azra.

Greek ἀγρός; ἄγριος. **Lat.** ager. **Teut.** akr-s.

---

2. Field.

Sk. padá, n.

Greek πέδον, πεδίον. **Lat.** pedum; *Umbr.* perum; op-pidum. **Slav.** *Lit.* pėdà, vestigium.

Wheel, Cart.

Sk. rathá. **Zend** ratha.

Lat. rota. **Teut.** *OHG.* rad. **Slav.** *Lit.* ráta. **Celt.** roth.

Wheel.

Sk. *k*akrá. **Zend** *k*akhra.

Greek κύκλος. **Lat.** circus, circulus. **Teut.** *AS.* hveohl.

Yoke.

Sk. yugá, n. **Zend,** *Mod. Pers.* yogh.

Greek ζυγόν. **Lat.** jugum, jûgerum. **Teut.** juk; *OHG.* joch. **Slav.** igo; *Lit.* jûnga. **Celt.** *Welsh* iau.

Waggon.

Sk. vấhana, n. **Zend** vâsha.

Greek ὄχος. **Lat.** vehiculum, via. **Teut.** *OHG.* wagan; *Goth.* vig-s, way. **Slav.** vozŭ. **Celt.** fén.

Axle.

Sk. áksha, m.

Greek ἄξων. **Lat.** axis. **Teut.** *OHG.* ahsa. **Slav.** osĭ. **Celt.** *Welsh* echel.

---

1. Corn.

Sk. dhânấ. **Zend** dâna.

Slav. *Lit.* dŭna, bread.

---

2. Corn, ground.

Sk. (*gîrna*). **Zend,** *Pushtu* zarai; but **Sk.** *k*ûrna, powder, flour.

Greek γῦρις, γρῦ. **Lat.** grânum. **Teut.** kaúrn; qaírnus, mill. **Slav.** zrŭno; zrŭny, mill; *Lit.* girna, millstone. **Celt.** grán, Lat.

Mill, to grind.

Sk. malana, n. = mardana, rubbing.

Greek μύλη (μελίνη, millet). **Lat.** mola (milium, millet). **Teut.** malan; muli, mill; melo, flour. **Slav.** melją; *Lit.* malnà, miller. **Celt.** melim, I grind.

Kinds of Corn.

1.

Sk. yáva, barley; yávasa, n. fodder; *Hind.* jau, barley. **Zend** yava, fodder; *Mod. Pers.* jav, barley.

Greek ζειαί (ζείδωρος), spelt. **Slav.** *Lit.* java, corn. **Celt.** eórna.

2.

Zend, *Pehl.* gurt-ak; *Mod. Pers.* zurd, fodder.

Greek κριθή, barley. **Lat.** hordeum. **Teut.** *OHG.* gersta.

3.

Sk. sasá, grass; sasya, n. (sown ?), grain. **Zend** hahya, grain.

Greek ἦια, chaff. **Celt.** *Welsh* haidd, barley.

IX.

SEASONS.

Spring.

Sk. vas-antá. **Zend** vaṅhra; *Mod. Pers.* bihâr.

Greek ἔαρ. **Lat.** ver. **Teut.** *ON.* vár. **Slav.** *Lit.* vasarà. **Celt.** *Welsh* gwanwyn; not errach.

Spring, Year.

Zend yâre, n. year.

Teut. jer, year. **Slav.** jarŭ, spring.

Summer.

Sk. sámâ, summer, season, year. **Zend** ham or hama.

Greek τρί-ενος. **Teut.** *OHG.* sumar. **Celt.** sam; *Welsh* hâf.

Autumn.

Sk. saråd. **Zend** saredha; *Mod. Pers.* sâl, year.

Greek καρ-πός. **Lat.** Ceres. **Teut.** *OHG.* her-bist.

Winter.

Sk. himá, n. snow; hímâ, winter; hemantá. **Zend** zyam, gen. zemo; hima, winter; *Mod. Pers.* zamistân, winter.

Greek χειμών, winter; χιών, snow. **Lat.** hiems. **Slav.** zima, winter. **Celt.** gem.

Snow.

Zend snizh, to snow.

Greek νίφ-α, acc. **Lat.** nix, nivis. **Teut.** snaív-s. **Slav.** *Lit.* snĕga. **Celt.** snechta; *Welsh* nŷf.

Ice.

Zend isi or isu; *Mod. Pers.* yakh.

Teut. *OHG.* îs.

X.

WEAPONS.

1. Weapons of Bone.

Sk. parasú; cf. parsu, rib. **Zend** peresu; *Mod. Pers.* pehlû.

Greek πέλεκυς.

Sk. asthi, bone. **Zend** asti, arrow.

2. Weapons of Wood.

Sk. dru, wood. **Zend** dru, spear.

Greek δόρυ, spear.

---

3. Weapons of Stone.

Sk. ásan, n.; ásman, n. **Zend** asan; *Mod. Pers.* âs, mill-stone.

Greek ἄκων. **Teut.** *OHG.* hamar? **Slav.** kamenĭ?

Stone Implements.

Anvil.

Sk. ásman, m. stone. **Zend** asman.

Greek ἄκμων, anvil.

Oven.

Sk. ásna, stone.

Greek ἰπνός. **Teut.** auhn-s.

Mill.

Sk. grấvan, stone.

Celt. bró, gen. broon, quern.

Sword.

Sk. asi.

Lat. ensis.

Shaft.

Sk. sâlya, n.

Greek κῆλον; κήρ.

Arrow.

Sk. íshu. **Zend** ishu.

Greek *ἰός*.

Bow-string.

Sk. *gyâ*. **Zend** *gya*.

Greek *βιός*.

Scraper, Razor.

Sk. kshurá.

Greek *ξυρόν*.

XI.

METALS.

Gold.

1. **Sk.** hír-a*n*ya. **Zend** zar-anya.

---

2. **Sk.** hárita, yellow, gold. **Zend** zairita.

Slav. zlŭtŭ, yellow; *Lit.* gelta, yellow.

---

3. **Sk.** hari*ná*, yellow. **Zend** zairina.

Greek *χλουνός*, gold. **Slav.** zelenu, yellow.

---

4. **Sk.** *haritya.

Greek **χερτιος*, **χρυτιος*, *χρυσός*. **Teut.** gulth. **Slav.** zlato, gold.

SILVER.

Sk. ra*g*atá, white; ra*g*ata*m* hira*n*yam, white gold; ra*g*atam, silver, Ath.-veda. **Zend** erezata; *Arm.* artsath.

Greek ἄργ-υρος. **Lat.** arg-entum; *Osc.* aragetud. **Celt.** (argat).

THIRD METAL.

Sk. áyas. **Zend** ayaṅh.

Lat. aes. **Teut.** aíz; *AS.* ar, ore.

XII.

GOVERNMENT.

FATHER, KING.

Sk. *g*anaka.

Teut. *OHG.* chunig.

MOTHER, WIFE, QUEEN.

Sk. *g*ani, wife. **Zend** *g*éni.

Greek γυνή. **Teut.** quinô. **Slav.** zena.

LORD.

Sk. páti. **Zend** paiti.

Greek πόσις. **Slav.** *Lit.* pat-s.

LORD OF CLAN.

Sk. vispáti, fem. vispatnî. **Zend** vîspaiti.

Slav. *Lit.* vészpati, fem. vészpatene; *Pruss.* waispattin.

Leader, King.

Sk. rāg.

Lat. rex. **Teut.** reik-s. **Celt.** rí, gen. rig; *Welsh* rhi.

Law (settled).

Sk. dhâ, to settle; dhấman, law. **Zend** dâta; *Mod. Pers.* dâd, law.

Greek *θέμις*. **Teut.** dom, judgment, doom.

Right.

Sk. *rig*u. **Zend** erezu.

Lat. rectus. **Teut.** raiht; garaicht, just.

Law (proclaimed).

Sk. dis, to indicate; dish*ta*, n. ordered. **Zend** dis.

Greek *δίκη*. **Lat.** ju-dex.

Law (agreed).

Sk. yos. **Zend** yaos, pure.

Lat. jus, ju-dex.

Custom.

Sk. éva, course, custom, law.

Teut. *OHG.* êwa, law; ê-haft, echt, lawful, genuine.

Sin.

Sk. ấgas.

Greek *ἄγος*.

To punish.

Sk. *k*i; apa*k*iti, reward; *k*aya, punishing. **Zend** *k*itha, penance; kaêna, vengeance.

Greek τίω, τίσις. **Slav.** cěna, price.

XIII.

BODY.

Body.

Sk. k*ri*p, form. **Zend** kehrp, body; *Arm.* kerp.

Lat. corpus. **Teut.** *OHG.* hrĕf. **Celt.** crí.

Bone.

Sk. asthí, asthán. **Zend** asti, asta (body).

Greek ὀστέον. **Lat.** os. **Celt.** *Welsh* asgwrn.

Marrow.

Sk. ma*gg*an. **Zend** mazga, brain.

Teut. *OHG.* marg. **Slav** mozgŭ.

Head.

Sk. síras. **Zend** sara.

Greek κάρ. **Lat.** cere-brum.

Foot.

Sk. pad, páda. **Zend** padha.

Greek πούς. **Lat.** pes. **Teut.** fôtu; *OHG.* fuoz. **Slav.** *Lit.* páda, sole.

HIP.

Sk. *sróni.* **Zend** sraoni.

Lat. clûnis. **Teut.** *ON.* hlaunn. **Slav.** *Lit.* szlaunì. **Celt.** *Welsh* clun.

ARMPIT, GIRTH.

Sk. káksha, side ; kakshâ, armpit. **Zend** kasha, shoulder.

Greek *κοχ-ώνη* ? **Lat.** coxa, hip. **Teut.** *OHG.* hahsa, hough or hock. **Celt.** coss, foot ; *Welsh* coes, leg, from Lat.

NAVEL.

Sk. nấbhi.

Greek *ὀμφαλός.* **Lat.** umbilicus. **Teut.** *OHG.* nabolo. **Slav.** *Old Pruss.* nabi. **Celt.** imbliu.

KNEE.

Sk. *g*ânu, *g*ñu. **Zend** zhnu.

Greek *γόνυ, πρόχνυ.* **Lat.** genu. **Teut.** kniu.

HEEL.

Sk. pấrsh*n*i. **Zend** pâshna.

Greek *πτέρνα.* **Teut.** fairzna. **Slav.** plesna.

ARM.

Sk. bâhú. **Zend** bâzu.

Greek *πῆχυς.* **Teut.** *OHG.* buoc.

NAIL.

Sk. nakhá.

Greek *ὄνυξ.* **Lat.** unguis. **Teut.** *OHG.* nagal. **Slav.** nogŭtĭ. **Celt.** inga.

Right.

Sk. dákshi*n*a, right and south. **Zend** dashina.

Greek δεξιός. **Lat.** dexter. **Teut.** taíhsva; *OHG.* zěsawâ, right hand. **Slav.** desĭnŭ. **Celt.** dess, right and south; *Welsh* deheu.

Mouth.

Sk. âs. **Zend** âoṅh.

Lat. ôs.

Nose.

Sk. nas. **Zend** nâoṅha.

Lat. nares, nasus. **Teut.** *OHG.* nasa. **Slav.** nosŭ.

Jaw.

Sk. hánu.

Greek γένυς, chin. **Lat.** gena; dentes genuini. **Teut.** kinnu. **Celt.** giun.

Tooth.

Sk. dat, dânta. **Zend** dañtan.

Greek ὀδούς. **Lat.** dens. **Teut.** tunthu. **Slav.** *Lit.* danti. **Celt.** dét; *Welsh* dant.

Brow.

Sk. bhrû. **Zend** brva*t*.

Greek ὀφρύς. **Teut.** *OHG.* brâwa. **Slav.** brŭvĭ. **Celt.** brai.

Eye.

Sk. ákshi, akshá, akshán. **Zend** ashi.

Greek *ὄσσε*. **Lat.** oculus. **Teut.** augô. **Slav.** oko. **Celt.** aged, face.

Tear.

Sk. ásru? **Zend** asru.

Greek *δάκρυ*. **Lat.** lacruma. **Teut.** tagr. **Celt.** dér; *Old Welsh* dacr.

Heart.

Sk. hrid, hrídaya. **Zend** zaredhaya; *Mod. Pers.* dil.

Greek *καρδία*. **Lat.** cor. **Teut.** haírtô. **Slav.** srĭdĭce; *Lit.* szirdì. **Celt.** cride.

Liver.

Sk. yakrit. **Zend**, *NE.* yakare; *Mod. Pers.* jigar.

Greek *ἧπαρ*. **Lat.** jecur. **Slav.** *Lit.* akni.

Spleen.

Sk. plîhán. **Zend**, *NE.* spereza; *Mod. Pers.* supurz.

Greek *σπλήν*; *σπλάγχνον*. **Lat.** lien. **Teut.** *OHG.* lungâ. **Slav.** slezena. **Celt.** selg.

Intestines.

Sk. antrá, n.

Greek *ἔντερον*. **Lat.** intestinum. **Teut.** *OHG.* innâdiri. **Slav.** jętro, jecur. **Celt.** inathar.

XIV.

MIND.

Mind.

Sk. mánas; man, to think; manú, man. **Zend** manaṅh.

Greek *μένος*; *μάντις*. **Lat.** mens; memini. **Teut.** mun-s, mind; manna, man; *OHG.* minna, love. **Slav.** mĭněti. **Celt.** menme, mind.

Memory.

Sk. smar, to remember; smará, remembrance, love. **Zend** mar.

Greek *μέρμηρα*; *μάρτυρ*. **Lat.** memor.

Will.

Sk. v*ri*, to choose; vára, wish. **Zend** var, to choose.

Greek *βούλομαι*. **Lat.** volo. **Teut.** viljan. **Slav.** voliti, to will.

Knowledge.

Sk. vid, véda, vidyâ. **Zend** vidhya.

Greek *οἶδα*, *ἵστωρ*. **Teut.** vait. **Slav.** věděti. **Celt.** rofetar, i. e. ro-fed-sar, Aor. in s.

To know.

Sk. *g*ânâmi, I know; *g*ñâna, n. knowledge. **Zend** zan.

Greek *γιγνώσκω*, *γνῶσις*. **Lat.** gnosco, notio. **Teut.** kann, I know; kunthi, knowledge. **Slav.** znati, to know. **Celt.** adgén-sa, I have known.

To perceive.

Sk. bódhâmi, I perceive; buddhi. **Zend** bud, to perceive.

Greek *πυνθάνομαι, πύστις.* **Teut.** ana-biudan, to make perceive, to bid; faúr-biudan, to forbid. **Slav.** bŭdĕti, to wake.

To believe.

Sk. *s*rad-dadhâmi; *s*raddhâ (not connected with h*r*id, heart).

Lat. credo, credidi. **Celt.** cretim, credo.

XV.

RELIGION AND MYTH.

Dyu, Dyaús, sky.

Sk. Dyu, nom. dyaús, dyaúshpitâ.

Greek *Ζεύς.* **Lat.** Juppiter, Jovis; Dius Fidius; **Diana**; Janus. **Teut.** *OHG.* Zio.

Devá, bright, god.

Sk. devá. **Zend** daêva, evil demon.

Greek *θεός? δῖος,* heavenly. **Lat.** deus. **Teut.** *ON.* tivar, gods. **Slav.** *Lit.* dëva, god. **Celt.** día, god; *Welsh* duw, god.

Agni.

Sk. Agní, fire.

Lat. ignis. **Slav.** ognĭ; *Lit.* ugni.

Apa-var.

Sk. aporнuván, removing, opening.

Greek Ἀπέλλων, Ἀπόλλων θυραῖος; cf. ἀπέλλαι, ἀπελλάζω; ἀλία.

Ærksha.

Sk. *ri*ksha, bear.

Greek ἄρκτος, Ἀρκτοῦρος. **Lat.** Ursa major. **Celt.** *Welsh* arth.

Ærbhu.

Sk. *Ri*bhú.

Greek Ὀρφεύς?; see Ra*g*as.

Ahanâ.

Sk. Ahanấ, morning, day.

Greek Ἀθήνη.

Aharyu.

Sk. *Aharyu, from ahar, day; cf. Ahalyâ, dawn; ahanî, day and night.

Greek Ἀχιλλεύς; Ἀχιλλήα, other name for Leuke, the island of the blessed.

Ahi.

Sk. Áhi, dragon. **Zend** Azish dahâka, Ash dahâk, Zohák.

Greek ἔχις, Ἔχιδνα.

Amrita.

Sk. am*ri*ta, n. immortal, nectar.

Greek ἀμβροσία.

Arguní.

Sk. Ar*g*unî, bright, dawn.

Greek Ἀργυννίς, name of Aphrodite.

A*s*man.

Sk. á*s*man, nom. á*s*mâ, stone. **Zend** asman, stone, sky.

Greek Ἄκμων, father of Uranus.

Bhaga.

Sk. Bhága, giver, one of the Âdityas. **Zend** bagha, god; *Old Pers.* baga, Bagaios, Zeus Phrygios.

Slav. bogŭ, god.

Bh*ri*gu.

Sk. Bh*rí*gu, Bh*rí*gavas, discoverer of fire; bhárgas, light.

Greek Φλέγυς; Φλεγύας. **Lat.** fulgeo; fulgur; *Osc.* Juvei flagiúí, Jovi fulguratori.

Bhura*n*yu.

Sk. bhura*n*yú, flickering flame.

Greek Φορωνεύς, discoverer of fire.

B*ri*haspati.

Sk. B*rí*haspâti = Vâ*k*áspáti, lord of speech.

Lat. verbum = b*r*ih. **Teut.** waúrd.

Brisaya.

Sk. B*r*ísaya; the offspring of B*r*ísaya, conquered by Pa*n*i.

Greek. Βρισηΐς, if for Βαρσηΐς, the offspring of Brises, conquered by Greeks, given to Achilles.

Dahanâ.

Sk. *Dahanâ, for Ahanấ, dawn.

Greek Δάφνη.

Dâsahantar.

Sk. *Dâsahantar, killer of Dâsa, evil spirit.

Greek Λεωφόντης, name of Bellerophon.

Dâsyanârî.

Sk. *Dâsyanârî, wife of a Dâsya or demon.

Greek Δηϊάνειρα, wife of Herakles, carried off by Nessos, etc.

Dyunisya.

Sk. *Dyunisya, son of Dyu-nisau, heaven and earth.

Greek Διόνυσος, Νυκτέλιος.

Dyâvan, see Dyu.

Sk. *Dyâvan and *Dyâvana.

Greek Ζήν, Ζῆνος. **Lat.** Janus, Januspater, Juno=Zênôn, fem.

Dyâvâ.

Sk. Dyâvâ in Dyấvâ-prithivî́, heaven and earth.

Greek Δηώ, Δημήτηρ=Dyâvâ mâtâ.

*G*ÂHUSHA.

Sk. *G*âhushá, setting sun.

Greek Ζέφυρος; cf. ζόφος.

HARIT.

Sk. Harít, Harítas, red, light of morning.

Greek Χάρις, Χάριτες. **Lat.** Fors Primigenia; *Osc.* Herentat = Venus; cf. Protogeneia, prathama*g*ấs. **Teut.** *OHG.* Gerda, beloved of Freyr.

HIMÂ.

Sk. hímâ, hiems.

Greek χίμαιρα, from χίμαρος = χειμέριος, winter, but also goat, one winter old; like vatsá, calf, ἰταλός; *ON.* gymbr, lamb one year old; *Scot.* gimmer; cf. Gymir.

I*D*, I*D*Â, IRÂ.

Sk. I*d*, I*d*â, Irâ, earth, daughter and wife of Manu.

Greek ἔρα. **Teut.** airtha, earth; *ON.* iörd, daughter and wife of Odin.

KSHAM.

Sk. Ksham, Kshấmâ, earth.

Greek χθών, θεοὶ χθόνιοι. Χαμύνη, epithet of Demeter. **Slav.** *Lit.* Žemýna, goddess of the earth.

MANU.

Sk. Mánu.

Greek Μίνως for μινϝοτ, Sk. manvat. **Teut.** Mannus.

Mahî.

Sk. Mahî, the earth.

Greek Μαῖα, i. e. *mahyâ. **Lat.** Maja. Magna mater = mahí mâtá.

Marut.

Sk. Marut, storm-god.

Lat. Mars, Marspiter; *Osc.* Mamers. **Greek** Ἄρης?

Mâs.

Sk. mâs, mása, moon, month. **Zend** máoṅh.

Greek Μήν, Lunus; Μήνη, Luna. **Lat.** Mena. **Teut.** mêna. **Slav.** mĕsęcĭ. **Celt.** mí, gen. mís.

Nak.

Sk. Nas, nákti, nis, nisâ, night.

Greek Νύξ. **Lat.** Nox. **Teut.** naht. **Slav.** noštĭ. **Celt.** in-nocht, hac nocte.

Naryâ.

Sk. náryâ, manly, strong.

Lat. Neria, wife of Mars.

Nâsatya.

Sk. Násatyau, the Asvínau, the constantly returning.

Greek νόστιμος, Νόστοι. **Teut.** nas-jand, σωτήρ.

Nyavâ.

Sk. *nyavâ, snow, from nyu = niv, for snu.

Greek Νιόβη; νίφα, acc. **Lat.** nix, nivis. **Teut.** snaív-s. Chione, also killed by Artemis, because she abused the children of Leto.

PRIK.

Sk. pṛik, to mix, to plat.

Greek πλέκειν. **Lat.** Parcae; cf. Κλωθώ from κλώθειν, to spin.

PARGANYA.

Sk. Párganya, storm and rain.

Slav. *Lit.* Perkúna, god of thunder. **Teut.** fairguni, n. mountain.

PRIS.

Sk. pris, to sprinkle, also prish, prush; prisni, sprinkled, speckled. **Celt.** erc.

Greek Πρόκρις; πρώξ, dew-drop.

PAVANA.

Sk. Pávana, wind.

Greek Πάν, son of Hermes and Penelope, or of Odysseus and Penelope.

PRAMANTHA.

Sk. pramantha, fire-stick, for kindling fire by rubbing.

Greek Προμηθεύς?

RAGAS.

Sk. rágas, mist, darkness; raganí, night.

Greek Ἔρεβος; ὀρφ-νός, Ὀρφεύς.

*S*ARBARA.

Sk. *s*árvara, dark ; *s*árvarî, night ; *s*abala, son of Saramâ.

Greek Κέρβερος.

---

*S*ARAD.

Sk. *S*arád, harvest, autumn.

Greek καρ-πός, ripe fruit. **Lat.** Ceres, Cereris.

SARAMÂ.

Sk. Sarámâ, peep of day, dog of the gods, carried off by Pa*n*is.

Greek 'Ελένη.

SÂRAMEYA.

Sk. Sârameyá, son of Saramâ.

Greek 'Ερμείας, 'Ερμῆς.

SARA*N*YÛ.

Sk. Sara*n*yú, dawn.

Greek 'Ερῑνύς.

SVAR.

Sk. svar, sky ; sū́ra and sûrya, sun. **Zend** hvare.

Greek 'Ηέλιος and 'Ηλιος, or=aushasya. Σείρ, sun ; σέλας, Σελήνη=svarâ*n*â. 'Ηρα=svâryâ or vasrâ ; 'Ελλη. **Lat.** Sol. **Teut.** sauil. **Slav.** slŭ-nĭca. **Celt.** súil.

Staras.

Sk. star, st*ri*. **Zend** stare.

Greek ἀστήρ. **Lat.** stella. **Teut.** staírnô. **Celt.** *Corn.* steyr, plur. **Welsh** sêr.

Talâtala.

Sk. talâtala, one of the hells.

Greek Τάρταρος.

Tan, stan.

Sk. tanyatú, thunder.

Lat. tonitru. **Teut.** *ON.* Thôrr.

Trita.

Sk. Trita, West.

Greek Τριτώ, Τριτογένεια; Τρίτων?

Uru, urvî.

Sk. Urvasî, urû*k*î, urvî, wide, dawn, earth.

Greek Εὐρυδίκη, Εὐρυμήδη, Εὐρυνόμη, Εὐρυφάεσσα, Εὐρώπη.

Ushas.

Sk. Ushás, ushásâ, dawn; usrá, matutinus; usriya=αὔριος.

Greek Ἠώς, ἠριγένεια, Aeol. αὔως. **Lat.** Aurora. **Teut.** *OHG.* Ostan, East; Austrô, Easter. **Slav.** *Lit.* Auszrâ.

Vadhan.

Sk. vadhá, striker; vádhatra, thunderbolt.

Teut. *Old Sax.* Wuodan; *AS.* Woden; *OHG.* Wuotan; *ON.* Óđinn.

Váruna.

Sk. Váruna, sky.

Greek Οὐρανός; Οὐρανίωνες.

Varsha.

Sk. varshá, rain.

Greek Ἐρση, ἐέρση, dew. **Celt.** frass, shower.

Vartikâ.

Sk. vártikâ, quail, the returning bird.

Greek Ὀρτυγία = Delos. **Lat.** Vert-umnus.

Vas, see Ushas.

Vâk.

Sk. Vâk, speech, wife of Vâta, wind; see Brihaspati.

Greek Ὄσσα, i. e. ϝοκja.

Vritra.

Sk. Vritrá, demon of darkness, cloud, etc.

Greek Ὄρθρος, double-headed dog, killed by Herakles; ὄρθριος, at day-break.

VAR*K*AS.

Sk. vár*k*as, light; ulkâ, meteor.

Lat. Vulcanus.

YAVISH*TH*A.

Sk. yávish*th*a, the youngest; yávish*th*ya; yavish*th*a Agni, fire just born.

Greek Ἥφαιστος.

YAVYÂ.

Sk. *yavyâ, young.

Greek Ἥβη.

APPENDICES.

I.

Letter from Sir George Birdwood on the Aryan Fauna and Flora.

In the course of a controversy which arose lately with regard to the original home of the Aryas, it seemed to me important to ascertain from a competent authority whether there are certain animals and trees which are restricted to the countries traversed by the North-Western or South-Eastern Aryas *after* their first separation, and which in consequence ought not to have common names in the Aryan vocabulary. I therefore requested Sir George Birdwood to give me his opinion. His exhaustive answer, here printed with his permission, though it seems to exclude all hope of our being able to determine the original home of the Aryas by means of the names of animals and trees either known or unknown to them, will save us infinite trouble in future, and will, it may be trusted, make those who have lately assigned the first Aryan home to Germany, Lituania, or Scandinavia more careful in their statements as to the presence or absence of certain trees and animals in various zones of Europe or Asia, whether in the nineteenth century after or before our era.

'You ask :—"Is there no animal or tree of common occurrence which exists only N.W. of Samarcand or S. E. of it ?" or, in other words, in "Western Turkestan" (Sogdiana and Bactriana), and the Panjáb ("Vedic India"), respectively.

I find it extremely difficult, and in regard to trees quite impossible, to answer you Yes or No. In maps of physical geography the globe is ruled round from the poles to the equator with blue, green, yellow, orange, and red zones of floral and faunal life. The *first* zone of vegetation is the northern glacial zone—called Wahlenberg's—of mosses and lichens and low tufted alpine plants, extending from about 80° to about 70° of northern latitude. The *second* is the zone of winter cold—named after Linnaeus—extending from about 70° to about 50° and 45′ of northern latitude, and marked by the predominance of firs, pines, larches, and such deciduous trees as the willow, birch, ash, alder, elm, maple, poplar, aspen, and 'British' or, as you would say, 'German Oak,' and by the cranberry, cloudberry, berberry, currant, and other edible berries; and also, in its more temperate areas, by the holly, beech, chestnut, sycamore, plane, hawthorn, and such almost sub-tropical climbers as the ivy, hop, and clematis. The *third* is Decandolle's zone of winter verdure, extending from about 45° to about 25° of northern latitude. It is the zone of the Caucasian range, stretching from the Pyrenees and the Atlas mountains on the West, to the termination of the Kuen-lun mountains in northern China on the East. It is the enchanting Cestus of our Earth-mother, broidered with umbrageous trees, and all the fruits and flowers of the poetry of the Caucasian races, viz. the laurels and myrtle blooms and citron worts, with dark shining evergreen leaves; the vine, fig, olive, walnut, mulberry, pomegranate, peach, apricot, date palm, and tea-plant; the rose, oleander, hyacinth, narcissus and tulip; and the sweet-leaved Labiates, and sweet-seeded Umbellifers. The *fourth* and *fifth* are the tropical and the equatorial zone, together extending from about 20° northern latitude to the equator: and repeated from the equator to about 20° of southern latitude. In the Old World, to which I am confining myself, these duplicated zones include Bengal and the Deccan in India, and Ceylon, and

Further India, and the Indian Archipelago, with northern Australia, and are characterised by such magnificent tree-forms, most of which are indigenous to India (exclusive of Rajputana and Sindh), as the cocoa-nut, "Palmyra tree," areca-nut, and other palms; the "Indian Fig" trees; the teak, ebony, sandalwood, and satinwood trees; the jack-fruit and bread-fruit trees; the silk cotton trees, and the *pulas* tree (*Butea frondosa*) which gives its name to the field of Plassey; the spice-bearing laurels, cinnamon, cloves, and nutmeg; and the pepperworts and gingerworts. But these zones lie beyond the limits of your question, and are excluded from further consideration in my reply.

'The zones indicated do not everywhere run parallel with the lines of latitude within which they are painted on the charts, like five (or seven) straightly stretched ribbons. They would indeed have done so had this globe been a perfect sphere, and the land and water uniformly distributed over it. But it presents the greatest confusion in the division of its land from its water, and in the contours and levels of its land; circumstauces all tending everywhere to deflect the lines of equal temperature, and with them the zones of similar vegetable and animal life, from the roughly corresponding lines of northern and southern latitude. This is particularly the case in the northern hemisphere, more especially in the Old World, and most emphatically in the very regions to which your query refers. Here all the chains of mountains by which the highly integrated configuration of Europe, Asia, and northern Africa has been determined converge in the stupendous steppe of the Great Pamir, known locally as the *Bam-i-Dumiah*, or "Roof of the World," as in the mighty axle of a six-spoked wheel: from which the Ural mountains stretch northward; the Suleiman mountains southward; and eastward the Himalayas and Kuen-lun mountains, holding up between them the elevated tableland of Thibet; and north-eastward, almost continuously to Behrings Straits, the Thian-shan and Altai mountains, leaving between them and the Kuen-lun mountains the wide extended depression of the desert of Gobi, presenting a waterless valley of even greater area than the corresponding basin of the Mediterranean sea; while westward the Caucasian range of the Hindu Kush, Elburz, Caucasus and Taurus mountains stretches continuously to the western coasts of Asia Minor, where it divides into the Balkans, the Alps, and the Pyrenees on the north, and the Lebanon and far projected Atlas mountains on the south; these northern and southern branches of the Caucasian range holding between them the vast valley, which, probably, within the mythical memory of the Caucasian races (Hamitic, Semitic, and Aryan), if we may so read the Samothracian legend preserved by Diodorus, became converted, by the bursting of the waters of the presumptive Aralo-Caspo-Euxine sea through the Bosphorus and the Hellespont, into the Mediterranean sea.

'Comparing the zones of vegetation to ribbons, it may be said that they are all brought together about the N.W. frontier of India, and intertwisted into an almost inextricable knot. Indeed you can no longer here arrange the development of vegetable life on the globe in zones (*Vegetations-zonen*); but must divide it into regions (*Florenreiche*). India is in latitude within the tropical zone; but the Himalayas and the high plateau of Persia bring down to the plain of the Ganges the climate and vegetation of the zones of Wahlenberg, Linnaeus, and Decandolle. The southern slopes of the Himalayas, marked by the prevalence of oak (*Quercus incana*) and the *deodar* pine, constitute Wallich's Kingdom. Central India and the Deccan, characterised by the tropical plants already enumerated, form Roxburgh's Kingdom; while beyond it, in the Indian Archipelago, is Blume's Kingdom. Persia is Gmelin's Kingdom, and carries the vegetation of Decandolle's zone eastward into the valley of the Indus, i.e. the Panjáb (Vedic India) and Sindh, and northward into Western Turkestan, which is also overlapped by the flora of the Siberian Kingdom of Pallas. There is thus at once a great similarity between the flora of Western Turkestan and of the Indus valley (*India alba*), and a great contrast between the flora of Western Turkestan and of India west and south of the Indus valley—that is, of the Ganges valley and the Deccan (*India nigra*). So many medicinal herbs indigenous to the Panjáb grow spontaneously on the sides of the famous Koh Umber, north of Kunduz, that the Turkomans believe this mountain to have been miraculously translated into their country from India. It is difficult therefore to discriminate between the flora N. E. and S.W. of Samarcand by naming plants either exclusively Inner Asian or exclusively Indian: meaning, that is, plants existing only either in the plain of the Oxus or in the valley of the Indus. It is easy enough to enumerate the assemblage of plant-forms which make up the vegetable physiognomy of each of these countries, and even to name a single plant-form predominant in either of them. But even so, I know of no "kenspeckle" plant, of no plant that would take hold of the popular eye and the memory of wandering barbarians, that is characteristic of Western Turkestan. I mean, for instance, in the same way as the "glutinous birch" and "Weymouth pine" are characteristic of the Highlands of Scotland, and northern Sweden, and Finland; the oak of Ulster, England north of the Humber, and Scotland south of the Forth, and of southern Norway and Sweden, and of western and central Russia; the beech of southern Ireland and England and northern France, Denmark, and Germany; *Amygdalus nana* and various species of *Stipa* (grasses) of the Russian Steppe region from the Black Sea, into upper Inner Asia; and the birch, willow, larch, and fir of the whole of Siberia; the oriental plane of Anterior Asia; the tragacanth and assafoetida of northern Persia; and the date-palm of Mesopotamia, southern Persia, Baluchistan, and Sindh. In this way botanists cite the *Borszczowia Aralo-Caspica* as characteristic of Western Turkestan; but it is a plant conspicuous only by the protracted cacophony of its scientific nomenclature. Wood, Schuyler, and Lansdell repeatedly describe the vegetation of Turkestan from the popular point of perception, and over and over again they repeat the names of the same plantation trees, the plane, poplar, birch, elm, willow, ash, fir; and of the same fruit-trees, the apple, plum, peach, apricot, fig, mulberry, pistachio, and the vine; and of the same flowering plants, the rose, poppy, and larkspur: plants which are everywhere found growing in natural or cultivated patches amid the undulating heathlands of grass, furze, broom, wormwood, and liquorice scrub. The assafoetida plant is found all over Western Turkestan, but it is more characteristic of northern Persia. In the Indus Valley the date-palm abounds; but it grows still more luxuriantly throughout southern Persia, Mesopotamia, and Syria. The natives of India are peculiarly apt in identifying countries by their distinguishing plants. In Rajputana they have a famous saying:

"*Aonla, aonla*, Mewar;
Bawul, bawul, Marwar."

They thus identify the *Phyllanthus Emblica* with the sub-tropical province of Mewar, and the *Acacia Arabica* with the Mediterranean province of Marwar; and, if compelled to name a single plant as predominantly characteristic of the Indus valley, and which, although not exclusively found there, does not exist in Turkestan, I should have to name the *Acacia Arabica*. Similarly, if forced to identify a universally popular plant with Western Turkestan, taken in connection with Central Asia generally, I should instance (for I know of none better for the purpose) the thorny shrub which yields the manna called *turanjabin* throughout the East. It is the "Hyrcanian tree," "occhus" of Pliny, the *Alhagi Maurorum* of botanists. Its area extends from Nepaul and the Southern Mahratta Country to Syria, but it yields its manna, for which alone it is "kenspeckle" only in Western Turkestan.

'In regard to the geographical distribution of animals, Mr. Alfred Russell Wallace, the most philosophical authority on the subject, divides the entire Euro-Asiatic continent into but two regions, namely, the *Palaearctic*, including all Europe, with northern Africa, and all Asia, excepting southern Arabia, Yemen, India, Further India, and the Indian Archipelago, which, with all Australasia, he includes in his *Oriental* region. The Palaearctic region he again subdivides into four sub-regions, namely the European or trans-Alpine, the Mediterranean or cis-Alpine, including northern Africa, Asia Minor, Syria, Northern Arabia, Afghanistan, and the western Panjáb; the Siberian or trans-Himalayan; and the Mongolian, including Mongolia, Manchuria, northern China, and Japan.

'Your question has strictly to do only with that portion of the Siberian region immediately north-west of the Hindu Kush, and that portion of the Mediterranean region immediately south-west of it. But it will be observed that immediately south-west of these mountains you have, as in the case of plant-life, to deal with two distinct regions of animal life; that is, the Mediterranean west of the Indus, and the Indian sub-region of the Oriental region east of that river. But as animals exercise something of volition in their movements, and it is easy for animals of the Ganges valley to extend their range into the Panjáb, while it is scarcely practicable for any of the larger Indian or Siberian mammals to pass respectively northward or southward through the lofty recesses of the Himalayas, each into the other's natural region, it should be somewhat less difficult than it is in regard to plants, to name some animal of common occurrence which exists only north-west of Samarcand or south-east of it. Wallace names four animals as absolutely restricted to the Siberian sub-region—a peculiar mole, two antelopes, and the *yak*. But deer and moles are found everywhere, and the *yak* is almost entirely confined to the tableland of Thibet. He does not name the dromedary, which is of common occurrence only in Western Turkestan, its original country; and as in a popular sense it is a most conspicuous and memorable animal, and with its double hump would never be confounded even by the most barbarous of mankind with the single-humped camel of Arabia, I would cite it, "the Bactrian camel," as the exclusively representative animal of Western Turkestan. For India, i. e. Vedic India, I would name "the Bengal tiger." It is the distinctive animal of Oriental rather than of Mediterranean India. But it is occasionally seen roaming along the southern slopes of the Himalayas and the Hindu Kush and Elburz mountains as far westward as the Caspian Sea. Pliny tells us that "Hyrcania and India produce the tiger"; and it was as an Hyrcanian rather than an Indian beast that he first appears in English literature. Shakespeare speaks only of "tigers of Hyrcania," and "the Hyrcan tiger," the "Hyrcanian beast" of the players in *Hamlet*; and before him, Daniel, in one of his *Sonnets*, which was probably in Shakespeare's mind when composing *Macbeth*, writes:

> "Restore thy fierce and cruel mind
> To Hircan tigers, and to ruthless bears."

Unfortunately the range of the tiger extends also northward along the Thian-shan, Altai, and Kuen-lun mountains into China and Japan, and through the eastward confines of Western Turkestan. Still I should not hesitate to name it as the distinctive animal of Vedic India; and with its dazzling colouring, in black and yellow stripes, and its terrific ferocity, so "kenspeckle" a beast, once encountered by "the undivided Aryas," should never have been forgotten by them. I find it stated however in standard ethnological works, I know not on what philological authority, that neither the tiger[1] nor the dromedary[2] were known to them, nor the loud-roaring king of beasts, the lion[3]; which, although an African animal, is common to the whole Mediterranean region as far eastward as Sindh and Kattiwar; and is the same lion in India and Mesopotamia as in Africa. This is strange, if "the Home of the Aryas" was, as I believe, in and about Western Turkestan. We must not however forget the great physical changes undergone by the whole of the Uralo-Caspian region in past ages, and which it is still undergoing. The country has visibly altered within the historical memory of its present inhabitants, among whom there is a tradition that in ancient times it was so well wooded that the *bulbul* (Persian nightingale) could flit from tree to tree all the way from the mountains of Kasghar to the Aral Sea. What I however most rely on, after the (to me) sufficiently conclusive arguments of the philologists, is the circumstance that all the traditions of the historical races of mankind, Turanian as well as Caucasian, refer back to Higher Asia as their primitive historical (I will not say ethnologically aboriginal) home; from which all the leading mountain-ranges of Europe and Asia radiate north, south, east, and west, pointing like road-posts the direction taken by the Turanian nations eastward and northward, and by the Caucasian nations southward and westward, when they first went forth from this universal "officina gentium" to divide the world between them.

'Moreover, man himself modifies nature, and, before he has evolved a scientific civilisation, nearly always injuriously; and it is not simply because the temperature of northern

[1] The tiger, unknown in the Rig-veda, is known in the Atharva-veda.—F. M. M.

[2] If the dromedary could be the ush*t*ra, it would have been known to the Vedic Indians. The v*ri*shabhá*h* kakúdmân is taken for the humped ox.—F. M. M.

[3] The lion, si*m*ha, is well known in the Rig-veda. The Greek λέων might be the Sanskrit ravan, roaring.—F. M. M.

Europe is milder than that of Central Asia and southern Europe that it is greener than these regions, but because it has not been so long subjected to the corroding influences of the presence of barbarous and semi-civilised humanity. Under these influences India was being gradually reduced, during the decline of the Moghul Empire, to the blighted condition of Central Asia, and was only saved from this impending doom by the British conquest. Similarly, were extended irrigation and scientific forestry introduced into Khiva, Bokhara, and Samarcand, their pristine verdure and prosperity would gradually be restored to them; and it would be found that in the apparently purposeless subjugation of these countries Russia had fulfilled her highest destiny.'

II.

The Original Home of Jade.

The following letters were written in order to ascertain whether the jade implements found in the lacustrian dwellings of Switzerland could be considered as a tangible proof of the ancient migration of races from the East to the West. The final verdict on this point must rest with mineralogists, and they seem to agree more and more both on the chemical constitution of jade and on the places in Asia where alone real jade has been found. If it should turn out that such wrought jade as is found in the lacustrian dwellings of Switzerland and elsewhere in Europe must have been brought from Asia to Europe, we should have a new indication of migrations from East to West at a time which may be called prehistoric, whether we place it before or after the Aryan immigration. It is possible that these jade implements may have been carried into Europe by non-Aryan races, but in any case they would tend to show that our belief in an ethnic movement from East to West, from Asia to Europe, is not based solely on the old proverb *Ex Oriente lux*, nor on the old assumption derived from the theological prejudice of a past age according to which all human migration must be from the East to the West, nor lastly on the more recent and more popular assumption that man must have had his origin in a country formerly abounding in apes.

The following paragraph appeared in the *Times*:—

'Switzerland. Geneva, *Dec.* 15, 1879.

'In the course of some excavations now going on in the bed of the Rhone near Geneva, many interesting objects, assigned by archaeologists to the age of polished stone, have been brought to light, the most curious of which is a scraper of jade, highly finished, and in a condition as perfect as when it left the hands of the workman. The question arises, and is being warmly discussed by the learned in lacustrine lore, how this instrument, made of a mineral which exists in a natural state only in Asia, can have found its way into the Rhone gravel at Geneva. Was jade ever an article of trade between the West and the East in prehistoric times, or is this scraper a solitary specimen brought by Aryan wanderers from the cradle of their race on the Hindu Kúsh? As yet no satisfactory solution of the problem has been suggested.'

On the 17th December, 1879, I sent the following letter to the *Editor of the Times*:—

'SIR,—The account sent by your correspondent at Geneva (December 15), of a scraper made of jade, lately found in the bed of the Rhone, is very important. But your correspondent is hardly quite right in calling this scraper a solitary specimen. Scrapers or cutting instruments made of real jade are very rare, in Switzerland and elsewhere, but I have myself seen several beautiful specimens—among the rest, one found by Dr. Uhlmann of München-buchsee, whose collection of lacustrine antiquities, all taken out by his own hand from one and the same small lake, the Moossee-dorfsee, is perhaps the most authentic and most instructive collection in the whole of Switzerland.

'Your correspondent asks whether, as true jade is never found in Europe, the Aryan wanderers could have brought that scraper from the cradle of their race in Asia. Why not? If the Aryan settlers could carry with them into Europe so ponderous a tool as their language, without chipping or clipping a single facet, there is nothing so very surprising in their having carried along, and carefully preserved from generation to generation, so handy and so valuable an instrument as a scraper or a knife, made of a substance which is *aere perennius*.

F. MAX MÜLLER.'

This letter elicited several replies. I here reprint one letter from Professor Story-Maskelyne which contains some important information on jade.

'SIR,—The space you have given in your columns to the curious question discussed by Professor Rolleston and Mr. Westropp regarding the sources of pre-historic jade, emboldens me to hope that you may not reject another letter on the subject.

'I believe Professor Rolleston is right in asserting an Oriental, possibly a single Oriental, source for the pre-historic jade of the Europ-Asiatic continent. I think so for these reasons:—Jade celts are very rare; they are found, however, few and far between, from Mesopotamia to Brittany; and they evince the passion of every race of mankind for the possession of green stones as objects endowed with an intrinsic preciousness. Now, if jade was a native product of all or of several of the numerous countries in the buried dust of which these jade implements are thus sporadically scattered, how comes it to pass that so remarkable a mineral has never been lit upon by the races of men who have lived and died in those countries since the "old men" wandered over them? One does, indeed, see a small jade celt once worn in a necklace by a Greek girl still pendant, as a talisman probably, from that specimen of antique gold jewellery in the British Museum. But it is a celt, not an object of Roman workmanship. One single cylinder among the hundreds of Assyrian and Babylonian cylinders in the same great repository attests the exceptional character of jade as a material among the peoples who inhabited Mesopotamia, where, however, jade celts have been found of still older date. But among the numerous materials of Egyptian ornamental and sacred art, jade is, I believe, unknown. There is no evidence that Greeks or Romans ever employed jade or (*pace* Mr. Westropp) had even a name for it. Had it been a product of the rivers or of the quarries of the Roman world, specimens of it would certainly have survived as the material of gems or in some other form of art. It may seem a startling proposition to maintain that the jade mines of the Kara Kash river, in the Kuen Luen range, north of the mountains of Cashmere, should have been the sources of the jade celts found over the whole of Europe. The difficulty of believing this seemed all the greater, for that, while white as well as green jade may be quarried there, it was only the green jade, and not the white, which thus permeated the pre-historic world. But a few months ago Dr. Schliemann asked me to look at some of the strange stones which he had lit upon in the oldest of the cities of Hissarlik, and there, with several specimens of green jade—one of them being a beautifully translucent specimen of the stone—was a single celt of fine white jade, just such as might have been dug from one of the pits above the Kara Kash, or fashioned from a pebble out of its stream.

'In contemplating these venerable treasures from that old town or fortress, one had to recognize that Dr. Schliemann had lit upon a place of importance, perhaps a sort of emporium planted on the stream of a pre-historic commerce, and situated just at one of the points where Asiatic products might collect previously to their being distributed by a process of barter among the peoples of the West. Or was it a halting-place at which some great wave of emigration was arrested for a time by the barrier of the Dardanelles? At any rate, there in considerable numbers were the green jade celts, the kind, no doubt, more valued on account of their colour; and there too was this solitary white celt, their companion probably from a common far-distant home in the Kuen Luen Mountains.

'To what cause is the failure in the supply of jade to the world lying to the south and west of the Pamir, after prehistoric times, to be attributed? I do not attempt to answer this question; I would only suggest the apparent evidence of such a failure. It is far from improbable that the green jade implement had in some sense a sacred character in pre-historic times, and was borne westwards by emigrating peoples, as they might bear their household gods, while by a slow process of barter specimens might have penetrated from the Hellespont to the Atlantic sea-board. And it may be that in even that remote age, or towards the close of it, people of Chinese race came to dominate over the district that produced the jade and closed the rugged passes that led south and west from that inhospitable region; and so, while China has from time immemorial had jade in plenty, the rest of the Asiatic continent may have been cut off from the source of its supply. Or, possibly, the geological changes that have raised the level of the lands to the north and east of Persia may have been still in action, and were gradually increasing the inhospitable features of the district towards the close of the period which we call the pre-historic period in Asia. It is probable that other sources of jade further north may have contributed some of the material borne westward in the form of celts. The Amoor in the far north rolls down jade pebbles from the Yablono Mountains of the Trans-Baikal district of Siberia, and the Chinese have probably some sources of green jade unknown to us. Their jadeite, a different mineral from jade, is supplied, though probably not exclusively, by mines in the mountains to the north-west of Bhamo in the Lao State of Burmah.

'The introduction of jade, or at least its use as a material for artistic workmanship, in India, dates almost from yesterday, since it belongs to the time of the early Mogul Emperors of Delhi. "The magnificent son of Akbar," Jehanghir, and Shah Jehan seem to have taken pleasure in jade cups and ornaments; and the art of inlaid work that found such exquisite expression in the Taj Mahal was copied under their munificent auspices in the most precious materials, rubies and diamonds and other precious stones being inlaid in jade of various colours, which was cut in delicate openwork and adorned with enamels, in the production of which India is still unrivalled. The collection of these beautiful productions of Indian art contained in the India Museum is the finest ever brought together. It was purchased, at a suggestion from myself, when the present Chancellor of the Exchequer [Sir Stafford Northcote] was Secretary of State for India; a selection having been made by the late Sir Digby Wyatt and me from an unique collection of jade vessels of all sorts, formed at great expense and trouble by the late Colonel Charles Seaton Guthrie.

'But these may be said to be the only forms in which civilized man beyond the confines of China has made jade the material for carving artistic creations.

'The Mexicans worked a kind of jadeite. The Maoris worked jade, which is a native mineral in their hornblendic rocks; and the inhabitants of New Caledonia, and indeed of Polynesia generally, have fashioned jade or some varieties of jadeite into implements, useful, ornamental, and perhaps too, in some sense, sacred.

'Jade is erroneously supposed to be a very hard substance. It is by no means so. Its most remarkable property—a property eminently fitting it for an implement—is an extraordinary toughness. Like well-tempered steel, in which toughness is combined with only enough hardness to do the work of cutting and to retain an edge, the implement of jade shared with the implement of fibrolite an unique combination of these qualities, essential alike in a weapon and in a working tool.—I am, Sir, your obedient servant,

'NEVIL STORY-MASKELYNE.'

'*British Museum*,
Dec. 30, 1879.'

In January 1880 I summed up the whole subject in another letter to the *Times*:—

'SIR,—The interesting and instructive letters on jade tools to which you have lately granted admission in your columns, will, I hope, have convinced most of your readers that the theory which I tried to uphold in my letter, published in the *Times* of December 16, was not quite so wild as at first sight it may have appeared. What are called wild theories are in many cases very tame theories. Students at first laugh at them, turn their backs on them, and try every possible exit to escape from them. But at last, when they are hemmed in by facts on every side, and see that there is no escape, they tamely submit to the inevitable, and after a time the inevitable is generally found to be the intelligible and the reasonable also.

'The problem of the jade tools is really very simple. Mineralogists assure us that jade is a mineral the identity of which, if properly tested, admits of no doubt, and they tell us with equal confidence that Europe does not produce true jade. These two statements I accept as true till they are upset by competent authorities. If, therefore, jade tools of exquisite workmanship are found in Europe during what is called the Stone age, I do not see how we can escape from the conclusion that these tools were brought from those well-defined areas in Asia—I suppose I may leave out of consideration America and Oceania—where alone jade has been found, and where it is still worked to the present day. Some of these are not so very distant, for true jade is found in the Caucasus and the Ural Mountains. I do not deny that at first one feels a little giddy when, while handling one of those precious scrapers, one is told that the identical scraper was the property of the first discoverers of Europe. And it was chiefly in order to remove that feeling of giddiness that I wished to call attention to another class of tools, equally ancient, possibly even more ancient, which were likewise brought into Europe from Asia by our earliest ancestors, and which we use every day without feeling the least surprise. Though no one nowadays doubts that our language came from the East, yet we do not always realize the close continuity between ancient and modern speech and the unbroken chain that holds all the Aryan dialects together from India to Ireland. We wonder how jade tools should have been brought from the East and passed from hand to hand during many thousands of years, "before pockets were invented," and yet every word of our language came from the East and must have passed from hand to hand during thousands of years before pocket-dictionaries were invented. If we take such useful tools as our numerals, and consider what is presupposed by the fact that, making allowance for a certain amount of phonetic wear and tear, these numerals are the same in Sanskrit and in English, we shall, I think, feel less upset, even when brought face to face with the jade tools in the lacustrine dwellings of Switzerland. Aye, I go a step further. Let us look at the fact that, of all the numerals from one to ten in Sanskrit, saptá (seven) and ashtáu (eight) alone have the accent on the last syllable, and then turn our eyes to ancient and even to modern Greek, and observe exactly the same exceptional accentuation there. Any one who can look without a tremor into the depth thus suddenly opened before our eyes, will hardly feel a swimming of the head when examining the wildest theories that have been founded on the jade tools unearthed in Switzerland and other parts of Western Europe.

'It is not necessary to enter here on the question, whether these jade instruments were brought into Europe by Aryan or pre-Aryan colonists. It is certainly strange that there is no ancient Aryan name for jade, but neither is there a pre-Aryan or Turanian name for it in any of the ancient Indo-European languages. I have collected elsewhere (*Lectures on the Science of Language*, vol. ii. p. 251, 9th ed.) some facts which make it seem not unlikely that Aryan languages were spoken in Europe during the age of stone and the prevalence of the Scotch fir, and I may add that the nature of the arguments brought forward against that hypothesis has strengthened rather than weakened my own confidence in it. Yet it is an hypothesis only. But, whether brought by Aryan or pre-Aryan settlers, certain it is that these jade tools were not made in Europe, and that, though jade is softer *in situ*, they testify to a high degree of humanity and mechanical skill among the people who made them.

'My friends Professors Rolleston and Maskelyne have left me but little to add in support of the foreign origin of the jade tools. Two facts only I may still mention, because they may help others, as they helped me, in forming their own opinion on the subject.

'It is a fact, I believe, that with a few and somewhat apocryphal exceptions, such as the finds at Potsdam and Schwemsal, no raw or unworked jade has ever been met with anywhere in Europe. This, to my mind, speaks volumes.

'It is another fact that there is in Europe no ancient name for jade. If on page 311 of H. Fischer's excellent work on *Nephrit und Jadeit*, 1875, we consult the chronological list of writers by whom jade is mentioned, we find in ancient times the name of jaspis, jaspis virens, jaspis viridis, but nothing to enable us to identify that name with true jade. Jaspis itself is a name of Semitic origin. In Chinese, on the contrary, we find from the most ancient to the most recent times the recognized name for jade—viz. yu or chiû. It is mentioned as an article of tribute in Professor Legge's translation of the Shû-King (*Sacred Books of the East*, vol. iii. p. 72), and it is curious to find in that, as we are told, most ancient among ancient books, articles such as "gold, iron, silver, steel, copper, and flint stones to make arrow-heads," all mentioned together as belonging to the same period, and all equally acceptable as tribute at the Imperial Court. *Forsan et haec olim meminisse juvabit!* The word jade is not met with before the discovery of America. The jade brought from America was called by the Spaniards piedra de yjada, because for a long time it was believed to cure pain in the side. For similar reasons it was called afterwards lapis nephriticus (nephrite), lapis ischiadicus, lapis divinus, piedra de los reñones, piedra ischada, pietra del fiancho, kidney-stone, Lendenhelfer, etc. The first who introduced this new nomenclature into Europe seems to have been Monardes, in his *Historia Medicinal de las Cosas que se traen de las Indias Occidentales*; Sevilla, 1569. The name which he uses, piedra de yjada, is meant for piedra de ijada, i.e. groin-stone, or a stone supposed to remove pain in the groin. The Spanish ijada is, according to the Dictionary of the Spanish Academy, il lado del animal debaxo del vientre junto al anca, and there can be little doubt that it is derived from the Latin ilia. Iliaco in Spanish is il dolor colico. As the name ijada, jada, or jade, and the belief in its healing powers, came from America, it can only be an accidental coincidence if, as Professor Skeat tells us in his excellent *Etymological Dictionary*, there existed in Sanskrit Buddhist texts the word yedâ as a name of a material out of which ornaments were made. I have never met with such a word.

'This is the state of the question of the jade tools at the present moment. To those who wish to study its history in all its bearings, Fischer's exhaustive work on *Nephrit und Jadeit* will give the necessary information. His survey of the literature on a subject apparently so abstruse and remote from general interest fills no less than 248 pages.—Your obedient servant,

F. MAX MÜLLER.'

I cannot resist the temptation of adding here one more letter on the subject of jade-tools, which I received from Mr. James Lowell, at that time Minister of the United States at

Madrid, a man perhaps the most widely admired and the most widely loved among the Aryas, whether in Europe or on the other side of the Atlantic.

'LEGACION DE LOS ESTADOS UNIDOS DE AMERICA EN ESPAÑA.

'18 *Jan.* 1880.

'I read with great satisfaction what you wrote about *jade*. One is tempted to cry out with Marlowe's Tamburlaine, "How now, ye pampered *jades of Asia*?" One thing in the discussion has struck me a good deal, and that is the crude notion very intelligent men have of the migration of tribes. I think most men's conception of distance is very much a creature of maps—which make Crim Tartary and England not more than a foot apart, so that the feat of the old rhyme—"to dance out of Ireland into France"—looks easy. They seem to think that the shifting of habitation was accomplished like a modern journey by rail—and that the emigrants wouldn't need tools by the way or could buy them at the nearest shop after their arrival. There is nothing the ignorant and the poor cling to so tenaciously as their familiar household utensils. Incredible things are brought every day to America in the luggage of emigrants—things often most cumbrous to carry and utterly useless in the new home. Families that went from our seaboard to the West a century ago through an almost impenetrable wilderness, carried with them all their domestic pots and pans—even those I should be willing to wager that needed the tinker. I remember very well the starting of an expedition from my native town of Cambridge in 1831 for Oregon, under the lead of a captain of great energy and resource. They started in wagons ingeniously contrived so as to be taken to pieces, the body forming a boat for crossing rivers. They carried everything they could think of with them, and got safely to the other side of the continent—as hard a job, I fancy, as our Aryan ancestors had to do. There is hardly a family of English descent in New England that doesn't cherish as an heirloom something brought over by the first ancestors two hundred and fifty years ago. And beside the motive of utility there is that also of sentiment—particularly strong in the case of an old tool.'

I answered on the 3rd of February, 1880.

'OXFORD, *Febr.* 3, 1880.

'... Your remarks about jade are very true. I should have written once more to the *Times*, but I felt jaded, and I was afraid the readers of the *Times* might share that feeling. Otherwise I really felt it due to our troglodyte ancestors to say a few words for their common sense, and not to let people believe that they kept their green jade tools "because they reminded them of green fields." Why, the man or the clan who possessed one of those small jade scrapers or knives or scissors, was a Rothschild among beggars. You can cut an iron nail with those jade-chisels [1], and they show no dent. Diamond only will tell on them. A man who possessed one of those treasures could eat a dozen of oysters and crack ten times as many marrow-bones as his neighbours who had flint knives only, which broke at every blow, and had constantly to be renewed. It was like a Krupp gun compared with old Bess. Of course any swell or family of swells who possessed such a diploma of nobility would keep it as long as they could keep anything, and, as you say, even when it ceased to be useful, sentiment would protect it, as it protects an old razor, though it has long ceased to be useful.

The wonderful fancies about jade begin in the sixteenth century. If you should come across some of the books written by the Court physicians of Charles V and others,

[1] *Pace* Sir John Lubbock, for chisel has nothing to do with German Kiesel, nor is a chisel a survival of a flint.

the cures which they describe as effected by wearing jade are marvellous. These were men as great as Sir Andrew Clark and Sir William Paget, only three hundred years ago. They describe cases which they watched for ten years and more, and give the names of their patients, and describe how the calculi passed away in shoals as soon as the patient touched the jade! Are we so much wiser than our fathers?

'F. MAX MÜLLER.'

III.

The Original Home of the Soma.

The following notes on Soma contain another attempt at fixing the original abode of the Aryas, or at all events of the South-Eastern branch of the Aryas, by discovering, if possible, the true habitat of the famous Soma plant which formed so prominent a feature in the worship and religion of the still undivided South-Easterners, but is at present utterly unknown.

'Oxford, *Oct.* 20, 1884.

'It is a real pleasure for once to see an official paper devoted to a purely scientific subject. I say purely scientific, because, whenever science becomes practically useful, governments are willing enough to patronise it. But here, in *File No.* 118, *Government of India, Revenue and Agricultural Department*, we are presented with "Papers relating to the Soma Plant," which have nothing to do with the cultivation or the export of Soma, but are simply intended to identify, if possible, the Soma plant, which is mentioned in the Veda and the Avesta, to determine its original habitat, and thus to find the original home, if not of the whole Aryan family, at least of its South-Eastern branch, comprising the speakers of Sanskrit and Zend. . . . .

'It is well known that both in the Veda and the Avesta a plant is mentioned, called Soma (Zend haoma). This plant, when properly squeezed, yielded a juice, which was allowed to ferment and, when mixed with milk and honey, produced an exhilarating and intoxicating beverage. This Soma juice has the same importance in Vedic and Avestic sacrifices as the juice of the grape had in the worship of Bacchus. The question has often been discussed what kind of plant this Soma could have been. When Soma sacrifices are performed at present, it is confessed that the real Soma can no longer be procured, and that some *ci-près*, such as Pûtikâs, etc., must be used instead. Dr. Haug, who was present at one of these sacrifices and was allowed to taste the juice, had to confess that it was extremely nasty and not at all exhilarating. Even in the earliest liturgical works, in the Sûtras and Brâhma*n*as, the same admission is made, namely, that true Soma is very difficult to be procured, and that substitutes may be used instead. When it was procured, it is said that it was brought by barbarians from the North, and that it had to be bought under very peculiar circumstances.

'All these facts were stated in some papers contributed by Roth to the Journal of the German Oriental Society in 1881 and 1883, and in these papers the learned scholar pointed out how Russian or English emissaries in the northern region of the neutral zone might render useful service if, in their wanderings, they would look out for a plant resembling the Soma plant. Wherever that plant grew naturally, it would be safe to place the cradle of the Aryan race, or, at all events, of the ancestors of the people who, when they had migrated south, spoke either Sanskrit or Zend.

'These papers were translated by Mr. Charles James Lyall, and forwarded to the Afghan Frontier Delimitation Commission. Mr. Lyall remarks:—

'"If we can find the Soma anywhere in the region of the Hindu-Kush, it at once fixes the region as the mother-country of Indians and Iranians, and locates them together, in the Vedic age, or at least its beginning."

'It seems that on this strong recommendation the Indian Government submitted Mr. Charles J. Lyall's papers and translations to Dr. G. Watt, a well-known Indian botanist. His answer has now been published, and though it is disappointing for the present, it is extremely instructive. Dr. G. Watt declares that no plant is known at present which would fulfil all the requirements, and he lays particular stress on the fact that the vague and poetical descriptions given of the Soma make any scientific identification almost impossible.

'Before it is too late, I take this opportunity of pointing out the oldest scientific description of the Soma plant which I know of. I published it so far back as 1855, in the Journal of the German Oriental Society. On p. xliii, after describing the peculiar rules for buying and rebuying the Soma from northern barbarians, as given in the Âpastamba-Ya*gñ*aparibhâshâ, I added in a note: "The only botanical description of the Soma plant which I know at present is found in an extract from the so-called Âyur-veda quoted in the Dhûrtasvâmi-bhâshya*t*îkâ." There we read: "The creeper, called Soma, is dark, sour, without leaves, milky, fleshy on the surface; it destroys phlegm, produces vomiting, and is eaten by goats."

'I added, that, according to the opinion of Sir J. Hooker, this description points to a Sarcostemma, which, alone of a large family, combines the qualities of sour and milky; but I remarked at the same time that the fact of this Sarcostemma growing in the Presidency of Bombay militated against this identification, because the true Soma must be a northern plant, which was replaced in India itself by Pûtikâs or similar substitutes.

'I cannot vouch for the exact age of the Âyur-veda, but I doubt whether we shall find any scientific description of the Soma of an earlier date. F. MAX MÜLLER.'

'TÜBINGEN, *Nov.* 9, 1884.

'Prof. Max Müller's letter in the *Academy* for October 25 calls the attention of your readers to the Soma, and to the arrangements recently made for searching after this plant in the region of the Hindu-Kush. Being interested in the matter, I beg you will allow me space for a few words which the occasion seems to demand.

'The learned scholar takes the opportunity of supplying an omission in my papers on the Soma (translated by Mr. Charles James Lyall, Secretary to the Chief Commissioner, Assam) by pointing out a passage of a certain *T*îkâ, that is, a commentary on another commentary, published by himself thirty years ago, which contains what Prof. Max Müller declares to be the oldest scientific description of the Soma.

'I did not, indeed, remember the passage referred to; but if it had been in my mind I should scarcely have mentioned it. The verses in question are stated to be taken from the Âyurveda, the exact age of which Prof. Max Müller says he cannot vouch for, but doubts whether any scientific description of an earlier date could be found.

'The Âyurveda, however, as Prof. Max Müller was not perhaps aware in the year 1855, but now, at any rate, knows as well as I, is not the title of a definite book, but the designation of the whole science of medicine, or rather, the medical literature. The expression used, "it is said in the Âyurveda," is equivalent to "it is said in a medical book." Thus no conjecture as to the date of the passage quoted is, on this ground, admissible. The wording, however, of the passage, sounds exactly like that of the descriptions of plants which we are accustomed to find in books of later, and even the latest date, especially in the so-called Ngha*nt*us, treatises containing the names of drugs, and enumerating their supposed effects. The definition of the Soma, for instance, as *s*leshmala, is based on the customary medical system. It states, however, not that the Soma destroys phlegm, but, on the contrary, produces phlegm. It is my opinion, moreover, that the verses cited contain an actual error, which is, perhaps, to be ascribed to the author of the *T*îkâ. The Soma plant is said to be vamanî, a word which can only be translated, as by Prof. Max Müller, "it produces vomiting." Now there is, in the first place, no instance of an adjective vamana; only vamanam, "an emetic," an abbreviation for vamana-dravyam, is current. Secondly, it is not to be supposed that the Soma, or its principal substitute in later times, should have caused vomiting. I conjecture that the correct reading was pâvanî, by which word an effect of the Soma plant is defined, for instance, in the Râganighantu, 3, 88.

'I consider it improbable, then, that an early date can be assigned to this description. It follows that the plant here intended is not the Vedic Soma for which we are seeking, but the Soma of later times which we know (that is, the *Sarcostemma acidum*), correctly described as bearing no leaves.

'These two verses, therefore, must not serve as a guide to the botanists of the Afghan Frontier Delimitation Commission. I am, indeed, still inclined to believe that the genuine original Soma, which will perhaps be discovered in the highlands beside the Oxus, will bear great resemblance to this, its later substitute.

'Dr. G. Watt opposes my conjecture most emphatically in "A Note upon Dr. Roth's Suggestion regarding the Soma Plant," dated Simla, August 20, 1884.

'Dr. Watt rejects the idea that the Soma must be a succulent plant, full of sweet sap. He would be much more inclined to regard the plant as one of the Compositae or Umbelliferae, which have from time immemorial afforded most of the prized products of the Afghan-Persian region. Dr. Watt even goes so far as to say there does not seem to be any evidence that the prized liquor was not a decoction.

'I am sorry not to be able to conform my views to those of the distinguished botanist. The Aryans no more drank a decoction of the Soma plant than they drank tea or coffee. It would be, indeed, a disgrace to the interpreters of the Veda and Avesta if Dr. Watt were right. Since this is not the place to enter into details, I will call attention to one place in the Atharva-veda, V, 29, 12. The wish is there expressed to a convalescent, that all the flesh which his disease has stripped off, may be replaced on his body; "that his limbs may increase in roundness; that he may grow plump like the shoot (amsu) of the Soma."

'I trust that the botanists of the Afghan Frontier Commission will not be diverted from directing their attention to other plants than the Compositae and Umbelliferae, and in particular that they will not bring us home, as Soma, the *Asafoetida*, which there obtrudes itself upon one's notice, or any other *Ferula*. R. ROTH.'

'OXFORD, *Nov.* 17, 1884.

'I think Prof. R. Roth has slightly misunderstood a sentence in my letter on the Soma Plant, published in the *Academy* of October 25. I said that I wished to take the earliest opportunity "of pointing out the oldest *scientific* description of the Soma plant which I knew of." By scientific I meant, of course, botanical; and I have had several letters from botanists, who recognised at once the scientific botanical character of that description, so different from all other descriptions, and wrote that "there was more to guide a botanist in that paragraph than in all that has hitherto been written on the Soma." No better scientific description of the Soma plant has as yet been pointed out, and, till that is done, the passage which I published in 1855 will remain the classical passage on the subject.

'I was careful to remark that the description in question was found in the *T*ikâ on the Bhâshya of Dhûrtasvâmin, that it was quoted from the so-called Âyurveda, but that I could not vouch for the age of that so-called Âyurveda. Why I could not vouch for the age of the so-called Âyurveda, Prof. Roth knows probably better than anybody else. I had the same impression which he seems to have had, namely, that the description of the Soma plant was taken from one of the Nigha*nt*us; but I have hitherto not been able to find it either there or in *K*araka, the Sau*s*ruta Âyurveda, *K*akradatta, or in other medical books.

'Whether by *s*leshmala is meant a plant that produces or one that destroys phlegm, I do not feel competent to decide.

I took it in the sense of sleshmaha, and was under the impression that certain medicines destroyed or carried off phlegm by first dissolving or, if you like, producing it. Medicines for producing phlegm in the ordinary sense of that term seem to me very doubtful.

'I grant Prof. Roth that our dictionaries contain no adjective vamana, from which vamanî could be formed. But that applies to many Sanskrit words; and adjectives in ana, forming their feminines in anî, like *k*odana, *k*odanî, &c., are perfectly regular. To replace vamanî by pâvanî is quite uncalled for. If we must needs conjecture, vâminî would be far better than pâvanî, as suggested by Prof. Roth. The learned professor must be aware how precious the adjective vamanî or vâminî is, for it expresses the one peculiarity of the Soma for which there is ancient Brâhma*n*ic authority, namely, that it produced vomiting in persons who were not accustomed to it, while it agreed with the Brâhmans. I need not quote passages in support of this, for they must be perfectly familiar to so distinguished a student of the Veda as Prof. Roth is known to be, nor need I refer him to his own dictionary, s.v. somavâmin. I am quite prepared to admit that this oldest scientific description of the Soma plant which I know of, may refer to one of the later substitutes of the Vedic Soma. But even if that plant could be identified once for all, something would have been gained. As to the Soma which the Brahmans knew (Rv. X, 85, 3, yam brahmâ*n*a*h* vidu*h*), I shall welcome it whenever it is discovered, whether in the valley of the Oxus or in that of the Neckar.

F. MAX MÜLLER.'

'KEW HERBARIUM, *Nov.* 15, 1884.

'I should like to say a few words in this discussion from a botanist's point of view. Since the matter was first mooted in your columns by Prof. Max Müller it has been definitely arranged that Dr. Aitchison should go with the Afghan

Boundary Commission as naturalist. Dr. Aitchison has twice visited the country already upon exploring expeditions, and has done more than any man living to increase our knowledge of the Afghan flora. From each previous expedition he has sent home to England large and beautifully prepared collections of plants, which have been reported upon in detail by himself and Mr. W. B. Hemsley in the Journal of the Linnean Society. Of these specimens type-sets have been retained for our Government herbaria at home, and the duplicates have been distributed to other public and private herbaria in Europe, India, and America.

'A very great deal has been done in other directions during the last twenty years to increase our knowledge of the botany of Central Asia. Working from Turkestan as a basis Dr. Albert Regel and other Russian explorers have collected most diligently; and now, in Boissier's *Flora Orientalis*, of which the fifth and concluding volume has been issued very recently, we have gathered up in one book all the scattered records that relate to Persia and the neighbouring regions.

'The Âyurveda description of the Soma plant, which was cited in your columns by Prof. Max Müller, appears to me to point distinctly in the direction of Sarcostemma. So far as I remember there is no other old-world climber with leafless fleshy stems which yields an abundant supply of milky juice. Sarcostemma is a genus of very wide distribution, of which about ten distinct species are known, all of which fulfil the above definition. Working from the Indian Peninsula as a centre it extends to Australia, Abyssinia, and Cape Colony. There is an endemic species in Scinde (*Sarcostemma Stocksii*). Two from the highlands of Arabia (*S. stipitaceum* and *Forskahlianum*) are described in Forskahl's *Flora Ægyptiaco-Arabica*, with a considerable amount of detail as to their uses, and Arabic and Persian names. One of the two, at any rate, appears to be eaten at the present day, both by men and animals.

'No Sarcostemma is known to grow anywhere in the neighbourhood of Central Asia, but other plants which belong to the same very limited group of leafless Asclepiads have been traced up to a considerable altitude. *Periploca aphylla*, which Dr. Aitchison reports as common in Afghanistan, has been traced up by Dr. Haussknecht to 3000 feet in the mountains of Persia. Of this the stems are used as cordage, and Dr. Stocks says that in Beluchistan the fragrant flowers are eaten by the natives, and taste like raisins. *Periploca hydaspidis* has been traced up by Mr. C. B. Clarke to 4000 feet in Kashmir, and nearly as high by Dr. Aitchison in the Kuram valley.

'In his letter in your issue just received, Dr. Roth demurs to the description of the Soma plant cited by Prof. Max Müller as being deficient in authenticity and antiquity. If then he will undertake to condense the authentic scattered notices of it which are to be found, into a brief definite description, and print this in your columns, we will take care that when Dr. Aitchison's plants come home and are being worked out this shall be kept in memory. But Central Asia has now been so well explored that it does not seem likely that any distinctively marked new plant-type still remains to be discovered. J. G. BAKER.'

'ROYAL GARDENS, KEW, *Nov.* 28, 1884.

'The discussion as to the identity of the original Soma plant has not brought to the front what appeared to me the most interesting point in my friend Dr. Watt's note, included in the papers printed by the Government of India on the subject. I quote the passage containing it:—

'"Is it not natural to suppose that, prior to its having come to be the most sacred offering, the Soma was viewed as a luxury, and by religious sentiment was extolled into the mythical emblem of perfect happiness? Can any one who has examined the bitter milky sap of the *Asclepiadeae* (such as *Calotropis gigantea*, the *Akanda* or *Madar*) suppose that such a liquid could ever be used for more than a medicinal purpose, and still less become the Soma of the Vedas? It is much more likely that the oblong fruit of the Afghan grape (often not unlike in shape and size the joints of the human finger) were described as the joints of the stem of a succulent plant, and were thus refused the position of being regarded as fruits, and that these, imported into the plains as they are at the present day, afforded the sweet and refreshing cup of which our Aryan ancestors became drunk while wrapt in the oblivion of religious enthusiasm."

'Now Dr. Roth is "still inclined to believe that the genuine original Soma will perhaps be discovered in the highlands beside the Oxus." A. de Candolle, on the other hand (*Origine des Plantes Cultivées*, p. 152), gives the ancient Bactria, Cabul, Cashmir, and Badakshan—pretty much the same ground—as the "eastern part of the area in which the vine is probably indigenous." And the neighbourhood of Cabul produces to this day grapes which are sent over India in little wooden boxes[1]. The imagery of the *Atharvaveda* quoted by Dr. Roth—"that his [a convalescent's] limbs may increase in roundness; that he may grow plump like the shoot of the Soma"—would be equally sustained by the swelling berries of the vine. At the time this was written one may presume that the morphological difference between a shoot and a fruit did not seem as profound as it does to us.

'That the primitive Soma was something not less detestable than anything that could be extracted from a *Sarcostemma* I find it hard to believe. When, however, the original Soma was unprocurable, and the use became purely ceremonial, the unpalatableness of the Soma substitute was immaterial. To quote De Gubernatis (*Mythologie des Plantes*, ii. 352):—

[1] Grapes and the sweet grape juice of Kapisa, North of Cabul, are referred to in Pânini's Grammar, iv. 2. 99.—F. M. M.

'"Dans les temps védiques et postérieurs, en chantant les louanges du Soma divin, on présentait aux dieux pour la forme quelque breuvage économique, que personne ne buvait, non pas seulement parce qu'il était réservé aux immortels, mais très probablement aussi parce qu'aucun mortel n'en aurait voulu. Dans l'histoire des sacrifices on trouverait un grand nombre de substitutions de ce genre."

'It is curious, however, to notice that, under the article "Vigne" (p. 369), he remarks, "il est très probable que le culte védique du *Soma* a été appliqué au vin dans la Perse, dans l'Asie Mineure, et en Grèce.' Now, supposing the cult of the Soma originated near the sources of the Oxus, and that the vine was used, then as its indigenous area extends westward—at any rate to Armenia—its sacred character would be likely to have been preserved towards the west, though the meaning of the cult itself might have changed. Towards Hindostan it was possibly exactly the opposite: the cult retained its integrity, and the plant was forgotten because the plains of India were too hot for it. In fixing on the *Sarcostemma* for a substitute, it must be remembered that succulent plants are rare in the Indian flora, and that there is a faint resemblance in texture and appearance, though not in form, between the joint of a *Sarcostemma* and an unripe green grape.

'I may mention, in conclusion, that I drew Prof. Max Müller's attention privately to this solution of the difficulty. He replied by saying that the passage in the *Âyurveda* quoted by him would not fit in with it. This is perfectly true; but I see that Dr. Roth considers "it improbable that an early date can be assigned to this description," and that it applies not to the Vedic Soma but to that of recent times. I do not presume to offer an opinion as to whether Dr. Roth's view is sustainable or not, but, at any rate, it diminishes my presumption in again urging the claims of the vine on Prof. Max Müller's attention. W. T. THISELTON DYER.'

'OXFORD, *Dec.* 8, 1884.

'Mr. W. T. Thiselton Dyer's letter in the *Academy* of December 6 once more moots the question whether the Vedic Soma might not be the vine. I do not deny the possibility of this identification, and I actually ventured to hint in my last letter that the Soma might possibly be found in the valley of the Neckar as well as in the valley of the Oxus. The same idea had been started before, and even the similarity of the names Soma and οἶνος had, I believe, been dwelt on by some venturesome scholar. It is true the difference between the two is only the spiritus; but that is enough.

'When Mr. Thiselton Dyer called my attention, in a private letter, to Dr. Watt's suggestion that Soma might have been the grape, I replied that the passage in the *Âyurveda* would not fit. But that was not my only difficulty. As to the date of the *Âyurveda*, I should probably assign a much later date to it than Prof. Roth, considering that I have tried to prove in my *India, what can it teach us?* that the whole of Sanskrit literature which we possess, with the exception of the Vedic and early Buddhistic, cannot be older than about A.D. 400. Being alone responsible for that heresy, I am not likely to claim for the *Âyurveda* an earlier date than any other Sanskrit scholar; but I still hold that it is the oldest accessible passage which gives a truly botanical account of the Soma. It is the classical passage, and must be taken into account, if only for determining what was supposed to be the Soma, before we go any farther.

'The question of the Soma is extremely complicated, and it was so even at the time when the Vedic hymns were written, if we may judge from a passage which I quoted in one of my former letters, and in which it is said:—"He who drinks, thinks it is Soma, and likewise when they beat the plant: the Soma whom the Brahmans know, of him no one eats."

'The fact is that Soma was originally a divine name, like Savitar, both derived from the root su, to squeeze, to beget. Long before it became a name of the moon, it was a name of the sun in his generative, fructifying, nurturing, vivifying, and exhilarating character. This name of Soma grew rapidly among the Vedic Rishis. It became one of the most prominent deities, and there is hardly anything in the life of nature that could not be ascribed to Soma. Rain, light, warmth, life, vigour, both bodily and mental, all were supposed to be manifestations of Soma.

'From the same root su, in the sense of pouring out, many names connected with the libations of the Vedic sacrifice were derived, and here, no doubt, one plant in particular, which was used for drink and sacrifice, became known by the name of Soma. It was collected on the mountains, its stems or shoots were bruised and squeezed, and the juice, after undergoing various processes, was called, like the plant, Soma. Unfortunately, that Soma plant was so well known, and possibly varied so much in different localties, that we find no botanical description of it in any of the hymns. On the contrary, the similarity of the name of the god and the name of the plant, and the idea which underlies the whole of the Vedic sacrifice, namely, that the sacrifice is an imitation of certain processes in nature, produced the most fantastic confusion between the two—the god and the plant. All the passages in the Veda bearing on the Soma have been carefully collected by Burnouf, Windischmann, Muir, and, lately, again by M. Bergaigne. One of the few tangible things said about the Soma-juice is that it was mixed with corn (yava), probably barley, and with milk. This statement, resting on the authority of the hymns themselves, makes, I am afraid, the grape impossible.

'But, if guessing be allowed, this fact may possibly point to hops, and a venturesome etymologist might not shrink even from maintaining that hops and Soma are the same word.

He would argue that the Sanskrit name came to the West through Persia, and in Persian Soma is haoma. In this form the Greeks heard of the Soma, for Plutarch (*De Iside et Osiride*, p. 46) speaks of the sacred plant as ὅμωμι. Hops came to Western Europe at a late time (see Hehn, *Kulturpflanzen*, p. 410). In the ninth century we find for hops the mediaeval Latin name humolo, humelo, and umlo. If we take lo as a later derivative, we have humo instead of homo, which, for a foreign word, brought from Persia into Europe, is tolerably near. I need not add other names of hops, as they can all be found in Hehn's book, such as the Finnish humala, the Slavonic chmelĭ, the Hungarian komló, mediaeval Greek χουμέλη, modern Geeek χουμέλι, &c. Now hops mixed with barley would give some kind of beer. Whether milk would improve the mixture I am not brewer enough to know. In fact, I am willing to wait, and not to disturb the fermentation, till Dr. Aitchison returns from the Oxus, where, I am glad to say, he has now been sent by Government.

'F. MAX MÜLLER.'

'*Dec.* 27, 1884.

'In common with many of your readers I have been impressed by Professor Max Müller's very original idea that the Soma plant was simply hops. Any confirmation of this, drawn from such a very disreputable source as gypsy, is, indeed, not worth much; yet it may be borne in mind that the Romany contains many odd and ancient fragments of old Sanskrit—like gems imbedded in petrified mud and gravel. In this tongue, soma or sumer (the pronunciation is not fixed) means a scent, smell, or flavour. Thus the hop gives the sūma or soma to the beer, as the lemon to punch. The fact that the hop is not found south of a certain range, or where the Hindus now dwell, rather proves than disproves Professor Max Müller's theory. Having left the plant far behind, while yet retaining its tradition, it is extremely possible that the early Indians attached the latter first to one and then to another vegetable with a bitter or acrid juice. The common gypsy word for hops is levinor (German Romany Löwina), which is also the name for beer.

'CHARLES G. LELAND.'

'TEHERAN, *Dec.* 20, 1884.

'In view of the correspondence on the Soma plant published in the *Academy* on October 25 and on November 15 and 22, a few facts regarding the Soma of Persia may be of interest.

'When travelling in 1879 between Bender Abbas and Kermân, and at an altitude of over 7000 feet, I was shown the Hûm shrub, from which the Pârsis of Persia get the juice Hûm or Hômâ, the Indian Sôma. It was, as far as I could make out, a Sarcostemma or Asclepias, growing to a height of four feet, and having circular fleshy stalks of whitish colour, with light brown streaks. The thickest stalks were about a finger thick; the leaves had fallen off as well as the flowers, which, I was informed, were small and white; some seeds adhered to the ends of some stalks; the seeds had long tufts of fine hair attached to them like the seeds of nearly all Asclepiads. The juice was milky, of a greenish white colour, and had a sweetish taste. A Pârsî who was with me, as well as others in Kermân and Yezd, told me that the juice turns sour after being kept for a few days, and that the colour of the juice, as well as that of the stalks, turns to a yellowish brown[1]. The plant I saw was not a creeper; but I was assured that when it grew near a tree it twined around it. The stalks break easily at the joints, the internodia, and then form small cylindrical pieces.

'Of Hûm mixed with the juice of many (forty) plants, as mint, thyme, asparagus, kangar (gundelia Tournefortii), &c.,

[1] Cf. Yasna, 11. 3, regarding the evil of keeping Soma and thereby causing it to get spoiled.

the juice of seven fruits, and the urine of a young pure cow, the purifying liquid Nîrengi[1] is prepared by the Pârsis. The priests drink a few drops of this every two or three days, and particularly when they have been to an impure place or have eaten anything prepared by an impure person, and the other Pârsîs drink a few drops, never more than twelve or sixteen, daily during their Birishnû time of purification. The liquid is also given as a remedy against sickness; a few drops are poured into the mouth of a newly-born child, and into that of a dead person before carrying the body to the Dakhmah, &c.; when taken in greater quantities, that is, more than twelve or sixteen drops, it is said *to cause vomiting*. The Hûm itself is used by the Pârsís in their religious ceremonies.

'The plant is at present not very plentiful round about Kermân; and many shrubs being cut by woodcutters when collecting firewood, it daily gets rarer. The mobeds of Kermân pay the woodcutters to preserve ten or twelve shrubs yearly[2]. The plant is also found on the mountains near Yezd, and a Pârsî told me lately that he had found it near Teherân on the Bîbî Shehrbânû mountain (the Kûh i Tabarek of Rey). I daresay it grows on all high mountains of Persia. The plant was, as the Avesta says, brought from the mountains, but this statement does not preclude its having grown in plains. The best plants—that is, those giving most juice—were, however, certainly only found on the mountains, exactly like other Persian juice containing plants; for instance, the Astragalus, which is common all over Persia, contains more juice and exudes more gum (Tragacanth) the higher it is found. The Hûm grows also in plains, but is then stunted and contains little juice.

[1] Dictionaries give the meaning of the word Nîreng, sorcery, incantation, talisman.

[2] Cf. Roth, *Zeitschrift DMG.* xxxv. 687. Soma must be bought from a *S*ûdra who brought it from the mountains.

'The Avesta says that the plant which gives the Soma grows on the mountains. Anquetil says it grows in Gîlân, Mazanderân, and Shîrvân[1]; Spiegel says that the Pârsîs of Bombay get their Homa from Kermân and send their priests from time to time to get it[2].

'The Pârsîs of Persia say that the Hûm they now use is the same that is mentioned in the Avesta.

'The thicker stalks are sometimes dried and straightened and used as a walking-stick on festive occasions, or kept in a room as a talisman against bad luck. The botanical description of the plant quoted by Professor Max Müller coincides very nearly with the Persian Hûm plant. The description says: "The *creeper* called Soma is *dark*, *sour*, *without leaves*, *milky*, *fleshy on the surface*; it destroys (or produces) phlegm; produces vomiting, and is eaten by goats." This is a description a person would give who had not seen the plant growing, who had details regarding it from the persons collecting it, and had seen it *several days after it had been collected*. The statement that it was eaten by goats would originate with the woodcutters or people sent to the mountains to collect the plant. They might have tried to account for its scarcity by saying that goats ate it. The plant is a *creeper*; the colour of the stalks would by the time the Hûm reached the describer have been brownish (*dark*), the juice would have been *sour*, the plant would have had *no leaves*, and the juice was *milky*, and the stalks had a *fleshy surface*. All this coincides with what I have said of the Kermân Hûm. Then, the plant was slesh-mala and vamanî. The term sleshmala, phlegm-destroying or phlegm-producing, is medical. The term vamanî would be medical, producing vomiting, or may mean that the Soma was used as an offering to the god Agni. Hûm, as a part

[1] Cf. Firdûsî, relation of Afrâsiâb's fight with Hûm in Âzerbâijân.
[2] Spiegel, *Eranische Alterthumskunde*, iii. 572.

of Nîreng, produces vomiting when taken to excess, and is also used as an offering during incantations, &c. The solving of this question, however, appertains to scholars like Professor Max Müller and Professor von Roth.

'Different Persian dictionaries describe the plant as follows:—Hûm, a small tree, growing everywhere (in Persia); its stems have many knots; its flowers are yellow and resemble those of the jessamine; its leaves are small, and they are formed like those of the jessamine; the Zardushtis (Zoroastrians) take a piece of it in their hands during their prayers; it is also used by them at incantations and sacrifices, and thrown into the fire. Arabs call it Hûm-Majûs (Hûm of the Maji, Zoroastrians), and explain it as a plant with branches full of knots. Others say that the plant is a deadly poison; its juice is used for poisoning arrow-heads; its fruit is very much liked by partridges; it resembles a tamarisk tree, &c. The latter qualities evidently refer to another plant. A. HOUTUM-SCHINDLER.'

'KEW, *Feb.* 31, 1885.

'The Hûm described by Mr. A. Houtum-Schindler in his letter in the *Academy*, January 31, p. 83, agrees sufficiently well with a *Sarcostemma*-like plant. The Parsis appear, however, to use other plants as the soma. Dr. Watt has recently sent me from India a scrap of one of these, and my colleague Professor Oliver, finds it indistinguishable from *Ephedra vulgaris.* This abounds in Afghanistan, and extends thence westward to the Mediterranean. It is a small rigid shrub, with what would be popularly regarded as leafless jointed branches, which are sometimes knotted. It bears in profusion small red berries, which are sweet and eaten on the Sutlej.

'M. Houtum-Schindler mentions that the Persian dictionaries recognise a second Hûm beside the *Sarcostemma*,

He says, "the fruit is much liked by partridges; it resembles a tamarisk tree." Perhaps the latter remark would be near enough for *Ephedra* in the case of *Tamarix articulata*. But he also says it is "a deadly poison" (though apparently not to partridges). This does not agree with *Ephedra*, which is browsed by goats. W. T. THISELTON-DYER.'

Note on the preceding Correspondence.

'Professor Max Müller, having thought these letters worth preserving in a more permanent form, has done me the honour of enquiring if I have anything to add to them. All I can speak about is, of course, the botanical aspect of the question.

'1. I find that in such authorities as I am able to consult there is a general agreement that whatever the Soma may have been originally, it was certainly in later times a fermented drink made from grain, to which the Soma plant itself was only added as an ingredient.

'Most books make the plant used in India *Sarcostemma brevistigma*. As far as I can make out this is based upon Roxburgh's identification with this species of the "Soma-latâ in Sanskrit" (*Flora Indica*, ii. p. 31). He adds: "This plant yields a larger portion of very pure milky juice than any other I know; and what is rare, it is of a mild nature and acid taste. The native travellers often suck the tender shoots to allay their thirst." One must admit therefore that the juice of a *Sarcostemma* is not necessarily nauseous. I also think it more than probable that the description in the Âyurveda applies to it. No *Sarcostemma* is however found in Asia farther north than Sind, and therefore the primitive Soma must have been something else.

'2. The examination of the fine collections made by Dr. Aitchison while attached to the Afghan Delimitation Commission has now been completed at Kew, and they throw no further light on the question. In the meantime Dr. Watt has procured from Dr. Dymock, of Bombay, a specimen of the Soma plant used by the Parsis. It is undoubtedly *Ephedra vulgaris*.

'3. Then there is the Hûm shrub used by the Parsis of Persia according to Mr. Houtum-Schindler. I am disposed to think that his description fairly answers to *Periploca aphylla*, a not uncommon Persian shrub. In the latter part of Mr. Houtum-Schindler's letter he quotes from Persian dictionaries the description of the Hûm, in which, as he sees, two different plants are confused. Dr. Aitchison, I think, supplies the key to that riddle in a note on *Periploca hydaspidis* in Afghanistan (*Journ. Linn. Soc. Bot.* xix. p. 176). He describes it "as a large semiscandent shrub with bright yellow flowers. Except when in flower and fruit it is quite impossible to distinguish it as it grows from *Ephedra ciliata*, a common plant of the same region."

'Now it is remarkable that all these plants have something in common in their naked and leafless stems and branches. Both *Periploca* and *Sarcostemma* are slightly addicted to climbing. Indeed Sir George Birdwood[1] sees the conventionalised form of *Sarcostemma* (though it is not clear where it came from) in the Assyrian Honeysuckle ornament, and the suggestion is plausible, though I have my doubts about it. He copies from Rawlinson, *Ancient Monarchies*, ii. p. 236, a figure in which it is twined about the date, and adds, "Possibly the date was substituted for the original *Hom* in Assyria, in consequence of the Aryas finding that they could not naturalise the true Hom plant, or because the date yields a more abundant intoxicating juice .... Later the vine took its place in Asia Minor and Greece."

'4. Dr. Aitchison himself inclined to the belief that the vine was the original Soma plant (see *Daily News*, March 13,

[1] *Industrial Arts of India*, pp. 336, 337.

1885). In that case in the plains of India the alcoholic basis of the Soma had to be found in fermented grain, and the green succulent shoots of the *Sarcostemma* were added as a ceremonial reminiscence of the grape. I must admit however that the apparently corresponding practice in Persia is hard to explain in the same way. It looks as if the essence of the matter was the *addition* of a Soma plant to more effective ingredients. The manufacture of "beer" from grain of different kinds is a widely diffused, and must have been a very early practice; certainly more general and perhaps earlier than the manufacture of wine from the grape. As De Candolle remarks (*L'origine des plantes cultivées*, pp. 129, 130), "Les Celtes, les Germains, d'autres peuples du Nord et même des peuples du Midi *qui avaient la vigne* faisaient de la bière soit d'orge, soit d'autres grains fermentés, avec addition, dans certains cas, de matières végétales diverses, par exemple d'écorce de Chêve, de *Tamarix*, ou du fruit de *Myrica Gale*[1]." I should not wonder therefore if the Hop were really a Soma plant, though widely remote in character and geographical position from its prototype.

'W. T. THISELTON DYER.'

[1] According to Lightfoot, *Flora Scotica* (vol. ii. p. 614), *Myrica* was used as a substitute for hops in the Highlands of Scotland in the last century (1777), and it may be still so employed.

IV.

PHILOLOGY *versus* ETHNOLOGY.

Letter to H. H. Risley, Esq.

'I HAVE read with real interest and pleasure the papers referring to an *Ethnological Survey of India* which you have done me the honour to send to me. Both from a practical and scientific point of view the inquiries which, with the sanction of the Indian Government, you have set on foot will, I have no doubt, be productive of most valuable results. They will enable the statesman to understand more thoroughly many of the traditional beliefs, local customs, and deep-rooted prejudices of those whom he has to influence and to control,—nay, they may possibly help the native inhabitants of India also to gain a truer insight into the meaning of many of their own apparently irrational customs, and a more correct appreciation of the original purport of their religious faiths and superstitions.

'But apart from the practical utility of such a survey as is contemplated by you and your colleagues, its value to the scholar and the student of ethnology can hardly be overestimated. India, with the immense variety of its inhabitants, representing almost every stage, from the lowest to the highest, in the progress of civilisation, is the most promising country for a scientific study of the devolopment of the human race. Ethnology, though a science of very ancient date, has of late attracted very general attention, and has extended its influence over very many important branches of philosophy. The words of Charron, repeated by Pope, "*La vraye science et le vrai étude de l'homme c'est l'homme,*" seem at last to have come true, and there is hardly a problem connected with the origin of man and the faculties of the human mind which has not been illuminated of late by fitful rays proceeding from the science of ethnology.

'But, as you truly observe, "many of the ethnological speculations of recent years have been based far too exclusively upon comparatively unverified accounts of the customs of savages of the lowest type," and, as an inevitable result, the whole science of ethnology has lost much of the prestige which it formerly commanded. It has almost ceased to be a true science in the sense in which it was conceived by Prichard, Humboldt, Waitz, Tylor and others, and threatens to become a mere collection of amusing anecdotes and moral paradoxes. It is a science in which the mere amateur can be of great use, but which requires for its successful cultivation the wide knowledge of the student of physical science and the critical accuracy of the scholar.

'The questions which you have drawn up, and the leading principles which you recommend for the guidance of your *collaborateurs*, seem to me excellent. If you could consult the Annual Reports of the American Bureau of Ethnology, and more particularly the excellent papers of its Director, Mr. J. W. Powell, you would find them, *mutatis mutandis*, very useful for your own purposes.

'If I may point out some dangers which seem to me to threaten the safe progress of ethnological inquiry in India and everywhere else, they are the same to which you yourself have called attention. Foremost amongst them I should mention the vagueness of the ordinary ethnological terminology, which has led to much confusion of thought and ought to be remedied *ferro et igne*. You are fully aware of the mischief that is produced by employing the terminology of Comparative Philology in an ethnological sense. I have uttered the same warning again and again. In my letter to the Chevalier Bunsen, "On the Turanian Languages," published as far back as 1853, I devoted a whole chapter to pointing out the necessity of keeping these two lines of research—the philological and the ethnological—completely separate, at least for the present. In my later works, too, I have protested as strongly as I could against the unholy alliance of these two sciences—Comparative Philology and Ethnology. But my warnings have been of little effect; and such is the influence of evil communications, that I myself cannot help pleading guilty of having occasionally used linguistic terms in an ethnological sense. Still it is an evil that ought to be resisted with all our might. Ethnologists persist in writing of *Aryas*, *Shemites*, and *Turanians*, *Ugrians*, *Dravidians*, *Kolarians*, *Bântu* races, &c., forgetting that these terms have nothing to do with blood, or bones, or hair, or facial angles, but simply and solely with language. Aryas are those who speak Aryan languages, whatever their colour, whatever their blood. In calling them Aryas we predicate nothing of them except that the grammar of their language is Aryan. The classification of Aryas and Shemites is based on linguistic grounds and on nothing else; and it is only because languages must be spoken by somebody that we may allow ourselves to speak of languages as synonymous with peoples. It takes away my breath when I am asked whether a Celt who has ceased to speak Cornish and learnt English is on that account less of a Celt than a Welshman. Welsh, Cornish, Celtic are all names of languages, not of race, and when we use our scientific terminology accurately we predicate nothing of Welshman, Cornishman or Celt, but that he speaks Welsh, Cornish, or a Celtic language in general.

'In India we have, first of all, the two principal ingredients of the population—the dark aboriginal inhabitants and their more fair-skinned conquerors. Besides these two, there have been enormous floods of neighbouring races,—Scythians from the North-West, Mongolians from the North-East, overwhelming from time to time large tracts of

Northern India. There have, besides, been inroads of Persians, Greeks, Romans, Mohammedans of every description, Afghans, and last, but not least, Europeans,—all mingling more or less freely with the original inhabitants and among themselves. Here, therefore, the ethnologist has a splendid opportunity of discovering some tests by which, even after a neighbourly intercourse lasting for thousands of years, the descendants of one race may possibly be told from the descendants of the others.

'We must not allow ourselves to be deceived by sacred Law-books. The very fact of their forbidding intermarriages between different classes shows that human nature was too strong for them. Intermarriages, whether forbidden or sanctioned by the law, took place; and we know that the consequence of one single intermarriage might tell in a few generations on thousands of people. Here, then, there is a promising field for the ethnologist, if only he will shut his ears to the evidence of language. As the philologist classifies his languages without asking a single question by whom they were spoken, let the ethnologist classify his skulls without inquiring what language had its *habitat* in them. After each has finished his classification, it will be time for the ethnologist or the linguist to compare their results, but not till then; otherwise we shall never arrive at truly scientific conclusions.

'To give one instance. When Mr. Hodgson had published his valuable vocabularies of the non-Sanskritic dialects spoken in India, he, like Lassen, seems to have been so convinced that the people who spoke them in the interior of India must have been either the aboriginal races or their fair-skinned Brahmanic conquerors, that in spite of most characteristic differences, he referred that whole cluster of dialects which we now call *Munda* or *Kolarian* to the Dravidian family of speech. Trusting simply to the guidance of language, and without paying the slightest regard to the strangely conflicting accounts as to the physical characteristics of these Munda tribes, I pointed out in 1853 that these dialects differed as much from the Dravidian as from the Sanskritic type, and that they must be admitted as a separate family of speech on the soil of India. Everybody accepted my discovery, but unfortunately very soon the term *Munda* or *Kolarian*, which was intended as a linguistic term only, was used ethnologically; and we now constantly read of a Kolarian race, as if we knew anything to prove that the people who speak Kolarian languages share all the same unmixed blood.

'If you were to issue an interdict against any of your *collaborateurs* using linguistic terms in an ethnological sense, I believe that your *Ethnological Survey of India* would inaugurate a new and most important era both in the science of language and in the science of man. And while I am speaking of the confusion of terms with regard to language and race, may I point out a similar danger which seems to me to threaten your researches into the origin of castes and tribes in India. On this point also you have to a certain extent anticipated my apprehensions, and I need not fear that you will misapprehend my remarks, though they can only be very short and imperfect.

'*Caste* is a European word, but it has become so completely naturalised in India that the vagueness of its meaning seems to have reacted even on the native mind. The Sanskrit word for caste is varna, literally "colour," or *g*âti, literally "breed" or "kith." But though the original meaning of these words is clear, it is well known how much their meaning has varied during different periods in the history of Indian society. As to colour, there are now true Brahmans in the south of India as black as Pariahs; as to kith and kin, whatever the orthodox doctrine may be, the Brahmans themselves are honest enough to confess that even in the earliest times Kshatriyas became Brahmans, such as Visvâmitra; nay more, outsiders, such as the carpenters under Bribu, were admitted to the Brahmanic community and endowed with Brahmanic gods, the *Ri*bhus (see *Chips from a German Workshop*, ii. p. 131, and my article on *Caste*, ibid. pp. 301–359). What took place during the Vedic period is taking place, as Sir Alfred Lyall has so well shown, at the present day, only we must take care not to ascribe to the proselytising spirit of the Brahmans what is simply the result of the religious and social flunkeyism of the lower races of India.

'Caste ought to be carefully distinguished from school, *k*ara*n*a—from race and family, gotra and kula. This subject is beset with many difficulties, and I do not myself profess to see quite clearly on the many intricate questions connected with it. With regard to the early history of races and families there is a rich literature in Sanskrit, and it would be very desirable if you could secure the assistance of a really learned pandit to give you a clear and full account of what can be known from these sources. Some of them are of very ancient date. Thus you will find in the Vedic G*ri*hya-sûtras a list of Brahmanic gotras (see my *History of Ancient Sanskrit Literature*, pp. 379–388), and, strange to say, you will see that the interdict against marriages between members of the same gotra is by no means so universal as it is supposed to be. Some of the statements set forth in these Brahmanic treatises may seem to represent *pia vota* rather than real facts, but we must not forget that even such theories have often very powerfully influenced the later development of social life in India. I have no doubt that with proper precautions you might derive most valuable help from educated natives, who know the meaning of the terms taken from their own language, and how far they really correspond with the terms which we use in English.

'It seems to me a dangerous habit to transfer terms which have their proper and well-defined meaning in one country to similar objects in other countries. It is, of course, very tempting when we see in India—nay, almost in every country of the world—two or more vertical stones with another on the top of them to greet them as cromlechs. But a cromlech is a stone monument erected by Celtic people, and to speak of cromlechs in India is apt to be misleading. It is far better to describe each class of rude stone monuments by itself, and, if possible, to call them by their own local name. In that way their individual features will not be overlooked; and this is of great importance,—nay, often of greater importance than to perceive the general similarity of such stone monuments in the most distant quarters of our globe.

'I am even afraid of such words as *totemism*[1], *fetishism*, and

[1] 'Unluckily the word totem is wrongly made. Professor Max Müller has called attention to the remark of the Canadian philologist, Father Cuoq (N. O. Ancien Missionaire), that the word is properly ote, meaning "family mark," possessive otem, and with the personal pronoun nindotem, "my family mark," kitotem, "thy family mark."'—E. B. Tylor.

Assikenack, one of the Ottawa chiefs who accompanied Mrs. Jamieson, gives the following account of the so-called totems:—'The inhabitants were divided into tribes, and a tribe was again sub-divided into sections, or families, according to their ododams, that is, their devices, signs, or what may be called, according to the usage of civilised communities, "coats of arms." The members of a particular family kept themselves distinct, at least nominally, from the other members of the tribe; and, in their large villages, all people claiming to belong to the same ododam, or sign, were required to dwell in that section of the village set apart for them specially, which, from the mention of gates, we may suppose was enclosed by pickets or some sort of fence. At the principal entrance into this enclosure there was the figure of an animal, or some other sign, set up on the top of one of the posts. By means of this sign everybody might know to what particular family the inhabitants of that quarter claimed to belong. For instance, those whose ododam was the bear would set up the figure of that animal at their principal gate. Some of the families were called after their ododam. For example, those who had the gull for their ododam were called the Gull family, or, simply, the Gulls; they would, of course, put up the figure of that bird at their gate. Others did not adopt this custom; for instance, the family who set up the bear were called the Big Feet. Many of the village gates must have been adorned with very curious carvings, in consequence of parts only of different animals being frequently joined together to make up the ensigns armorial of a family; for instance, the ododam of one par-

several other *isms*, which have found their way into ethnological science. They are very convenient and commodious terms, and, if used with proper care, quite unobjectionable. But they often interfere with accurate observation and distinction. A fetish, from meaning originally something very definite in the worship of the Negroes on the west coast of Africa, has become a general name of almost any inanimate object of religious worship. The Palladium, the Cross, the black stone of the Kaaba, have all been called fetishes as much as the tail of a dog worshipped on the Congo,—as if we could arrive at any sound conclusions by throwing together, regardless of their antecedents, objects of worship belonging, it is supposed, to the earliest and to the latest phases of religious belief.

'Again, if there is anything like *totemism* in India, let us have a full and detailed description of each individual case, instead of hiding all that may be really enlightening under the large bushel of totemism. Almost anything that outwardly distinguishes one race from another is now called *totem*, though what seems to be the same, and even what answers the same purpose, is by no means always the same in its origin. This habit of generalising and exaggerating has done infinite mischief. The North-American Indians have their *totems*, wrongly so spelt, and we know what they mean by these symbols. We find similar family symbols in many parts of the world, but to call them all *totems* is most inaccurate. And what is the result? Because in some parts of the world marriages between members of the same *totem* are forbidden, statements that in Australia members of the same *totem* are encouraged to marry are received with incredulity. Because certain races abstain from eating animals which form their totems, we are told that the pig may in

ticular section consisted of the wing of a small hawk and the fins of a sturgeon.'—See Letter from Rev. J. Hoskyns Abrahall in *Academy*, Sept. 27, 1884.

ancient times have been the totem of the Jews. *Si duo faciunt idem, non est idem.* Think only of the different Nâgas or snakes in India. People are called Nâgas, they worship Nâgas, they use emblems of Nâgas, and we may believe that they do not eat Nâgas. Is the Nâga or serpent therefore to be simply classed as a *totem*? There are *fagots et fagots,* and any one who has lived in India knows that in India, as elsewhere, nothing has such various antecedents, and nothing serves such different purports, as Nâga, the serpent.

'I have written down these few remarks, not with a view of offering you advice in the prosecution of your ethnological inquiries in India, but in order to show to you how entirely I agree with the spirit in which you have hitherto conducted your *Ethnological Survey of India,* and I hope will continue it and bring it to a successful issue.

'Yours, very truly,

'F. Max Müller.'

V.

The Third Metal,

COPPER OR IRON.

Whether the Aryas before their separation were acquainted with iron, and knew how to extract it from the ore and work it into tools and weapons, has been a question often asked and often answered. At first, nothing seemed easier. Áyas in later Sanskrit does certainly mean iron, and as áyas is the same word as Latin aes[1], and Gothic aiz[2], no one hesitated to ascribe to the undivided Aryas an acquaintance with iron. I did so myself in 1856 in my Essay on 'Comparative Mythology.'

When, however, we were told by archaeologists that several of the Aryan nations were ignorant of iron tools and weapons even during historical times, it seemed difficult to believe that they should have forgotten the usefulness of iron, if they had once discovered it. Examined from that point of view, the mere evidence of language was found to be less strong than it had been supposed. The Sanskrit áyas means certainly iron in the later periods of literature, but there is no passage in the more ancient hymns of the Rig-veda where it *must* mean iron. The same applies to the Zend ayañh, though Spiegel[3], following the uncertain lead of the Parsi tradition[4], is inclined to assign to ayañh

[1] Aes in Latin is used for copper in general, whatever its admixture in various localities may have been, and more especially for copper as mixed with tin, i.e. bronze.

[2] In German, it is difficult to say whether Gothic aiz, OHG. êr, AS. âr, are meant for copper, bronze, or metal in general. In English, ore has assumed a very general meaning, being, like the German Erz, applicable to every kind of metal in its raw state.

[3] 'Die Arische Periode,' p. 34.

[4] Commentators are apt to introduce the ideas of their own time into

the meaning of iron in the Gâthâs, the most ancient portions of the Avesta.

While a recent controversy on the original home of the Aryas and on the state of civilisation which they had reached before their dispersion was carried on, I was challenged to give my reasons for saying that áyas in the Rig-veda *may* mean iron, but that there is no passage where it *must* have that meaning. This distinction between *may* and *must* is very important, though it was neglected by my friendly antagonist, Professor Sayce. Roth in his Dictionary explains áyas by Erz, Metal, insbesondere Eisen, but this does not prove, what it has been supposed to prove, that in the Rig-veda áyas has ever of necessity the meaning of iron. We cannot be too careful in these matters, for the slightest ambiguity may give rise, as it has done in this case, to the most far-reaching but misleading theories.

Whether a knowledge of iron preceded a knowledge of copper, or whether the copper age preceded the iron age, are questions hotly debated by students of antiquity, and both sides have tried to avail themselves of the evidence of language in support of their theories. I doubt, however, whether the evidence of language can settle these questions, though I think it may help to point out the right way for their solution. Language supplies us with words, but not with scientific definitions, and as little as at the present day a mere peasant could tell the difference between the ores of gold, silver, copper, iron, lead, or tin, can we expect that language should from the very beginning have clearly distinguished between these metals.

the ancient traditions which they have to explain. Thus when Kâtyâyana (*S*rauta Sûtra, V, 2, 17) speaks of a loha-kshura, a razor made of loha, the native commentator explains it by an iron razor set in copper (lohena tâmre*n*a parishk*ri*tam ayomayam eva kshura*m* hastena g*ri*hitvâ. Loham atra tâmram u*k*yate, lohita ivâgnir iti va*k*anât). In the *S*atap. Brâhm., on the contrary, loha*h* kshura*h* is explained by Sâya*n*a as a razor made of copper, tâmramaya*h*.

The great mistake which antiquarians seem to me to have committed in discussing the priority of copper or iron, arises from their not distinguishing sufficiently between the various localities in which certain metals are present or absent, and the conditions under which they are found. Livingstone (*Neue Missionsreise*, 1866, i. p. 123) tells us that the natives west of Lake Nyassa worked iron, while the oxydised copper which is found in abundance is not used, because, according to their notions, it is more difficult to treat than iron. Percy (*Trans. Ethn. Soc.*, N. S. iv. pp. 2, 195) states that from a metallurgic point of view the so-called age of iron ought to have preceded that of bronze. It is well known how strongly that view has been advocated in Germany by Lindenschmit, Hostmann, and others, and how it is scouted by the most eminent representatives of the Scandinavian school of archaeology.

That in Greece iron was supposed to be difficult to work, we learn from its being called *πολύκμητος*, wrought with much toil, while in Sanskrit iron, and iron only, is called a*s*masâra*h*, girisâram, *s*ilasâram, i.e. the sap or inside of stone, thus indicating the difficult process by which it was obtained. On the contrary, in the Bundahi*s* (*S. B. E.*, v. p. 56) the working of iron is described in a very primitive way: 'And first, a clothing of skins covered them; afterwards, it is said, woven garments were prepared from a cloth woven in the wilderness. And they dug out a pit in the earth, and iron was obtained by them and beaten out with a stone, and without a forge they beat out a cutting edge from it; and they cut wood with it, and prepared a wooden shelter from the sun.'

All this tends to show that the working of iron was more or less difficult in different countries, though it was not so difficult as to be altogether beyond the reach of people unacquainted as yet with copper and bronze.

But if, on the other side, it is argued that copper could

never have been efficiently used for tools and weapons, because it was too soft a metal, this too is by no means so certain as is commonly supposed. Geoffroy (*Recueil d'Antiquités de Caylus* i. p. 239) writes as follows: '*J'ai cherché à imiter pour la dureté et pour le tranchant une épée romaine, et je crois n'y avoir pas trop mal reussi dans celle que j'ai remise à M. le comte de Caylus.*' The testimony of Proclus, Tzetzes, and Moschopulos on the well-known passage in Hesiod leaves little doubt that the ancients were acquainted with a method of hardening copper by means of what they call βαφή or immersion.

It seems to me therefore that neither the supposed difficulty of working iron nor the supposed difficulty of hardening copper can help us to decide the question of the priority of the use of iron or copper among the ancient Aryan nations.

If, then, we turn for help to the evidence of language, what do we find? Dr. Schrader[1] thinks that the evidence of language shows that the Aryas, before they separated, were acquainted with one metal only, namely copper. This, again, is far too positive an assertion.

The radical identity of the names for gold and silver seems to me to make it more than probable that the yellow and the white metal, gold and silver, were known before the Aryan Separation. In addition to these, a third metal had been named, but I am not prepared to say that it was copper, at least not in the strict scientific sense which that word has assumed in our language.

If I am right in this, the idea that the Greeks borrowed their name for gold from Semitic neighbours falls to the ground. It seems to me contradicted likewise by the wide influence which the word χρυσός has exercised in the mythological phraseology of Homer.

That the Romans had their own name for gold, aurum

[1] 'Handelsgeschichte,' p. 121.

for ausum, and preserved no trace of a name derived from the root HÆR, is, no doubt, a weighty argument on the other side, but it is not decisive, as there are many cases of the same kind in Latin. The Celtic nations borrowed their names for gold from Italy; whether the Prussian ausis, the Lit. auksas, came from the same quarter, is less evident.

Silver seems to us so entirely different from gold that we can hardly imagine that the two should ever have been confused. But, barring its colour, silver in ancient times seems to have served very much the same purposes as gold. We must also remember that in some countries gold and silver are found mixed, and that the Greeks in later times used the name ἤλεκτρος, masc., whenever silver constituted the fifth part of gold[1]. In Japan, I am told, no difference was made till the beginning of this century between a gold and a silver coin.

In the Taittirîya-Samhitâ (I, 5, 1, 2), where silver is mentioned for the first time as an inferior metal, it is called ragatám híranyam, i.e. white gold (λευκὸς χρυσός, Herod. I, 50). In later times, when su-varna, i.e. 'of good colour,' had become the recognised name for gold, dur-varna, i.e. 'of bad colour,' became the name of silver. The Afghans to the present day call silver white gold, spîn zar.

It is quite true that the Teutonic and Slavonic languages do not share in any of the names for silver, derived from the root ÆRG, such as Sk. ragata, Greek ἄργυρος, Lat. argentum, while the Celtic nations clearly borrowed their name for silver from Italy. But to say, as Schrader does (l. c. p. 264), that silver cannot have been known to the Indo-Germans before they separated, is far too strong an assertion. In Gothic we find silubr, in Old Slavonic sĭrebro, in Lituanian sidabras, words of very obscure origin, which Victor Hehn ventures to derive from the town 'Αλύβη in Pontus, changing

[1] Lepsius, 'Abhandl. der Berl. Akademie,' 1871, p. 129; Schrader, 'Sprachvergleichung,' p. 263.

'Αλύβη into 'Αλύβη, and this into Σαλύβη. But though Homer (Il. II, 857) refers to 'Αλύβη,

τηλόθεν ἐξ 'Αλύβης, ὅθεν ἀργύρου ἐστὶ γενέθλη,

it would be difficult to imagine how the name of that city, even if it had been Salybe, could have supplied the German nations with their common name for silver, such as Gothic silubr.

It is curious also to observe that a similar name, that of the Chalybes (σιδηροτέκτονες), is supposed to be the origin of the Greek name of hardened iron or steel, namely χάλυψ[1].

If now we turn to the third metal, we may say, as in the case of silver, that it was known as soon as it had been named, and distinguished from gold and silver. But even when it had been named and known, it need not have been known at first as anything beyond a metal, different from gold and silver. To say that it was copper, is going too far, for we must remember that copper too is not always found in a pure state, and that some of the natural alloys of that metal have often been selected on account of their fitness for the manufacture of weapons and tools. Nor would the colour be enough to distinguish copper from other metals. It is generally supposed that when áyas is called loham[2] or lohitam, red, it must be meant for copper, and that, if called syâmam, black, it can be intended for iron only. But even that is not so certain as it seems. Copper, as found in the earth, is often quite black, while iron ore (oxide of iron) is very decidedly red. In Finnish, copper is called pataroh[3], which means black copper. The third metal, áyas, so far as we can judge, meant originally no more than metal in general, though different from gold and silver. If derived from I, to go, its etymological meaning would have been what goes, or yields, or melts. But there was nothing

[1] Schrader, l. c. p. 291.
[2] Loha, masc., Amarakosha; neut., Halâyudha, means iron.
[3] Schrader, 'Sprachvergleichung,' p. 267.

to prevent the meaning of áyas from being specialised into either copper or iron. We see how Sk. drus, which meant originally a tree which can be stripped of its bark, shaped into a shaft, or hollowed out so as to serve for a boat, came to mean oak in Greek and Irish, pine in Lituanian, its general meaning becoming specialised at different times and in different countries. Sometimes the opposite process also took place, as when we see how *oak*, after it has become the name of a special tree, is used in Icelandic as eik for trees in general. Áyas therefore might likewise have been used, not only in the general, or rather as yet undefined meaning of metal[1], but also as a name for special metals, whether copper or iron.

So long as we meet with three metals only, it is extremely difficult to determine the exact nature of the third metal. Thus if we read in the Atharva-veda, V, 28, 1, of hárita, ra*g*atá, and áyas, we may be quite certain that hárita stands for the yellow metal or gold, ra*g*atá for the white metal or silver, but we cannot speak with equal certainty as to áyas being meant specifically for either copper or iron.

It is different when we have to deal with four metals, for the ancient tetrad of metals among the Aryan nations seems always to have been gold, silver, copper (pure or alloyed), and iron[2].

Thus when we find in Greek the word σίδηρος by the side

[1] In such expressions as k*r*ish*n*âyas, syâmám áyas, áyas has clearly the general meaning of metal, iron being called black or dark metal, copper lóhitam, i. e. red metal. In Âpast. Dh. S. II, 16, 18, we find k*r*ish*n*âyasa*m* trapusîsam; in II, 14, 7, k*r*ish*n*am bhaumam.

[2] That where four metals are mentioned they are always meant for gold, silver, copper, and iron is to be taken *cum grano salis*. In fanciful comparisons, as, for instance, in Ath.-veda XI, 3, 1, 7, we find the flesh of a sacrificial offering represented as *s*yâmám áya*h*, black iron, the blood as lóhitam, red copper, the ashes as trápu, tin, the colour as hárita, gold. Here *s*yâmám áyas is generally, and probably correctly, taken for iron. In IX, 5, 4, *s*yâma is used with así in the sense of a black or iron weapon.

of χαλκός, we cannot doubt that σίδηρος or iron had been clearly distinguished from χαλκός, copper, more or less pure. The well-known passage of Hesiod refers of course to times much later than those we are here speaking of. It reads like the utterance of a thoughtful antiquarian, and no more:

> Τοῖς δ' ἦν χάλκεα μὲν τεύχεα, χάλκεοι δέ τε οἶκοι,
> χαλκῷ δ' εἰργάζοντο· μέλας δ' οὐκ ἔσκε σίδηρος.

It is strange that a Greek who knew that there was a time when the black iron did not exist, and when weapons, houses (i. e. their doors and bars), and tools were made of copper, should not have known that there was a time when copper did not exist, and weapons, houses[1], and tools were made of stone. Neither in Hesiod nor in Homer do we find any recollections of a stone age, and language alone is left to testify to its former existence in Greece also. I do not mean to claim the stones hurled by Polyphemus against Odysseus nor those thrown by Ajax or Hector in the heat of battle (Il. VII, 268; XII, 445), as evidence for the use of palaeolithic weapons in Greece. But there is a passage in the Odyssey, VIII, 190, where we can see quite clearly that the disk thrown by Odysseus was made of stone, for instead of δίσκος in one place, we have λίθος and λᾶς in another[2]. There is another passage in the Iliad, which seems to indicate, though it does not prove, that Homer looked on stone as he looked on χαλκός and σίδηρος as useful both for attack and defence. Hector, when calling on the Trojans not to be afraid of the Argeioi, says[3], 'Their skin is not stone or iron, so that it will withstand the χαλκός.' But far stronger is the evidence for the use of stone weapons, supported by such words as ἄκων and ἄκμων. Ἄκων in Greek

[1] *Satap.* Br. III, 1, 3, 11, asmapurâ.

[2] Od. VIII, 186, λάβε δίσκον; 190, βόμβησεν δὲ λίθος; 192, λᾶος ὑπὸ ῥιπῆς.

[3] Il. IV, 511,

> Ἀργείοις, ἐπεὶ οὔ σφι λίθος χρὼς οὐδὲ σίδηρος
> χαλκὸν ἀνασχέσθαι ταμεσίχροα βαλλομένοισιν.

means javelin, and no longer stone, but it is the same word as the Sk. *ásan*, which means stone, and afterwards weapon. Ἄκμων in Greek means stone and anvil, *ásman* in Sanskrit means stone only, and particularly a stone used as a weapon.

In this way language teaches us that the ancestors of the Homeric Greeks had passed through a stone age, and such evidence is far stronger than the evidence derived from Hesiod's archaeological theory that there was an age when iron was not yet known in Greece. I do not think we ought to attach much weight to Hesiod's remark. But what we may assert, quite independent of it, is that iron possessed a high value in the eyes of the Homeric Greeks, because in the games, when prizes are given of horses, mules, gold, women, etc., he who could throw a disk furthest, received a disk of iron (Il. XXIII, 826), σόλον αὐτοχόωνον, which will be enough for him, if he has wide acres, for five years, and neither his shepherd nor his ploughman will have to buy any in the town, but he will give it them. This iron (σίδηρος) was called by Homer πολιός, grey, ἰόεις, violet, αἴθων, bright; by Hesiod also μέλας, black.

But because iron, being harder than copper, was highly valued by the Homeric Greeks and probably scarce, it does not follow, strictly speaking, that it was at any time unknown in Greece. Still less does it follow, even supposing that Hesiod was right, that iron was either known or unknown during the earliest period of Aryan history. We must try to keep ourselves quite free from all these preconceived opinions, when trying to determine whether *áyas* in the Rig-veda means iron or any other metal. The fact that *áyas* means iron in later Sanskrit is important, but it is not decisive, and we shall find that in several passages taken from the Brâh-ma*n*as and the later Vedas, it is by no means certain that *áyas* has already the technical meaning of iron.

Thus we read in the *S*atapatha-Brâhma*n*a, VI, 1, 3, 5, that Pra*g*âpati creates water, from water comes foam, from foam mud, from mud sand, from sand gravel, from gravel stones, from stones áyas. Here áyas, as coming from stone, asmasâram, might certainly seem to be intended for iron. But the text goes on to say that from áyas comes gold, and therefore it is said that they blow, i.e. they smelt, áyas from stone, and gold from áyas, and when much blown or smelted, áyas becomes like gold (ayo bahudhmâta*m* hira*n*yasa*m*kâ*s*am ivaiva bhavati). Here therefore, if we consider the colour of copper and gold, áyas would seem to be meant for copper rather than for iron. The same remark applies to VI, 1, 1, 13.

In *S*atap. Br. V, 1, 2, 14, áyas means any metal that is not either gold or lead, for it is said, 'This is not áyas, nor gold, for it is lead[1]' (*S*atap. Br. XII, 7, 1, 7). The commentator adds, that lead is better than áyas, but worse than gold. In *S*atap. Br. V, 4, 1, 2, we read, 'This is not áyas, nor gold, for it is lohâyasam;' and this, according to the commentator, is tâmram, or copper. Here therefore áyas cannot be meant for copper, and was probably meant for iron.

There is a very difficult passage on metals in the Vâ*g*asaneyi-*S*a*m*hitâ XVIII, 13. We find there the following list of six metals: híra*n*yam, áya*h*, *s*yâmám, lohám, sī́sam, and trápu. The commentator takes hira*n*ya for gold, but he suggests that it may mean both gold and silver. He explains áyas by loham, by which he can only mean iron[2]. Then

[1] Lead is used here, not exactly as money, but as an article for which parisrut, an intoxicating liquor, is to be exchanged, when it would not be lawful to buy it with either gold or ayas. And a similar thought is expressed in Vâ*g*asaneyi-Sa*m*hitâ XIX, 80, where it is said that certain gods weave a sacrifice with sîsa, lead, and ûr*n*âsûtra, wool-threads, because the grass and other things requisite for it (Kâty. Sûtra, XIV, 1, 14) had been acquired in exchange for sîsa, lead, and wool, and threads (Kâty. Sûtra, XIX, 1, 19).

[2] Loha in lohamaya is explained by Roth as made of copper or iron. In the *S*atapatha-Brâhma*n*a, where we find the three words, hira*n*maya, lohamaya, and âyasa in juxtaposition, lohamaya would mean made of copper, if we could be quite certain that âyasa means made of iron.

follows syâmám, which he explains by tâmraloham, i. e. copper, adding, however, that it may also mean brass, silver, or gold. Lastly comes loham, which the commentator explains by kâlâyasa, that is, iron again. Here the commentator can hardly be right, as we should have iron twice. Professor Schrader has attempted a different explanation, but his interpretation of lohám by copper, and áyas by brass is purely conjectural. I feel by no means certain of my own interpretation as given in the following list. All I wish to conclude from it is that even at the time of the *S*atapatha-Brâhma*n*a áyas was by no means the recognised name for iron and for iron only.

	Comm.	Schrader.	M. M.
Híra*n*yam	Gold, etc.	Gold	Gold.
Áyas	Loham, iron	Brass (Erz)	(?).
*S*yâmám	Tâmraloham, copper	Iron	Copper.
Lohám	Kâlâyasam, iron	Copper	Iron.
Sísam	Lead	Lead	Lead.
Trápu	Tin	Tin	Tin.

In later Sanskrit eight metals are distinguished: Suvar*n*a, gold; ra*g*ata, silver; tâmra, copper; rîrî, white brass; kâ*m*sya[1], yellow brass; trapu, tin; sîsa, lead; dhîvara, iron[2].

If now we return to the principal and most important question, whether in the Rig-veda there are any passages where áyas can mean iron only and nothing else, what we ought to do is to examine every passage in which áyas occurs by itself, instead of saying, as Roth does, 'Erz, Metal, insbesondere Eisen.'

Rv. IV, 2, 17, áya*h* ná devấ*h* *g*ánima dhámanta*h*, means that the gods made all creatures, as if blowing, i. e. melting metal, not necessarily iron.

Rv. VI, 3, 5, *s*í*s*îta té*g*a*h*, áyasa*h* ná dhârâm, i. e. he sharpened the light, like the edge of metal.

[1] Made of trapu, tin, and tâmra, copper; see Rig-veda-prâti*s*. p. lxii.
[2] Hema*k*andra, 1039, note.

The same expression occurs VI, 47, 10, *k*odáya dhíyam, áyasa*h* ná dhắrâm, rouse and sharpen the mind, like the edge of metal. Here no doubt iron, or even steel, would to us seem a most appropriate rendering. Still when the question is whether the poets of the Rig-veda distinguished between metal in general and copper, or iron in particular, these passages are again of no avail.

Rv. I, 57, 3. Here áyase is not a dative of áyas, as Roth supposes, but the infinitive of the verb i, to go; see Kuhn's 'Zeitschrift,' xii. p. 342.

Rv. I, 163, 9, híra*n*yas*ri*ṅga*h* áya*h* asya pắdâ*h*, i.e. golden-horned, his feet are metal. Here we have only the common distinction and opposition between hira*n*ya, gold, and áya*h*, some kind of metal, of which we know nothing but that it is not gold. It may be copper, or iron, but there is nothing to enable us to prove that it was iron, and not copper.

The Vedic poets are very fond of contrasting hira*n*ya and ayas, e.g.

Rv. I, 88, 5, híra*n*ya*k*akrân áya*h*da*m*sh*t*rân, the Maruts with golden chariots, like boars with metal tusks, i.e. with strong tusks[1].

Rv. V, 62, 7, híra*n*yanirnik, áya*h* asya sthű*n*â, adorned with gold, its pillar was iron.

Rv. V, 62, 8, híra*n*yarûpam ushása*h* vyûsh*t*au, áya*h*sthû*n*am úditâ sűryasya, you mount the chariot (throne) which is gold-coloured at the dawning of the dawn, but has metal poles at the setting of the sun. Here, no doubt, if it is the intention of the poet to contrast the colour of the morning with that of the evening, we should imagine that aya*h*sthû*n*a, with metal poles, was used to indicate the dark colour of the metal, particularly if we consider that in India there is little twilight, and sunset is followed by immediate darkness. Still

[1] Even hira*n*yada*m*sh*t*ra, golden-tusked, is explained by abhagnada*m*sh*t*ra, with unbreakable tusks, *Kh*ând. Up. IV, 3, 7.

other explanations are possible; and the contrast between the colours of gold and copper would be equally appropriate, particularly in the North of India[1].

We have thus seen that the passages brought forward by Roth from the Rig-veda do not prove that áya*h* in the oldest hymns meant more than metal.

There are other passages in the Rig-veda, not quoted by Roth, in which áyas occurs, but again without any clear proof that it meant iron.

VI, 75, 15, yásyâ*h* áya*h* múkham, the arrow, the mouth, i. e. the point of which is metal; just as in the Mahâbhârata, *S*ântip. 262, ver. 46, the plough is called kâsh*th*am ayomukham, the pole with a metal mouth. Here, as in other cases, iron would give a welcome meaning, but as we know that arrows had points made of other metal besides iron, this passage again fails us, if we wish to prove that ayas in the Rig-veda *must* have meant iron.

The same applies to many compounds, such as áyas-agra, metal-pointed (arrow), Rv. X, 99, 6; áya*h*-apâsh*t*i, with metal claws (hawk), Rv. X, 99, 8; áya*h*-da*m*sh*t*ra, with metal tusks (Agni, or boars), Rv. I, 88, 5; áya*h*-hanu, with metal jaws (Savit*ri*), Rv. VI, 71, 4; áya*h*-*s*ipra, with metal jaws (*Ri*bhus), Rv. IV, 37, 4; áya*h*-*s*îrshan, with a metal head or helmet (dûta), Rv. VIII, 101, 3. In some of these cases áyas may have been used simply to imply strength; in others, where it is clearly metal, we have to confess our ignorance as to which metal was meant. Vessels are called áya*h*-hata, Rv. IX, 1, 2; 80, 2, i. e. struck, hammered out of metal, pots made of metal, also ayasmáya, Rv. V, 30, 15; but nowhere is there any clear indication to tell us whether the metal was copper, iron, or brass.

All therefore we are justified in stating positively is, that at the time of the Rig-veda, besides silver and gold, a third metal was known and named áyas; but whether that name

[1] For a different explanation see Schrader, l. c. p. 263.

referred to either copper or iron, or to metal in general, there is no evidence to show. I think we might venture to assert the same with regard to the period which preceded the Aryan Separation, though no doubt the evidence on which we here rely has been questioned by very competent judges.

The result of all this may seem to some of my readers very disappointing, but such disappointments are extremely useful, if they teach us that we can never be too careful, never too minutely accurate, never, if you like, too pedantic in our linguistic researches. It may seem to make but little difference whether we say that áyas *must* have meant iron in the Rig-veda, or whether we say that it *may* have meant iron; but in the controversy which has lately stirred the British Association at Manchester, and has found an echo even in the columns of the *Times*, we have seen what important issues depend on a simple *may* or *must*. It is sometimes supposed that in addressing a popular audience extreme accuracy and precision of language are hardly necessary. To me, on the contrary, it has always seemed that the commonest honesty requires us to be even more careful and conscientious in statements addressed to a popular audience than in communications sent to learned societies. The latter can defend themselves, the former cannot, and nothing is so difficult to stop than a vulgar error which has once taken possession of the public at large.

Truth is as sacred in science as it is anywhere else, and to represent the uncertain as certain, and the plausible as true, is as reprehensible where a mere various reading is concerned as it would be where life and honour are at stake. A scholar's work is not idle amusement, nor is its highest object either gain or fame. Just as the builders of the ancient pyramids when in the sweat of their brow they had placed a block of granite at the rightest angle, delighted in feeling that the work was done and done for ever, the true scholar also thinks nothing of himself, nothing of what he himself is doing, or what he himself has done, he only thinks of the work that is done, and well done, and done for ever.

We are trustees of the greatest treasures which the human race has accumulated by centuries of toil and travail, and it is our duty to keep these treasures safe, and to augment them, if we can, by hard and honest work. Whoever is without this sense of responsibility, without this consciousness of the high dignity of a scholar's calling, does not belong to our brotherhood. Let the world call us pedants by all means—we know how to glory in our shame.

INDEX.

T